Activities for First Grade

CH

Activities for First Grade

Hundreds of fun and creative activities that will help kids
advance in math, language, science, and more!

Naomi E. Singer & Matthew J. Miller

Adams Media Corporation
Holbrook, Massachusetts

Published by
Adams Media Corporation
260 Center Street, Holbrook, MA 02343. U.S.A.
www.adamsmedia.com

ISBN: 1-58062-275-5

Printed in the United States of America.

J I H G F E D C B A

Library of Congress Cataloging-in-Publication Data
Singer, Naomi E..
A+ activities for first grade / Naomi E. Singer and Matthew J. Miller.
p.   cm.
ISBN 1-58062-275-5
1. First grade (Education)—United States—Curricula. 2. Education, Primary—Activity programs—United States.
I. Title: A plus activities for first grade. II. Miller, Matthew J. III. Title.
LB1571 1st .S48   2000
372.19—dc21   00-036202

This publication is designed to provide accurate and authoritative information with regard to the subject matter covered. It is sold with the understanding that the publisher is not engaged in rendering legal, accounting, or other professional advice. If legal advice or other expert assistance is required, the services of a competent professional person should be sought.
—From a *Declaration of Principles* jointly adopted by a Committee of the American Bar Association and a Committee of Publishers and Associations

Cover photo by Jim Craigmyle/Masterfile.
Interior illustrations by Kurt Dobler and Kathie Kelleher.

This book is available at quantity discounts for bulk purchases.
For information, call 1-800-872-5627.

DEDICATION

To my parents, Herbert and Shirley Singer, with all
my love and thanks for a lifetime of inspiration.
—NAOMI

To my parents, Denny and Helaine Miller, for teaching me
that anything is possible . . . all my love.
—MATT

TABLE OF CONTENTS

INTRODUCTION / XIII

SKILLS LIST / XV

LANGUAGE ARTS ACTIVITIES / 1

A+ ACTIVITIES FOR FIRST GRADE

MATH ACTIVITIES / 65

SCIENCE ACTIVITIES / 127

SOCIAL STUDIES ACTIVITIES / 169

BIBLIOGRAPHY / 193

RESOURCES / 199

ABOUT THE AUTHORS / 200

INTRODUCTION

When given the opportunity to write a book of first grade activities, we enthusiastically agreed. Innumerable times in our experience as teachers, we have been asked by parents, "What can we do at home to support our child's learning?" *A+ Activities for First Grade* is our best effort to answer this question.

We teach in an inclusive school system that celebrates diversity. The parents, teachers, and administrators of our school communities have developed core values that emphasize a love of learning, respect for self and others, academic excellence, and commitment to school and community. Each of these values has been a driving force in the writing of this book and in the work we do each day with our students. Just as we embrace these values in our classrooms, so do parents embrace them at home.

We took on the challenge of writing this book because we truly believe that parents working in partnership with teachers make a huge and positive difference in the education of young children. The goal of *A+ Activities for First Grade* is to extend classroom learning to the world around you. As you use these activities, build on your child's strengths to enhance your first grader's self-confidence and positive self-image. Have fun and enjoy learning! By taking an active and participatory part in your child's learning, you not only support your first grader's developing skills, but also demonstrate the value that you place on learning.

Ask questions, explore, and observe together. Celebrate your child's learning by praising, encouraging, and valuing all efforts. In so doing, you create a safe environment for learning and share the joyful experience of discovery.

We want to thank the members, past and present, of the faculties of both the Cabot Elementary School and the John Ward Elementary School in Newton, Massachusetts. We appreciate and value their support. Of course, we thank all the children with whom we have worked and the parents who have entrusted their children to our care. Thanks also to all of our friends and to our families for their encouragement and patience. Finally, we acknowledge and thank Dr. Margery Miller (no relation), Director of the Graduate Reading Programs at Lesley College in Cambridge, Massachusetts, for recommending our authorship to Adams Media Corporation, and thank editors Cheryl Kimball, Linda Spencer, and Anne Weaver for their support.

SKILLS LIST

Generic skills covered in the range of activities presented include: visual discrimination, visual memory, auditory discrimination, auditory memory, listening comprehension, expressive language, receptive language, vocabulary development, fine motor skills (drawing, painting, cutting, coloring, writing), brainstorming, recording data, making comparisons, observation, and imaginative thinking. The language arts skills, by their very nature, are embedded in math, science, and social studies activities.

LANGUAGE ARTS

READING
Phonemic Awareness
Concepts of Print
Alphabet Awareness
Sight Word Recognition
Phonetic Analysis
Oral Reading
Silent Reading
Reading Comprehension
Literature Appreciation

WORD STUDY
Parts of Speech
Compound Words
Homonyms
Synonyms
Antonyms
Contractions
Plurals
Alliteration

WRITTEN EXPRESSION
Mechanics
Spelling
Sentence Structure
Writing Process
Story Form
Story Sequence
Poetry
Drawing

HANDWRITING
Letter Formation
Letter Recall
Spacing

MATH

NUMERATION & COUNTING
Number Awareness
Number Recognition
Connecting Math & Literature
Counting
Number Writing
Number Formation
Number Words
One-to-One Correspondence
Number Sequence
Calculator
Place Value
Equivalent Names
Number Patterns
Fractions

OPERATIONS & RELATIONS
Addition
Subtraction
Problem Solving
Number Relations

MEASURES & REFERENCE FRAMES
Time
Calendars
Ordinal Numbers
Length
Height
Weight
Temperature

EXPLORING DATA
Predicting
Estimating
Ordering
Tables & Graphs

GEOMETRY
Shapes
Symmetry
Polygons
Three-Dimensional Objects

MONEY
Coin Recognition
Coin Values
Dollars
Making Change
Coin Sorting

PATTERNS & ATTRIBUTES
Visual Patterns
Odds & Evens

SCIENCE
Brainstorming
Asking Questions
Observation
Surveying
Gathering Information
Identifying
Sorting
Classifying
Recording Data
Making Comparisons
Hypothesizing
Prediction
Experimentation
Measurement
Application
Symmetry
Constructing
Drawing Conclusions
Researching
Referential Writing
Connecting Science & Literature

SOCIAL STUDIES
Self-Awareness
Family Awareness
Community Awareness
Cultural Awareness
Respecting Human Differences
Interpreting Signs & Symbols
Map Skills

LANGUAGE ARTS

Welcome to first grade! It is September, the first day of school, and you are five or six years old. Mom and Dad hold your hand as you walk into your new classroom. Everywhere around you is print. You see your name on your cubby and desktop. You notice signs above the sink, on crates of books, beside the flag, above the windows, and next to boxes of pencils and crayons. Posters adorn the walls and colorful, inviting books stand open on shelves and tables. The clock ticks on the wall, the bell rings, Mom and Dad have to leave and it is time for you to learn new and exciting skills. You're a little scared, a bit overwhelmed. You wonder whether you'll be able to read those signs, posters, and books and whether you'll be able to write all those letters that come in two different shapes and sizes.

Can you remember the feeling you had as a first grader on the first day of school? We can. We had lumps the size of apples in our throats and needed to use every ounce of bravado to keep from crying and chasing our parents down the hall. Yet, we stayed and we learned and we thrived! Your child will, too!

First grade is a time of huge steps and quantum leaps. It is a time of joyful discovery and amazing firsts. It is a time to celebrate and nurture learning so that learning becomes a lifelong love. It is a time to join your child on a learning journey as your brave first grader sets out on a year of awakenings.

Formal instruction in language arts—specifically in reading, writing, spelling, and handwriting—begins in first grade. The goal of any language arts program is to develop and reinforce the array of skills necessary for purposeful and effective communication. With speaking and listening embedded in daily interactions at home, first graders continue to build not only confidence in speaking with others but also the ability to focus when others are speaking. This language that they have been using has been put to print, and grade one is the time to see that reading opens the world.

Learning to read begins with the belief that you can read. To develop fluent, excited, and successful readers, we present an integrated array of activities that encourages the use of rich literature and language, sight word recognition, phonetic analysis, and multisensory strategies. We emphasize that the best approach to teaching and supporting reading development is the balanced approach, the one that recognizes the developmental and learning needs of the individual child.

As you use the activities with your first grader, be aware of where your child is in the development of emerging literacy skills in both reading and writing. Select an alphabet activity to enjoy or find the rhymes in a bedtime story. Go fishing for short vowels or make a gameboard to reinforce the "stub-your-toe" /ow/ sound. Move from the concrete to the abstract as you draw conclusions or make straw puppets of a favorite book character. Build a diorama of a giant's castle or invite your child to a literary lunch. Make sandwich-bag sentences or write a story from a star.

Read, read, read, and write, write, write! Then read and write some more! Together, you and your child are certain to enjoy a rich and exciting year as you travel through first grade!

RHYME DOODLES

SKILLS: Phonemic Awareness/Rhyme/Drawing

Doodle a rhyme at any time to strengthen your child's ability to hear sounds, know their positions, and understand the role they play in words. Words that rhyme sound the same at the end.

Provide your child with drawing paper and crayons or markers. Show your first grader how to doodle a quick sketch to match a rhyming phrase. Try phrases such as "duck on a truck," "frog on a log," "mouse in a house," "cat in a hat," and "star in a jar"—one rhyme doodle per page.

Encourage your child to create more rhyme doodles independently. Then make a rhyme doodle book. Staple the pages together or punch a hole in the upper left corner of each page. Tie the pages together with yarn, ribbon, or string. Read the book together, saying the rhyming phrases as you turn the pages. Add this book to your child's library.

REQUIRED:
• Drawing paper
• Crayons or markers

OPTIONAL:
• Stapler
• Hole punch
• Yarn, ribbon, or string

FILL 'ER UP!

SKILLS: Phonemic Awareness/Rhyme

You can have great fun at home or on the road with this simple rhyming game. Make up a sentence in the form, "The basket is filled with cakes." Ask your child to repeat the sentence, replacing *cakes* with a word that rhymes. For example, your child may respond, "The basket is filled with steaks, rakes, snakes, mistakes . . ." Each participant takes a turn until no one can think of another rhyming word. Play again, changing the item in the basket. "The basket is filled with books, cooks, hooks, brooks . . ." To vary the game, change the container. Use the following sentences to get you started.

The pail is filled with rocks, socks, blocks, locks.
The sack is filled with rings, swings, strings, kings.
The trunk is filled with bugs, jugs, rugs, mugs.

REQUIRED:
• Your imagination

BEDTIME RHYME

SKILLS: Phonemic Awareness/Rhyme

Enjoy a few minutes together before lights out and build your child's sense of rhyme at the same time! Be ready at bedtime with a rhyming book that you've chosen from either your local library or your child's personal library. Some familiar favorites are *Sheep in a Jeep* by Nancy Shaw, *Is Your Mama a Llama?* by Deborah Guarino, *The Lady with the Alligator Purse* or *Skip to My Lou* by Nadine Westcott, or *Noisy Nora* by Rosemary Wells. Read the book once, enjoying the rhythm, rhyme, story, and illustrations. Read the book a second time, omitting rhyming words at the end of a line so that your child can fill in the missing word. From *Noisy Nora*, for example, you read,

Jack had dinner early,
Father played with Kate,
Jack needed burping,
So Nora had to _____.

REQUIRED:
• A rhyming book

OPTIONAL:
• Milk and cookies
• Library/bookstore visit

Your child chimes in, "Wait." Praise whatever suggestion your child makes. Sleep tight!

SOUND HUNT

SKILLS: Phonemic Awareness/Initial Consonant Sounds

Phonemic awareness is the awareness that a word is made up of individual sounds or phonemes. Strong phonemic awareness enhances reading development. Help your child master the sound of each consonant in the alphabet by having a sound hunt. Select eight to ten safe household items that begin with different consonant sounds. Show all the items to your child while identifying them by name and beginning sound. For example, hold up a basket and say, "Basket . . . /b/," "can . . . /k/," "dime . . . /d/," "fork . . . /f/," "gum . . . /g/," "hat . . . /h/," "jar . . . /j/," "lemon . . . /l/," "magazine . . . /m/," "notebook . . . /n/." Do not say the name of the letter but the sound that the letter makes. Ask your child to leave the room while you hide the items in a designated area. When your child returns, ask your sound hunter to find the item that begins with, for example, /b/, voice the sound of *b*. As each item is retrieved, your child names the item and voices the beginning sound. Happy hunting!

REQUIRED:
• A collection of safe household items

GIVE ME A BREAK!

SKILLS: Phonemic Awareness/Initial Sounds/Final Sounds

Imagine what life would be like if initial sounds decided to take a break! A trip to the *park* . . . visit the *ark!* Feed the *cow* . . . milk the *ow!* Wash the *dishes* . . . dry the *ishes!* Set the *table* . . . clear the *able!* Engage your child in creative wordplay by suggesting that the first sound heard in a word take a break!

Say a word. Ask your child to repeat the word. Then ask your child to repeat the word without the initial sound. For example, you say, "Noodle." Your child says, "Noodle." Now tell your child to say "noodle" without the /n/ . . . "oodle." You say, "Pizza." Your child says, "Pizza." Tell your child to say "pizza" without the /p/ . . . "izza."

For variation, let the final consonants take a break. Repeat the procedure, asking your child to say a word without the final sound. For example, tell your child to say "bark" without the /k/ . . . "bar."

When the letters take a break, you'll have lots of fun and build sound awareness, too!

REQUIRED:
• Your time

WHERE DO YOU HEAR . . .?

SKILLS: Phonemic Awareness/Initial Sounds/Medial Sounds/Final Sounds

It is important for beginning readers to hear where a sound occurs within a word. Sit beside your child at a table. Place three cups or bowls before you. Show your child that the cup on the left represents the beginning sound of a word; the cup in the middle, the middle sound; and the cup on the right, the ending sound.

Give your child a supply of game markers. Say a word, for example, "pig." Ask your child, "Where do you hear /p/?" Be sure you say the sound of the letter, not the name of the letter. Your child responds, "I hear /p/ at the beginning of 'pig.'" Your first grader then drops a marker into the cup on the left. Ask, "Where do you hear /i/?" Your child responds, "I hear /i/ in the middle of 'pig'" and drops a marker into the middle cup. Ask, "Where do you hear /g/?" Your child responds, "I hear /g/ at the end of 'pig'" and drops a marker into the cup at the right.

Present other three-sound words, requesting the sounds out of order to give your child practice in phonemic awareness.

REQUIRED:
• Three cups or bowls
• Beads, buttons, or raisins as markers

BREAKFAST BOOK BROWSE

SKILL: Concepts of Print

Lead your child to an understanding of concepts of print over breakfast! Sit down with your child, at home or in a restaurant, with a book. During the course of the meal, examine the book together. Look at the front cover and the back. Point out the title, the author's name, and, if applicable, the illustrator's name. Inside the book, examine and talk about concepts of print, including top of the page, bottom of the page, left side of the page, and right side of the page. Ask your child to point to a letter, a word, a sentence. Encourage your first grader to show you the beginning of a page and the end of the page. Look at the uppercase letter at the start of each sentence. View the punctuation at the end of each sentence—period, question mark, exclamation point. Look at the location of illustrations in relation to the print. Then, before finishing breakfast, read the story aloud.

REQUIRED:
- A book
- Breakfast

OPTIONAL:
- Library/bookstore visit

ALL ABOARD

SKILLS: Alphabet Awareness/Drawing

All aboard the Alphabet Train! Create an ABC train with 4″ × 6″ index cards and yarn. Begin with *Aa*. Draw a horizontal line to divide the index card in half. Clearly print *Aa* on the lower half. Ask your child to draw and color a picture of something that begins with *Aa* on the upper half. Make a hole in each corner of the card. Repeat the process for *Bb*. Connect the *Aa* car to the *Bb* car with yarn. Continue through the alphabet until twenty-six cars have been created, making two to three cars per day.

Finally, invite your child to make an engine and a caboose from construction paper. Punch a hole in the upper and lower right-hand corners of the engine to connect it to the *Aa* car. Punch a hole in the upper and lower left-hand corners of the caboose to connect it to the *Zz* car. Enjoy reading the Alphabet Train. Fold accordion style for easy storage.

REQUIRED:
- Index cards
- Yarn/string/ribbon
- Safety scissors
- Crayons/markers
- Construction paper
- Hole punch

ALL ON A PAGE

SKILLS: Alphabet Awareness/Letter Recognition

First graders need to become as familiar with letters as they are with crayons and pencils. The more exposure to print, the better! Send your child on an alphabet hunt without even leaving the room!

Open a newspaper or magazine on the table or floor. Ask your young explorer to search for each letter of the alphabet. Either call out the letters one by one and work as a team or have your child work independently on one page while you work on another. Circle all letters found, *Aa* to *Zz*. Review your findings to determine whether all 26 letters were found. Note those missing. Turn to another page and continue the exploration until the alphabet hunt is complete.

REQUIRED:
- Newspaper or magazine
- Pen, pencil, or marker

GIVE ME AN A

SKILLS: Alphabet Awareness/Letter Recognition

Three cheers for the ABCs! Spread letter cards or plastic, rubber, or magnetic letters in mixed order on the table or floor. Call out, in alphabetical order first and then random order, a letter name. For example, say, "Give me an *A*." Your child then searches for the *A* and hands it over. Continue in this manner, practicing individual letter names.

Add to the fun by calling out letters in order to spell a word. Keep blank letter cards and a marker handy for words with repeated letters. For example, spell your child's name, a letter at a time. As your first grader hands over the letters, place them in sequence on the table. Say, "Give me an *R*, an *A*, a *C*, an *H*, an *E*, and an *L*. What have we got? RACHEL!" Invite your child to call out the letters, spelling names and words he or she knows.

REQUIRED:
- Letter cards
- Marker

OPTIONAL:
- Plastic, rubber, or magnetic letters

AS EASY AS ABC

SKILLS: Alphabet Awareness/Letter Recognition

What letter is *lmno* or *ynz?* Children often sing or recite the alphabet by rote, not yet associating a letter name with a printed letter. Help your child to make that association! Sit beside your child at a table. Place 26 individual letter cards in sequential order across the table before you. Point to each letter as you sing the alphabet together. Point to each letter as you say the alphabet together. Now point to each letter as your child says the name of the letter.

When your child can name the individual letters in sequence, go a step further. Keeping the letter cards in sequence on the table, point to a letter at random and ask your child to tell you its name. Reverse the process as well. Ask your child to point to a letter so that you can name it! It's as easy as ABC!

REQUIRED:
• 26 letter cards

OPTIONAL:
• Plastic, rubber, or magnetic letters

ABC JUMBLE

SKILLS: Alphabetical Order/Letter Recognition

Putting the letters of the alphabet in order is like putting a puzzle together. Sit beside your child at a table. Start with *A.* Place the first six letters of the alphabet before you in alphabetical order. Use homemade letter cards or, if available, plastic, rubber, or magnetic letters. Call out, "ABC Jumble," and join your child in jumbling the order of the letters. Then ask your child to put the letters back in order. On completion, read the six letters together, pointing to each letter as it is named. Repeat the process, adding the next six letters of the alphabet. Work toward the goal of sequencing all 26 letters of the alphabet.

REQUIRED:
• 26 letter cards

OPTIONAL:
• Plastic, rubber, or magnetic letters
• Unpopped bag of microwave popcorn

To add to the fun, turn ABC Jumble into a race. Set a timer to an agreed upon limit and go! Or, to provide a big incentive, race a bag of microwave popcorn! Try to complete the reordering of the letters before the popcorn is done!

ABC LINEUPS

SKILLS: Alphabetical Order/Letter Recognition

Try a range of ABC Lineups to show your child that words in alphabetical order are listed in the order letters appear in the alphabet.

Begin with a telephone book or dictionary. Flip through the pages, pointing out that words on a page all begin with the same letter as the guide words at the top. Move from one letter to the next, asking your child to predict what will come next.

Next, print one uppercase letter on a piece of paper. Write four words beneath the letter, three that start with the letter and one that doesn't. For example, beneath *S* write, "sat," "sing," "red," and "soft." Ask your child to cross out the word that doesn't begin with *S*. Repeat the procedure with each letter of the alphabet.

Now write three words in a list, for example, "hop," "dog," and "tree." Ask your child to circle the word that comes first in ABC order. Then ask your child either to number the words or write the words in ABC order.

REQUIRED:
- Telephone book or dictionary
- Pencil and paper

Finally, challenge your first grader with lists of three words that begin with the same letter, "big," "ball," and "blue" or "flag," "foot," and "fan." Put each list in ABC order by the second letter!

LETTER IN THE LIMELIGHT

SKILLS: Letter Recognition/Map Skills/Drawing/Brainstorming/Classifying

Each letter of the alphabet deserves time in the limelight! Follow the alphabet in sequence or select letters in random order to strengthen your child's letter recognition ability by focusing on a letter a week.

Choose a letter. Print the letter clearly in both uppercase and lowercase on a piece of paper. Post in a place of prominence. Introduce your child to Mr. A, Mrs. B, Ms. C, Lord D, Lady E, Dr. F, Sir G. Bring the letters to life! Have fun with them. Then, during the course of the week, focus on the Letter in the Limelight. For example, during *Aa* week, eat apples and read books such as *Arthur's Tooth* by Marc Brown or *Amelia Bedelia* by Peggy Parish. Use maps or a globe to identify *A* states (Alaska, Alabama, Arkansas, Arizona), *A* continents (Asia, Africa, Australia, Antarctica), or *A* countries (Austria, Argentina, Antigua, Afghanistan). Look for pictures of things that begin with *A*. Talk about astronomy and astronauts. Draw pictures of things that begin with *A*. Brainstorm categories of words that begin with *A*—fruits, vegetables, animals. Anything goes! Have lots of fun over the course of 26 weeks!

REQUIRED:
- Your time

OPTIONAL:
- Library/bookstore visit
- Paper and pencil
- Crayons/markers

GRAB BAG O' LETTERS

SKILL: Letter Recognition

Every letter has a partner. For this game, you need 52 index cards, 26 for the uppercase letters and 26 for the lower. Clearly print, one letter per card, the uppercase letters from *A* to *Z*. Place them in a paper shopping bag. Clearly print, one letter per card, the lowercase letters from *a* to *z*. Spread these cards face up on the table or floor, either in sequential or random order. Shake up the letter cards in the bag. Have your child reach in, grab one uppercase letter, and name it. Provide assistance if needed.

Your first grader then finds the partner letter to make a match. Continue play until all letters have been matched.

As an option, put the lowercase letters in the bag and the uppercase letters on the playing area. As a second option, mix the upper and lowercase letter cards, putting half in the bag and half on the playing area. At the end of the game, ask your child to read the letters.

REQUIRED:
- Index cards
- Marker
- Bag

OPTIONAL:
- Plastic, magnetic, or rubber letters

LETTER SOUND DRILL

SKILLS: Phonetic Analysis/Symbol to Sound

Strengthen your child's knowledge of the relationship between sound and symbol with this Letter Sound Drill. Make a lowercase letter card for each letter of the alphabet. Sit opposite your child. Start with the cards in alphabetical order. Show a card. Ask your child to name the letter on the card and then say the sound the letter makes. For the vowels, focus on the short sounds: *a* as in "cat," *e* as in "bed," *i* as in "tip," *o* as in "hot," *u* as in "tug." For example, flash the *a* card. Your child says, "A says /a/." Flash the *b* card. Your child says, "B says /b/."

Try the same activity with cards presented in random order. In five minutes, you will have reviewed all letters and sounds, reinforcing the symbol-to-sound relationship.

REQUIRED:
- 26 index cards
- Marker

SOUND STREET

SKILL: Symbol to Sound

Travel Sound Street from start to finish to develop and reinforce your child's awareness of the sound of each consonant. Work with your child to make a gameboard from a file folder. Open the folder horizontally. In the upper left-hand corner, draw a one-inch square. Label it "Start." In the lower right-hand corner, draw another one-inch square. Label this square "Finish." Now build Sound Street by drawing 20 to 30 connecting squares between Start and Finish. Make the street a winding one. In five selected squares, write messages such as, "Good Thinking, Move Ahead 2" or "Oops, Miss 1 Turn." Next, make a deck of consonant cards, one card for each of the 21 consonants. Finally, use buttons or coins as game pieces.

Take turns drawing the top card from the deck of consonant cards. Say the name of the letter and voice the sound it makes. For each sound correctly voiced, roll the die and move that number of spaces. Alternate turns. The first player to reach Finish is the winner. Decorate the gameboard with drawings or stickers. Fold the file for easy storage.

REQUIRED:
- File folder
- Crayons/markers
- Buttons or coins
- Die

OPTIONAL:
- Stickers

LETTER BALL

SKILLS: Letter Recognition/Symbol to Sound/Initial and Final Sounds/Alliteration

A beach ball does more than bounce when you use it to heighten your child's awareness of letters and sounds! Blow up a beach ball. Use a permanent marker to write the letters of the alphabet, *Aa, Bb, Cc,* and so forth, in random order all over the ball. Then let the games begin!

Toss or roll the ball from player to player. The player catches the ball, names the letter under each hand, voices the sound of each letter, and says a word that begins with each letter. Or, catch the ball, name the letter under each hand, voice the sound of each letter, and say a word that ends with each letter.

For extra fun, try tongue-twister Letter Ball. Toss or roll the ball from player to player. The player catches the ball, looks at the letter under each hand, and chooses one of the letters to turn into a tongue twister. For example, find a *D* under your left hand and say, "Dizzy dogs dance!" When the initial sound of each word in a phrase is the same, you have created a figure of speech called alliteration.

REQUIRED:
- Beach ball
- Permanent marker

NOODLE NAMES

SKILLS: Letter Formation/Spelling

Choose a noodle and take out the glue! To help your child know and sequence the letters of his or her name, make Noodle Names together. Work on heavy cardboard. Begin by helping your child form only the first letter with glue. Place uncooked noodles on the wet glue before moving on to the next letter. Repeat the process until your child has "written" all the letters in noodles. You may want to make your noodle name as well. Dry on a flat surface.

Add pizzazz by painting or food coloring your noodles before or after writing the noodle names. You may also want to paint the cardboard area around the name. Your child may want to hang the noodle name on his or her bedroom door. You can hang yours on your bedroom door, too!

REQUIRED:
- Uncooked noodles
- Nontoxic glue
- Cardboard

OPTIONAL:
- Paint/paintbrush
- Food coloring

WRITE 'N' SHAKE

SKILLS: Letter Recall/Letter Formation

Let your fingers do the writing! Use the sense of touch to strengthen letter recall and letter formation. Cover the bottom of a rectangular plastic container with a quarter-inch layer of a granular substance such as salt. Be sure the sides of the container are no more than one inch high.

Seat your child at a table or desk appropriate for writing. Place the container vertically before your young writer. Hold up the index finger of your writing hand. Then say a letter, write the letter in the salt with your finger, look at the letter, and shake the box. Now ask your child to hold up his or her writing finger. Say a letter, specifying uppercase or lowercase. For example say, "Please write uppercase *B*." Ask your child to repeat the letter name and use his or her index finger to "write" the letter, forming it from top to bottom and left to right, in the salt. Confirm that the letter written is correct. Ask your child to shake the container gently to clear the salt for the next letter.

REQUIRED:
- Rectangular plastic container with cover
- Sugar, salt, sand, cocoa powder, dry Jell-O®, dry pudding

COOKIES A TO Z

SKILLS: Letter Recall/ Letter Formation/Letter Recognition

Munch and crunch from *A* to *Z* by making and baking cookies in the shape of the letters of the alphabet. Using slice and bake dough or a favorite sugar cookie recipe, roll the cold cookie dough into strips of varying lengths. Use the strips to form letters, uppercase or lowercase. For letters such as *O, C,* and *S,* use a single strip. For letters such as *A, M,* and *N,* use multiple strips. You may want to decorate your cookies before baking or frost them after baking. In either case, read before eating and enjoy!

REQUIRED:
• Sugar cookie dough

OPTIONAL:
• Colored sugar/ nonpareils/sprinkles
• Frosting

STICKY LETTERS

SKILLS: Letter Recall/Letter Formation/Letter Recognition

Use sight, touch, and creativity to build and strengthen your child's letter-recognition ability. Choose a medium and be creative!

Start with glue letters. Use nontoxic craft glue to form a letter on construction paper or oak tag. Allow the glue to dry and voila! You have a raised letter to touch and read. Make one for each letter of the alphabet, uppercase and lowercase.

Follow the same process and add flair to the letters while the glue is still wet. Sprinkle glitter on the glue. Try colorful confetti, beads, buttons, bits of cotton, or pieces of bright tissue paper. Display the letters for all family members to enjoy as your first grader recognizes and reads the letters from *A* to *Z*.

REQUIRED:
• Nontoxic glue
• Construction paper or oak tag

OPTIONAL:
• Glitter
• Confetti
• Cottonballs
• Tissue paper
• Beads, buttons

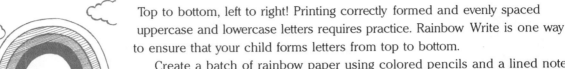

RAINBOW WRITE

SKILL: Letter Formation

Top to bottom, left to right! Printing correctly formed and evenly spaced uppercase and lowercase letters requires practice. Rainbow Write is one way to ensure that your child forms letters from top to bottom.

Create a batch of rainbow paper using colored pencils and a lined notebook or pad. Ask your child to choose three favorite colors, for example, orange, green, and purple. Use an orange marker or pencil to trace the first line of the paper, green to trace the second line and purple to trace the third.

Skip a line and begin again, following the same pattern to the bottom of the page. End with the last complete pattern of orange, green, and purple.

Now Rainbow Write! Show your child that the uppercase letters need to start at the orange line and come down to purple. Many of the lowercase letters, with the exception of *b, d, f, h, k, l,* and *t* start at the green line and move to purple. Some, *g, j, p, q,* and *y* move from green to below the purple line. The colors serve as a visual aid for writing upper and lowercase letters.

REQUIRED:
- Lined paper
- Colored pencils/markers
- Pencil

WHICH ONE IS B?

SKILLS: Letter Recall/Letter Formation/Letter Recognition/Visual Discrimination

If your child is confusing *b* with *d,* try these concrete helpers. More often than not, the letter reversals will disappear!

Place your hands, thumbs up, palms facing you, fingers touching, before you. Keeping your thumb up, close your left hand into a fist. Notice that your hand makes a lowercase *b.* Now do the same with your right hand to make *d!* Move your fisted hands together so that your knuckles touch. You've made a "bed," *b* the headboard, *d* the foot. Use the index finger of your right hand to trace the *b,* starting at the top of your thumb. Use the index finger of your left hand to trace the *d.*

Another self-check is to print a lowercase *b* on a piece of paper. Turn it into an uppercase *B* by adding a stroke at the top.

Finally, remind your child that *b* faces *d* and *d* faces *b.* Write *b c d* on a piece of paper. Draw a profile on *b,* adding an eye, a nose, and a mouth. Draw a profile on *d* in the same manner. Point out that *b* and *d* look at each other in the alphabet.

Encourage your child to use these helpers at home and at school.

REQUIRED:
- Paper and pencil

MIND YOUR *P*'S AND *Q*'S!

SKILLS: Letter Recall/Letter Formation/Letter Recognition/Visual Discrimination

Are *p*'s and *q*'s giving your first grader trouble? Share these concrete helpers to keep the letters straight!

Print *l m n o p q r s t* on a piece of paper. Draw an eye, a nose, and a mouth to make a profile on *p* and a profile on *q*. Now say this little rhyme along with your child while pointing to the letters.

l   m   n   o   p faces *q   r   s   t!*

Repeat the rhyme often enough so that your child automatically recites it when stuck on a *p* or *q* when reading or writing.

REQUIRED:
• Paper and pencil

A CAMEL CAN HELP

SKILLS: Letter Recall/Letter Formation/Letter Recognition/Visual Discrimination

Sometimes an *m* is inverted to *w* and an *n* is inverted to *u*.

A camel can help! Share these concrete reminders as your child reads and writes.

For *m*, remember that a ca*m*el has two rounded humps just like the humps on the *m* in "camel." Draw a long neck and head coming off the first stroke of *m*, and a tail coming off the final stroke of *m*. Draw four legs at the base of *m* to complete the camel.

For *w*, remember that *w*ater is inside a *w*ell. Note that the *w*, whether made with curves or sharp angles, needs to "hold the water." The opening must be on top!

For *n*, remember that a *n*urse is someone who always smiles. Draw a smiling face in the center of *n*, the sides of the letter making the hair. Add a hat to the top of the *n* and a bow tie at the base.

For *u*, remember that the *u* in the middle of every "c*u*p" needs to be open on top to hold a drink.

Encourage your child to use these helpful reminders at home and at school.

REQUIRED:
• Paper and pencil

TWO FINGERS

SKILLS: Handwriting/Spacing

Two fingers go a long way in helping your child produce well-spaced and organized written work. Children often write without paying attention to space on the line or the page. While ruled paper helps with the spacing on the page, two fingers help with placement of words on the line.

Whenever you join in a writing activity, encourage your child to place two fingers in vertical position at the end of one word to ensure proper spacing between words on the line. If right-handed, your child should use the index and middle fingers of his or her left hand to block out the space before writing the next word. If left-handed, your child should use the index and middle fingers of the right hand to block out the space before writing the next word. When your first grader gets into the habit of leaving spaces between words, two fingers can take a rest!

REQUIRED:
- Lined paper
- Pencil

NO FRILLS FLASH

SKILL: Sight Word Recognition

Beginning readers use many skills when learning to read. It is the balanced combination of these skills that makes an effective reader. Sight word recognition is just one of the developing skills in first grade. Children add daily to the treasury of words they recognize and read by their constant exposure to frequently occurring words.

No Frills Flash is a quick and easy way to support your child's sight word recognition ability. Be aware of the words your child sees regularly and reads. Write these words on index cards, one word per card. Keep them in a small box. Provide flash card drill often, selecting words at random from the box, holding them up, and asking your child to read.

No Frills Flash can also be used to practice words that follow specific phonetic rules. Make and use flash cards at any time for any skill.

REQUIRED:
- Index cards
- Marker
- Small box

WORD BANK: we, love, each, kind, by, give, from, out, of, high, then, there, was, little, under, this, around, where, mine, our, what, after, about, again, when, could, should, would, were, said, the, ever, you, went, many, because, every, again, about, today, walk

TREASURE CHEST OF WORDS

SKILL: Sight Word Recognition

Open up the treasure chest and pull out another gem! The gems are words that your child is learning to recognize by sight. All you need to get started are index cards and a small box. Gather materials your child can use to decorate the box as a treasure chest. Buttons, shiny wrapping paper, plastic beads, small shells, or any other kind of knickknack will excite your young reader. Completed, the treasure chest serves as an inviting tool for collecting, saving, reviewing, reinforcing, and mastering a growing list of personally chosen words. At any time and repeatedly, ask your child to add to the chest. The words printed on index cards by either you or your child can be words your child already knows, words your first grader is eager to learn, or words that you feel are important for your child to learn. Take the "gems" from the treasure chest often for sight word reading drills and practice.

REQUIRED:
- Index cards
- Box
- Buttons, wrapping paper, plastic beads, small shells, knickknacks
- Pencil/marker/crayon
- Nontoxic glue
- Safety scissors

PITCH-A-WORD

SKILL: Sight Word Recognition

Warm up your pitching arm for sight word recognition fun! This interactive game is easy to make, flexible, and an exciting way to reinforce early reading skills.

Divide a large piece of construction paper or poster board into six equal sections. Within each section, print one sight word. Write the word large enough for your child to see from several feet away. Now you are ready to play!

Place the gameboard on the floor three to five feet in front of you. Take turns pitching the beanbag so that it lands in one of the word squares. After the toss, the pitcher retrieves the beanbag and reads the word. If the beanbag lands on a line or misses the board, the pitcher can toss again. You may play for points, one point scored for each word read correctly. Select words from the word bank provided or use words that your child wants to know. Play often, using new words.

REQUIRED:
- Construction paper/ poster board
- Ruler/yardstick
- Marker
- Beanbag

WORD BANK: and, with, can, jump, down, here, said, up, I, look, big, go, we, is, red, for, me, the, my, oh, am, came, eat, good, she, he, they, was, pet, help, away, boy, girl

A+ ACTIVITIES FOR FIRST GRADE

SIGHT WORD SCAVENGER HUNT

SKILL: Sight Word Recognition

Search for word cards both indoors and out! Your child can reinforce sight word vocabulary and have a great time, too! To prepare for the hunt, write sight words on index cards, one word per card. Choose words from the bank below. Start with five to ten cards. Depending on the weather and time of year, hide the cards throughout your home or yard in safe and accessible places. Challenge your child to find each word as you say it. For example, if you say *"monkey,"* your child must find and return the "monkey" card. When your child has found all words, invite your first grader to challenge you by hiding the cards and asking you to find them. Play again, increasing the number of word cards hidden.

REQUIRED:
- Index cards
- Marker
- Plastic bag or index card box for storage

WORD BANK: know, surprise, to, again, bear, call, ball, from, head, monkey, two, water, one, friend, enough, grow, there, where, what, who, said, says, should, would, could, Mr., Mrs., some, come, put, any, whose, four, eight, have, done, gone, of, you, are, your, into, were, do, many, does, very, once, give, live

OLD FAVORITE WITH A NEW TWIST

SKILL: Sight Word Recognition

Everyone loves a good game of Go Fish, especially with a new twist. To strengthen sight word recognition, make a deck of 21 *pairs* of sight words using index cards cut in half. Select the words from your child's reading vocabulary.

Deal five cards to each player, placing the extras in the fish pile in the center of the playing area. Play begins to the left of the dealer and continues clockwise. In turn, each player asks a specific opponent for a word. If the opponent has the word, the opponent hands it over. The asker puts the pair face up on the table and goes again. If the opponent does not have the word, the opponent says, "Go fish." The asker takes a card from the fish pile in the center. Play continues until all cards from the fish pile are gone or one of the players uses all of his or her cards. The winner is the player with the most pairs. At the end of the game, enjoy reading all the words together.

REQUIRED:
- Index cards
- Safety scissors
- Marker
- Plastic bag for storage

As your child's reading vocabulary grows, add cards to the deck.

POLLY WANT TO READ?

SKILLS: Oral Reading Fluency/Oral Reading Expression/Sight Word Recognition

Parrots do a good job imitating language and children do, too! Parrot reading is a terrific way to build sight word vocabulary and to enhance your child's oral reading fluency and expression. Choose a book together, one that is written at a comfortable reading level for your child. Read the book aloud to your child, pointing to the words as you read. Read expressively, perhaps using different voices for the characters. Discuss the story while you are reading and at completion. Then begin Parrot Reading. Go back to the beginning of the book. Use a finger or marker to keep place across the line and down the page. Read a single line or sentence. Provide time for your child to repeat the line as you move your finger or the marker across the page. Continue in this manner, encouraging your young reader to follow your lead.

REQUIRED:
• A book
OPTIONAL:
• Library/bookstore visit

OOPS!

SKILLS: Phonetic Analysis/Oral Reading Fluency

"Oops! Mom, Dad, you made a mistake!" Let your child take the role of teacher! Choose a short book to read to your child. Be sure that your selection is one that your child can read with ease. Before you begin, tell your child that you are tired and might make some mistakes. You need help. Remind your child to follow the words across the line and down the page as you read aloud. As you read, insert an occasional mistake. For example, read the line, "Jam is the thing that I like most," from the book *Bread and Jam for Frances* by Russell Hoban, as "*Jum* is the thing that I like most." Your child should recognize from meaning, hearing the word, and looking at the text that you made a mistake in reading "jam" as "jum." If your child doesn't recognize the error, ask, "Did that make sense? Let's look again." These are mistakes you'll be glad to make!

REQUIRED:
• A book
OPTIONAL:
• Library/bookstore visit

CONSONANT CARD PLAY BEGINS

SKILL: Initial Consonant Sound Recognition

Twenty-one consonant cards go a long way! Strengthen your child's recognition of initial consonant sounds by playing this simple card game. Make a lowercase letter card for each consonant: *b, c, d, f, g, h, j, k, l, m, n, p, q, r, s, t, v, w, x, y,* and *z.* Sit opposite your child. Place cards face down in a pile. Pick a card. Don't show the card to your child. Say a word that begins with that letter. Ask your child to name the letter heard at the beginning of the word. For example, pick the letter *m.* Say, "What letter do you hear at the beginning of 'map'?" Your child responds, "I hear *m* at the beginning of 'map.'"

Continue until all cards have been used. You may want to take turns picking cards.

Variation: Pick a card. Show the card to your child. Ask your first grader to say the letter name, voice the letter sound, and say a word that begins with the letter. For example, hold up the *b.* Your child says, "*B,* /b/, boy." Continue until all cards have been used. You may want to take turns picking cards.

REQUIRED:
• Index cards
• Pencil/marker

CONSONANT CARD PLAY ENDS

SKILL: Final Consonant Sound Recognition

Where there's a beginning, there's an end! Strengthen your child's recognition of final consonant sounds by playing this simple card game. Make a lowercase letter card for each consonant: *b, c, d, f, g, h, j, k, l, m, n, p, q, r, s, t, v, w, x, y,* and *z.* Sit opposite your child. Place cards face down in a pile. Pick a card. Don't show the card to your child. Say a word that ends with that letter. Ask your child to name the letter heard at the end of the word. For example, pick the letter *t.* Say, "What letter do you hear at the end of 'hot'?" Your child responds, "I hear *t* at the end of 'hot.' Continue until all cards have been used. You may want to take turns picking cards.

Variation: Pick a card. Show the card to your first grader. Ask your child to say the letter name, voice the letter sound, and say a word that ends with the letter. For example, hold up the *d.* Your child says, "*D,* /d/, mud." Continue until all cards have been used. You may want to take turns picking cards.

REQUIRED:
• Index cards
• Pencil/marker

SUPERSTARS

SKILLS: Phonetic Analysis/Vowel Awareness/Vowel Recognition/Cutting

Without vowels there would be no words! Beginning readers need to remember for reading and writing that every word must include at least one of the five superstars: *a, e, i, o,* and *u.*

Put the vowels in the spotlight in several ways. First, write one on the tip of each finger of your child's hand. Introduce the superstars one at a time as your first grader holds up each finger. Second, write the alphabet on a piece of paper. Search for the five superstar vowels. Draw a star around each one. Next, write each vowel in the center of a separate piece of paper. Draw a star in glue around each vowel. Sprinkle the wet glue with glitter to emphasize star status. Finally, cut five stars from construction paper. In the center of each star, print one lowercase vowel. Punch a hole in the top point and hang in a place of prominence with yarn or ribbon. With this kind of publicity, the vowels are sure to make an impression!

REQUIRED:
- Construction paper
- Writing paper
- Markers/crayons/pencil
- Safety scissors
- Nontoxic glue
- Glitter
- Ribbon/yarn
- Hole punch

ABBY APPLE WITH AN A

SKILLS: Phonetic Analysis/Short *a*/Cutting/Drawing/Brainstorming

Abby Apple is eager to help your child master the sound of short *a* as in "Abby" and "Apple." Work with your child to bring Abby to life by cutting two 12″ × 18″ pieces of red construction paper into the shape of an apple. Staple, tape, or glue the two apples together, leaving the top open to make a pocket. Cut and attach a stem from brown paper and two leaves from green. Next add a face, either drawing or cutting and attaching eyes, nose, and mouth. Finally, print "Aa" on the stem or leaves.

Now brainstorm words with short *a* either at the beginning, as in "add," "alligator," "ant," and "avenue," or in the middle, as in "cab," "dad," "rag," "pal," "ham," "fan," "tap," and "sat." Print these words on index cards and use repeatedly for practice and reinforcement. Add cards often and store in the Abby Apple pocket.

REQUIRED:
- Red construction paper
- Green construction paper
- Brown construction paper
- Safety scissors
- Tape, stapler, or nontoxic glue
- Index cards
- Pencil/marker

ED ELEPHANT WITH AN *E*

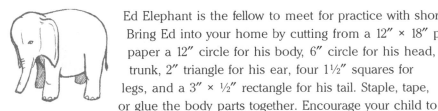

SKILLS: Phonetic Analysis/Short *e*/Cutting/Drawing/Brainstorming

Ed Elephant is the fellow to meet for practice with short *e* as in "Ed" and "Elephant." Bring Ed into your home by cutting from a 12″ × 18″ piece of gray construction paper a 12″ circle for his body, 6″ circle for his head, 5″ × 1″ rectangle for his trunk, 2″ triangle for his ear, four 1½″ squares for legs, and a 3″ × ½″ rectangle for his tail. Staple, tape, or glue the body parts together. Encourage your child to draw Ed's eye and mouth. Then cut and attach a 6″ square of brightly colored construction paper to the center of Ed's body, leaving the top open as a pocket. Print "Ee" on the center of the pocket.

Brainstorm words with short *e* either at the beginning, as in "egg," "end," "elf," and "elk," or in the middle, as in "bed," "leg," "sell," "pen," and "met." Print these words on index cards and use repeatedly for practice and reinforcement. Add cards often and store in Ed Elephant's pocket.

REQUIRED:
- Gray construction paper
- Colored construction paper
- Safety scissors
- Tape, stapler, or nontoxic glue
- Index cards
- Pencil/marker

IZZY INSECT WITH AN *I*

SKILLS: Phonetic Analysis/Short *i*/Cutting/Drawing/Brainstorming

Izzy Insect is one bug you'll want in your home! Create this short *i* helper by cutting two 12″ circles for the body from 12″ × 18″ colored construction paper. Staple, tape, or glue the circles together, leaving the top open to make a pocket. Next cut one 6″ circle for the head, two 4″ × 1″ rectangles for antennae, and six 2″ × ¾″ rectangles for legs. Staple, tape, or glue the body parts together. Use markers or crayons to make a face. Print "Ii" in the center of the body. Make your Izzy one of a kind by adding stripes, dots, or squiggles!

Now brainstorm words with short *i* either at the beginning, as in "inch," "igloo," "if," and "it," or in the middle, as in "big," "hid," "rip," "pin," "fib," "sit," and "trim." Print these words on index cards and use repeatedly for practice and reinforcement. For extra fun, hide the cards. Ask your child to find and read each one! Add cards often and store in the Izzy Insect pocket.

REQUIRED:
- Construction paper
- Safety scissors
- Tape, stapler, or nontoxic glue
- Index cards
- Pencil/marker

OSCAR OCTOPUS WITH AN O

SKILLS: Phonetic Analysis/Short *o*/Cutting/Drawing/Brainstorming

Eight tentacles are on hand as Oscar Octopus helps your child master the sound of short *o*. Cut two 12″ circles for the body from 12″ × 18″ colored construction paper to make this short *o* friend. Staple, tape, or glue the circles together, leaving the top open to make a pocket. Next cut eight 6″ to 10″ tentacles. Attach the tentacles to the base of the body. Print *"Oo"* in the center of the body to serve as Oscar's nose and a freckle. Add eyes and a mouth with construction paper or markers/crayons. Encourage your child to make Oscar special by adding dots, squiggles, or stripes.

Now brainstorm words with short *o* either at the beginning, as in "October," "olive," "ox," and "odd," or in the middle, as in "pod," "log," "mop," "cob," "hot," and "mom." Print these words on index cards to use for flash card practice. For extra fun, play short *o* hopscotch, substituting the word cards for the eight numbers on the hopscotch board. Store the cards in the Oscar Octopus pocket.

REQUIRED:
- Construction paper
- Safety scissors
- Tape, stapler, or nontoxic glue
- Index cards
- Pencil/marker

OPTIONAL:
- Hopscotch board

UMBY UMBRELLA WITH A U

SKILLS: Phonetic Analysis/Short *u*/Cutting/Drawing/Brainstorming

With Umby Umbrella you don't need a rainstorm to master the sound of short *u*. Cut one 12″ circle from 12″ × 18″ colored construction paper. Fold the circle in half. Staple, tape or glue the resulting semicircle, leaving the top open to make a pocket. Next cut an 8″ × 2″ handle in the shape of the letter *J*. Attach the handle to the base of the umbrella. Print "Uu" in the center of the umbrella. Add eyes and a mouth with construction paper or markers/crayons. Decorate the umbrella around the face.

Now brainstorm words with short *u* either at the beginning, as in "under," "up," and "us," or in the middle, as in "tub," "bud," "rug," "hum," "sun," "pup," "bus," and "hut." Print these words on index cards to use for flashcard practice. For extra fun, fling the cards in the air to make a short *u* rainstorm. Ask your child to pick up each card and read each one. Store cards in the Umby Umbrella pocket.

REQUIRED:
- Construction paper
- Safety scissors
- Tape, stapler, or nontoxic glue
- Index cards
- Pencil/marker

A+ ACTIVITIES FOR FIRST GRADE

UP, UP, AND AWAY

SKILLS: Phonetic Analysis/Short Vowels/Rhyme/Cutting

Fly high with five short vowels: /a/ in "cat," /e/ in "bed," /i/ in "pig," /o/ in "hop," and /u/ in "sun." Make short vowel kites to reinforce your child's awareness of short vowel sounds and strengthen his or her ability to read three-letter words with short vowels.

Cut a kite from construction paper. In the center of the kite, print "a." Attach a piece of string or yarn, 3′ to 5′ long, to the base of the kite. Next, cut paper bows for the kite string. The color of the bows should match the color of the kite. On the left side of each bow, write one three-letter word with short *a* in the middle. On the right side of the same bow, write a rhyming word. For example, the bows on the short *a* kite string might read "rag/bag," "ram/jam," and "map/tap." Attach the bows to the kite string. Hang the kite and encourage your child to read the words often. Add short *a* bows at any time. Repeat the process for each vowel.

REQUIRED:
- Construction paper
- Safety scissors
- String/yarn/ribbon
- Stapler/tape/nontoxic glue
- Marker/crayons

CATCH-A-WORD

SKILLS: Phonetic Analysis/Short Vowel Discrimination/Drawing/Cutting

You don't need to visit the pet store to have fun with fish! Use color-coded paper fish to strengthen your child's ability to discriminate the sounds of the five short vowels. Draw a fish, approximately 3″ × 5″, on a piece of cardboard. Cut out the fish and trace 10 times on a piece of colored oak tag or card stock. On one side, draw an eye and print a consonant-vowel-consonant short *a* word such as "bat," "can," or "sad." Flip the fish over. Draw an eye and place a 1″ magnetic strip or paper clip in the center.

Attach a 12″ string to a stick, dowel, or pencil. Tie a small magnet to the end of the string. Spread out the short *a* fish on the floor or table. Go fishing! Catch a fish and read the word.

What fun it will be to catch a "pat" fish or a "rag" fish!

Repeat the process for short *e, i, o,* and *u,* using a different-color set of fish for each short vowel. Play the game with one vowel, pairs of vowels, or all the vowels.

REQUIRED:
- Five sheets oak tag or card stock, each a different color
- Marker
- String
- Magnetic strips/paper clips
- Small magnet
- Stick/dowel/pencil

BRING ON THE RIDDLES

SKILLS: Phonetic Analysis/Initial Consonant Blends/Expressive Language

What is green and hops? A frog! What is wrapped and has a bow? A present! What travels on tracks and has a caboose? A train! Build your child's awareness of the sounds of the *r* consonant blends while strengthening thinking and language skills, too! Have fast-paced fun at home or on the go by making up *r*-blend riddles. Use the word bank below to get you started.

br: brain, brush, brother, broom, bridge, bride
cr: crown, crow, crab, crumb, crib, crane
dr: drum, drink, dragon, driveway, dress, drawer
fr: friend, frost, fruit, french fry, frame, freezer
gr: grape, grandmother, grass, green, ground, grade
pr: prize, president, prince, princess, pretty, proud
tr: trunk, trade, trampoline, truck, tray, trash

REQUIRED:
• Your time

Variation: Use the same procedure for the *l* blends: *bl* (blouse, blue), *cl* (cloud, clay), *fl* (flap, flower), *gl* (glass, glad), *pl* (play, plate), and *sl* (slow, slipper).

PASS THE *L*, PLEASE

SKILLS: Phonetic Analysis/Initial Consonant Blends

Set the table for two and sit down for an *l* blend meal! Cut twelve 3″ × 2″ cards from a piece of white construction paper. Clearly print lowercase *l* in the center of six cards. Clearly print *b*, *c*, *f*, *g*, *p*, and *s* in the center of the remaining cards, one letter per card. Put the *l* cards, faceup, on your plate and the other letter cards, facedown, on your child's plate. Ask your child to choose a facedown card, name the letter, say the sound the letter makes, and place the letter faceup on the table. Then your child says, "Pass the *l*, please." Pass your first grader an *l* card. Your child puts it beside the letter on the table and blends the sounds. For each *l* blend formed, both you and your child say a word that begins with the blend. Play until both plates are empty and all six *l* blends have been made.

REQUIRED:
• Two plates
• Marker
• Construction paper
• Safety scissors

Sample Words: *bl*anket, *cl*ock, *fl*ag, *gl*itter, *pl*um, *sl*ed

Variation: Use the same procedure for *br, cr, dr, fr, gr, pr,* and *tr* and play Pass the *r* Please.

STARS AND SLIDES

SKILLS: Phonetic Analysis/Initial Consonant Blends/Drawing

Start and finish with a star! Have fun sliding from top to bottom while reinforcing awareness of consonant blends made with *s.* Open a file folder horizontally. In the upper left-hand corner, draw a star. Label it "Start." Do the same in the lower left-hand corner. Label this star "Finish." To the right of Start, draw a 12″ × 1½″ rectangle. Divide it into four equal sections. Measure down 1½″, draw another 12″ × 1½″ rectangle, and divide it into four equal sections. Repeat the process until you have four rows. Label the boxes left to right, beginning with the Start line. Row one: *sc, sk, sl, sm.* Row two: *sn, sp, st, sw.* Row three: *sm, sl, sk, sc.* Row four: *sp, sn, st, sw.*

Connect rows one and two with a 1½″ slide from *sm* to *sw,* rows two and three, *sn* to *sm,* rows three and four, *sc* to *sw.* In row four, draw a slide from *sp* to Finish.

Alternating turns, roll the die. Move that number of spaces. Spell the blend, voice the sound, say a word that begins with the blend. Use the slides to move from row to row. The first to the finish wins!

REQUIRED:
- File folder
- Pencil/marker
- Ruler
- Die
- Game markers

BOOK LOOK

SKILLS: Phonetic Analysis/Initial Consonant Blends/Recording Data

Finding initial consonant blends in the books you share is lots of fun! Do a Book Look anytime. When you complete a page, work with your child to find and reread words that have initial consonant blends. Look for the *l* blends in words such as "black," "clip," "flake," "glue," "please," and "slice." Search for the *r* blends in words such as "brick," "crayon," "drizzle," "from," "grand," "press," and "trail." Find the *s* blends in words such as "score," "skip," "slide," "smell," "snap," "spot," "stop," and "swing." If you wish, make a three-column poster listing all the words you find. Add to the poster each time you complete a Book Look.

REQUIRED:
- A book

OPTIONAL:
- Construction paper
- Marker
- Library/bookstore visit

BLEND AT THE END

SKILLS: Phonetic Analysis/Final Consonant Blends/Recording Data/Brainstorming/Cutting

Next time you read and enjoy a book together, go back to find the words that end with a blend. Divide a piece of paper into several columns. Label the columns "mp," "sk," "nd," "nk," "nt," "st," "ft," "lk," and "ng." Find a word with a blend at the end. Write the word in the appropriate column.

Prepare strips of construction paper approximately 8″ × 2″. Make a paper chain for each ending blend. For example, to make an *mp* chain, write *mp* on the first strip. Join the two ends with glue. Using your list, copy the *mp* words onto paper strips, one word per strip. Insert the first *mp* word strip into the finished *mp* link and join the two ends. Repeat the process until the chain is complete. Add to the Blend at the End chains at anytime. Brainstorm words, or take them from your reading or from the word bank below.

REQUIRED:
- A book
- Paper and pencil
- Construction paper
- Safety scissors
- Nontoxic glue
- Marker

OPTIONAL:
- Library/ bookstore visit

WORD BANK:

mp:	camp, romp, lump	*nk:*	sank, think, honk	*ft:*	left, drift, soft
sk:	ask, desk, risk	*nt:*	pant, dent, hint	*lk:*	elk, milk, sulk
nd:	land, find, pond	*st:*	last, fist, cost,	*ng:*	sang, ring, long

SHARKS AND CHIMPS, THUMBS AND WHEELS

SKILLS: Phonetic Analysis/Initial Consonant Digraphs/Auditory Discrimination

When *h* is paired with *s, c, t,* and *w,* new sounds are formed. Help your child to recognize the sounds of these consonant digraphs, *sh* as in "sharks," *ch* as in "chimps," *th* as in "thumbs," *wh* as in "wheels." Place four paper plates on the table. In the center of each plate, write one consonant digraph.

Sit opposite your first grader. Set the consonant digraph plates on the table so that they face your child. Provide a bowl of Cheerios, raisins, jelly beans, or M&M's to use as game markers. Now, simply say words that begin with any one of the initial consonant digraphs. Tell your child to listen to the beginning sound of each word, repeat the sound, then put a game marker on the matching plate. For example, ask, "What sound do you hear at the beginning of 'shirt'?" Your child responds, "I hear /sh/ at the beginning of 'shirt'" and places a marker on the *sh* plate. Use the word bank below to get started.

REQUIRED:
- Four paper plates
- Marker
- Game markers

WORD BANK:

sh:	ship, shoe, shout, shelf, shell, shovel	*ch:*	children, chair, chain, chick, chart, chocolate
th:	thermometer, theater, thirty, thimble, thirsty, Thursday	*wh:*	whip, whisper, whiskers, whistle, wheat, whale

A+ ACTIVITIES FOR FIRST GRADE

CHICK CHOOSE

SKILLS: Phonetic Analysis/Consonant Digraph *ch*/Drawing

Fill a paper lunch bag with cherries, chops, and chocolate chips! Strengthen your child's ability to read words that begin with the digraph *ch*. Create a Chick Choose bag by placing a lunch bag on the table with the opening at the top. Draw two eyes at the top of the bag. Add a "V" just below the eyes for a beak. Below the beak, print "ch." At the base of the bag print a "W" in each corner for feet.

Write words that begin with *ch* on index cards. Place these word cards in the bag. Then, for practice and reinforcement, play Chick Choose. Your child reaches into the bag and chooses a word card. Ask, "Which chick word did you choose?" Your child answers by reading the word. Alternate turns, continuing until all cards have been read. Encourage your child to add new words to the bag often.

Variation: Add words that end in *ch*.

INITIAL CH WORD BANK: chap, chip, chat, chest, chin, chimp, cheese, chime, child, chess, check, chose, chomp

FINAL CH WORD BANK: rich, much, such, which, each, beach, peach, reach, pouch, couch, lunch, bunch, hunch, porch

REQUIRED:
- Paper lunch bag
- Markers/crayons
- Index cards

THIRSTY THERMOS

SKILLS: Phonetic Analysis/Consonant Digraph *th*/Drawing

Think of things to put into a Thirsty Thermos paper lunch bag! Strengthen your child's ability to read words that begin with the consonant digraph *th*. Place a lunch bag on the table with the opening at the top. Make the thermos by drawing two lines across the bag an inch from the top. Below the lines that make the lid, print "th."

Write words that begin with *th* on index cards. Place these word cards in the bag. Then, for practice and reinforcement, play Thirsty Thermos. Your child reaches into the bag and chooses a word card. Ask, "Which thirsty word did you choose from the thermos?" Your child answers by reading the word. Alternate turns, continuing until all cards have been read. Encourage your child to add new words to the bag often.

Variation: Add words that end in *th*.

INITIAL TH WORD BANK: third, think, thing, thank, thin, thumb, thorn, thought, thigh, thin, thick, thunder, this, then

FINAL TH WORD BANK: with, bath, math, path, both, oath, moth, myth, tooth, booth, teeth, fourth, fifth, tenth

REQUIRED:
- Paper lunch bag
- Markers/crayons
- Index cards

SHIP SHOW

SKILLS: Phonetic Analysis/Consonant Digraph *sh*/Drawing

Put shirts and shells in the Ship Show paper lunch bag! Strengthen your child's ability to read words that begin with the digraph *sh*. Place a lunch bag on the table with the opening to the right. Draw two parallel lines, 2″ long and 2″ apart, down from the center top of the bag. Extend these lines, outward to the left and right edges of the bag. Continue each line diagonally to the base of the bag. Draw portholes across the ship. Print "sh" below the portholes.

Write words that begin with *sh* on index cards. Place these word cards in the bag. Then, for practice and reinforcement, play Ship Show. Your child reaches into the bag and chooses a word card. Ask, "Which ship word can you show?" Your child answers by reading the word. Alternate turns, continuing until all cards have been read. Add new words to the bag often.

Variation: Include words that end in *sh*.

INITIAL SH WORD BANK: shop, sheep, shade, shin, share, shine, should, shove, shiver, shut, shower, shape, shook

FINAL SH WORD BANK: dish, fish, wish, cash, dash, flash, mash, rash, splash, fresh, push, wash, mush

REQUIRED:
• Paper lunch bag
• Markers/crayons
• Index cards

WHICH WHALE?

SKILLS: Phonetic Analysis/Initial Consonant Digraph *wh*/Drawing

Put a whistle and a wheelbarrow into a Which Whale paper lunch bag! Strengthen your child's ability to read words that begin with the digraph *wh*. Place a lunch bag on the table with the opening to the right. Draw an eye and a smile at the left edge of the bag. Print "wh" in the center of the bag. Now turn the bag so that the opening is at the top. Print a "V" from the left corner to the right corner to make the tail.

Write words that begin with *wh* on index cards. Place these word cards in the bag. Then, for practice and reinforcement, play Which Whale? Your child reaches into the bag and chooses a word card. Ask, "Which whale word did you choose?" Your child answers by reading the word. Alternate turns, continuing until all cards have been read. Encourage your child to add new words to the bag often.

WORD BANK: what, where, when, why, wheel, wheat, whip, whistle, whisper, white, whine, whirl, wharf, whim, whimper, whiskers, whopper, whiz, whisk

REQUIRED:
• Paper lunch bag
• Markers/crayons
• Index cards

DIGRAPH FIND

SKILLS: Phonetic Analysis/Consonant Digraphs/Recording Data

Go on a consonant digraph find! First graders enjoy finding letter elements in the books they read. To start, make a four-column chart. Label the first column "ch," the second column "sh," the third, "th," and the fourth, "wh." Choose a book to read and enjoy. Then reread the book and begin to look for consonant digraphs /ch/ as in "chick" and "rich," /sh/ as in "ship" and "wish," /th/ as in "thermos" and "bath," and /wh/ as in "whale." Write each word found in the appropriate column on the chart. Each time you do the Digraph Find, add words to the chart. Read the words on the chart for practice.

REQUIRED:
- A book
- Paper and pencil

OPTIONAL:
- Library/bookstore visit

WORD STRINGS

SKILLS: Phonetic Analysis/Initial Consonant Clusters/Auditory Discrimination

String three consonants together at the start of a word and you've made an initial consonant cluster! Ask your child to listen to the sound of *str* as in "string," "stretch," "strike," "straight," and "straw." Use magnetic letters, letter tiles, or letter cards to slide the consonants together as you say the sound. Then write "str" on an index card and, one word per card, any words you can think of that begin with *str*. Punch a hole in the left corner of each card. Keeping the *str* card on top, string the word cards together. Tie the ends in a bow so that you can add new words at any time.

Repeat the process, making word strings for *scr* as in "scrape," "screen," "scream," "scratch," and "scrawl"; *shr* as in "shrink," "shrimp," "shrug," "shred," and "shrank"; *spr* as in "spring," "spray," "spread," "sprout," and "sprint"; *thr* as in "throw," "threw," "thread," "through," and "thrust"; and *spl* as in "splash," "split," "splat," "splurge," and "splinter."

Look for consonant clusters in the books you read together. Add to the word strings often.

REQUIRED:
- Manipulative letters
- String, ribbon, yarn, or twine
- Index cards
- Marker
- Safety scissors
- Hole punch

VOWEL IN A BAG

SKILLS: Phonetic Analysis/Long Vowels/Auditory Discrimination/Rhyme/Counting

What's in a name? The sound! When a vowel says its own name, the vowel is long. You can hear *a* in "cape," *e* in "seal," *i* in "bike," *o* in "coat," and *u* in "mule." Help your child strengthen recognition and discrimination of long vowel sounds by playing Vowel in a Bag.

Put five paper bags on the table or floor, each labeled with one vowel. Give your child a supply of raisins. Say long vowel words, one at a time, as your child listens for the vowel sound. For example, you say, "Cake." Your child says, "I hear *a* in 'cake'" and puts a raisin in the *a* bag.

Variation: Ask your child for a rhyming word. Play as long as you like. At the end of the game, count the raisins in each bag. The vowel with the most raisins wins!

WORD BANK: *a:* bake, cake, mail, sail, ape, tape, train, brain
e: feet, meet, eel, peel, cream, dream, peep, sleep
i: rice, price, pine, dine, ride, side, dime, time
o: boat, float, load, road, mole, hole, cone, tone
u: cube, tube, cute, flute, rude, dude, tune, June

REQUIRED:
• Paper bags
• Marker
• Raisins

MAGIC *E* MONSTER

SKILLS: Phonetic Analysis/Long Vowels/Drawing

Magic *e* Monster isn't really a monster at all! In a concrete way, he'll help your first grader read long vowel words with silent *e*. He turns "tap" into "tape," "pet" into "Pete," "dim" into "dime," "hop" into "hope," and "cub" into "cube."

Draw a big, fuzzy ball on oak tag or poster board. Add two eyes, a nose, a big open mouth, two arms, and two feet. Cut a slit in the middle of the mouth. Make small *e* letter cards to fit through the slit. Use index cards to make silent *e* word cards.

Tell the story of Magic *e* Monster, a creature who looks for the letter *e* at the end of a word. If he catches a final *e,* he eats it. As a result, the *e* at the end of the word is silent while the angry vowel in the word yells its own name. Now flash a word card. Your child feeds the Magic *e* Monster an *e* letter card and reads the word. Any time your child gets stuck on a magic *e* word say, "Remember Magic *e* Monster!"

REQUIRED:
• Oak tag/poster board
• Markers
• Index cards
• Safety scissors

WORD BANK: rake, gave, line, time, joke, home, cute, huge

MAGIC E FLIP

SKILLS: Phonetic Analysis/Long Vowels

Do the Magic e Flip to change short vowel words into long vowel words. Make a series of consonant-vowel-consonant word cards. Write a three-letter short vowel word near the left edge of each card. Fold over the right half of the card so that the right edge just meets the last letter of the word on the card. Write "e" on the folded section so that the word becomes a four-letter word. For example, print "tap" on the left side of the card. Fold the card and print "e" as described. Open the card, your child reads "tap." Flip at the fold to see whether your child can switch to long a to read "tape." Try words that work and words that don't to strengthen reading and vocabulary.

WORD BANK: can-cane, man-mane, van-vane, fad-fade, mad-made, dim-dime, hid-hide, pin-pine, rip-ripe, bit-bite, hop-hope, rob-robe, not-note, mop-mope, cod-code, cub-cube, tub-tube, hug-huge, cut-cute, dud-dude, pet-Pete

REQUIRED:
• Index cards
• Pen/pencil

BIG MOUTH

SKILLS: Phonetic Analysis/Long Vowels/Drawing

"When two vowels are side by side, the first is long; the second silently tags along." Insert the word "usually" after the comma since with vowel teams, the rules are sometimes broken. Nonetheless, first graders benefit from knowing a rule that is often true. Big Mouth is a friendly creature who helps children read words that include vowel teams.

Draw a long oval on oak tag. Add two eyes, a nose, a big open mouth, and long arms. Cut a slit in the middle of the mouth. Make vowel cards small enough to fit through the slit. Include a, e, i, y, and w, which sometimes acts like a vowel. Use index cards to make vowel team word cards.

Tell the story of Big Mouth, who looks for two vowels together. When he finds a vowel team, he eats the second vowel and we can't hear it. The first vowel gets angry and shouts its own name.

Flash a word card. Your child feeds Big Mouth a vowel card to match the second vowel in the word and reads the word. Whenever your child gets stuck on a vowel team say, "Remember Big Mouth!"

WORD BANK: sail, beat, feet, toe, day, snow, pie, clue

REQUIRED:
• Oak tag
• Markers
• Index cards
• Safety scissors

TAKE CHARGE R

SKILLS: Phonetic Analysis/*r*-Controlled Vowels/Drawing

One morning we drove the *car* to the *park*. We looked at the *birds*, *ferns*, and *furry* animals. At lunch time we ate *corn* on the cob. Imagine how challenging it is for first graders to learn another sound for each of the vowels! Take Charge *r* comes along and changes everything!

Practice the *r*-controlled vowels by making *r*-word ladders. Draw ladders with six to ten rungs. Write "ar" on the top rung and an *ar* word on each successive rung. Words might include: "car," "jar," "star," "card," "dark," "farm," and "yarn." Make an *or* ladder using words such as: "for," "fork," "cord," "cork," "horn," "horse," and "storm."

Notice that *er, ir,* and *ur* sound the same. The *er* ladder could include "her," "herd," "clerk," "gerbil," "water," "teacher," and "father." Choose words for the *ir* ladder like "sir," "first," "third," "shirt," "skirt," "girl," and "thirst." The *ur* ladder words could be "fur," "burn," "turn," "curl," "curve," "hurt," and "turtle."

Start at the top of each ladder. Climb down by reading the words along the way. Then climb back up. Climb the *r* ladders anytime to enhance recognition of the *r*-controlled vowels.

REQUIRED:
• Paper and pencil

FROM OUCH TO WOW

SKILLS: Phonetic Analysis/Diphthongs/Drawing

What do you say when you stub your toe? "Ouch!" What do you say when you win a prize? "Wow!" While beginning readers recognize high frequency words such as *house* and *cow*, they also need to be exposed to the diphthongs *ou* and *ow*, as in "ouch" and "wow," so that they can apply the sound to read unfamiliar words.

Make the From Ouch to Wow gameboard from a file folder. Open the folder vertically. In the lower left-hand corner make a 1″ square. Label this square "Ouch." Do the same in the upper right-hand corner. Label this square "Wow." Connect the two squares by drawing 20 to 30 squares from Ouch to Wow. In four selected squares, write messages such as "Not Now, Miss 1 Turn," "Power, Move Ahead 2," "Cloudy, Go Back 1," or "Extra Turn Found." In the remaining squares, print *ou* and *ow* words. Use buttons or coins as game markers.

REQUIRED:
• File folder
• Marker
• Game markers
• Die

Place both game markers on Ouch. Alternate turns. Toss the die, move that number of spaces, read the word, and use it in a sentence. The first player to reach Wow is the winner. Fold the file for easy storage.

FROM COIN TO TOY

SKILLS: Phonetic Analysis/Diphthongs/Drawing

"Coin" and "toy" are frequently occurring words in the classroom and at home. Your first grader is likely to recognize both words from sight. Your child also needs to be exposed to the diphthongs *oi* and *oy*, as in "spoil" and "royal," to apply the sound in order to read unfamiliar words.

Make the From Coin to Toy gameboard from a file folder. Open the folder horizontally. In the lower left-hand corner, draw a 1″ circle. Label it "Coin." Do the same in the upper right-hand corner. Label this circle "Toy." Connect the two circles by drawing 20 to 30 circles from Coin to Toy. In four selected circles write messages such as "Enjoy, Take an Extra Turn," "Spilled Oil, Go Back 1," "Oh Boy, Move Ahead 2," or "Foiled, Miss a Turn." In the remaining circles, print *oi* and *oy* words. Use buttons or coins as game markers.

Place both game markers on Coin. Alternate turns. Toss the die, move that number of spaces, read the word, and use it in a sentence. The first player to reach Toy is the winner. Fold the file for easy storage.

REQUIRED:
- File folder
- Marker
- Game markers
- Die

BOOKS OR SCHOOL?

SKILLS: Phonetic Analysis/Diphthongs

Your beginning reader probably recognizes and reads "books" and "school" without ever stopping to wonder why the *oo* has a different sound in each word. Use word wheels to familiarize your child with both sounds for reading unfamiliar words with the diphthong *oo*.

Fasten a small paper plate to the center of a large paper plate with a paper fastener. If paper plates aren't available, cut two circles from oak tag or cardboard. Write "ook" to the left of the fastener on the small plate. Print "b," "br," "c," "cr," "h," "l," "n," "sh," and "t" along the edge of the larger plate. Turn the large plate so that your child can combine the initial consonants with "ook" to read "book," "brook," "cook," "crook," "hook," "look," "nook," "shook," and "took."

Follow the same procedure, writing "ool" on the small plate and "c," "f," "p," "sch," "sp," and "t" on the large plate. Read the words "cool," "fool," "pool," "school," "spool," and "tool." Point out that the letters *oo* make two different sounds. Make additional word wheels for "ood," "oof," "oom," "oon," "oop," and "oot."

REQUIRED:
- Paper plates
- Marker
- Paper fasteners

OPTIONAL:
- Oak tag or cardboard
- Safety scissors

DIPHTHONG COLLAGE

SKILLS: Phonetic Analysis/Diphthongs/Recording Data

Find pictures to reinforce the sound and spelling of diphthongs, the vowel pairs that break the rules! Draw a line down the center of a large piece of construction paper. Label the left side "ou" and the right side "ow." Look through recyclable magazines or catalogues for pictures to glue on each side of the collage. Under each picture, print the word. Repeat the process, making a collage for "oy/oi," and for "oo," one side as in "shook," the other as in "food." Use the word bank below to help you select pictures. Be sure to talk about the sounds of the diphthongs with your first grader as you search for pictures and say, write, and read the words.

WORD BANK:		
ou:	house, mouse, blouse, cloud, scout, trout	
ow:	clown, crown, flower, brown, gown, cow	
oy:	boy, toy, oyster, joy, annoy, royal	
oi:	coin, foil, soil, doily, oil, broil	
oo:	book, hook, cook, brook, hood, foot	
oo:	groom, pool, school, moon, spoon, broom	

REQUIRED:
- Construction paper
- Marker
- Safety scissors
- Nontoxic glue
- Magazines/catalogues

DRAW A NOUN

SKILLS: Nouns/Brainstorming/Drawing/Expressive Language/Categorizing

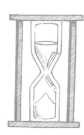

Farmer, farm, wagon. Teacher, school, book. Nouns can name a person, place, or thing. That's why we call them naming words.

Play Draw a Noun with your first grader to build awareness of the naming words. After brainstorming words that name people, places, and things, take turns drawing a picture of a noun and having other players guess the word. Give a category clue if necessary, for example, "It's a thing." Use a three-minute timer to speed up the fun. All you need is a pencil, a paper, and a quick sketch!

WORD BANK PEOPLE: boy, girl, baby, clown, firefighter, grandfather
WORD BANK PLACES: city, beach, forest, jungle, bank, field
WORD BANK THINGS: shell, car, house, cake, kite

REQUIRED:
- Paper and pencil

OPTIONAL:
- Timer

VERB CHARADES

SKILLS: Verbs/Brainstorming

Verbs are action words that can tell how people, animals, or things move. Play Verb Charades to build your child's awareness of the action words. To get ideas going, brainstorm a list of physical action words. Tell your child that you will act out an action word without using words. Then hop, skip, or jump to see if your child can guess the verb. Each player gets a point for a correct guess. Alternate turns and set a timer to one minute for fast-paced fun!

WORD BANK: wave, smile, frown, laugh, cry, eat, drink, sneeze, run, walk, skate, ski, wiggle, scratch, snore, sleep, yawn, read, write, paint, fly, yell, pedal, tickle, hug, kiss, chew, kick, blink, wink

REQUIRED:
• Paper and pencil
OPTIONAL:
• Timer

PAINT A WORD PICTURE

SKILLS: Adjectives/Expressive Language/Making Comparisons/Drawing

Adjectives are words that describe or tell about people, places, and things. Close your eyes and picture this: A seagull flies over the water. Ask your child to add a word to the sentence to tell about the seagull so that the words paint a better picture of how the seagull looks or acts. For example, "A white seagull (or a graceful seagull or a bossy seagull or a noisy seagull) flies over the water." Next ask your child to add to the word picture by telling about the water. Repeat the sentence including both adjectives, "A white seagull flies over the sparkling water."

Paint word pictures at any time by using colorful adjectives. As your child adds adjectives, you can, too! Then compare the different pictures that result. To get started, try the sentences that follow, using adjectives to describe the italicized nouns. As an option, draw a picture of the sentences created.

SENTENCE BANK:

The *puppy* chases the *ball*.
Michael rides his *bike* on the *road*.
A *mouse* ate the *cheese*.
Barbara draws a *picture* on the *paper*.
A *tiger* growls in the *jungle*.

REQUIRED:
• Your time
OPTIONAL:
• Paper
• Crayons/markers

WHO AND WHO?

Have you ever heard your first grader say, "Me and my friend played in the sandbox"? Have you ever seen your child write, "Me and my dad had popcorn at the movies"? All around us, on television and in daily conversation, the pronouns "I" and "me" are misused! Each time the "Me and my friend . . ." goes uncorrected, no matter how endearing it may sound, the incorrect form is validated so that the nonstandard form never sounds wrong.

Who and Who? is a quick and easy reminder to your child to reverse the order of the subject words and to use "I" instead of "me" as the subject of the sentence. There is no need, at this age, for a grammar lesson on nominative case pronouns. Rather, by reinforcing correct standard English, "My friend and I" as the subject will begin to sound correct!

Next time you hear your child say, "Me and my mom . . .," ask, "Who and who?" If your child repeats, "Me and my mom . . .," say, "Who and who?" again. Show your child that when you remove the second person, "Me had popcorn at the movies," the language sounds really funny!

REQUIRED:
• Your time

COMPOUND CONNECTION

SKILLS: Compound Words/Expressive Language

Sometimes, two words are better than one! This fast-paced game helps your child understand that often, two words put together make one word. Choose a compound word from the list provided. Say the first word of the compound word to your child. Ask your first grader to add a word to make a compound word. For example, you say "butter," your child says, "fly." You say "bath," your child says "tub" or "room." You say "straw," your child says "berry." You say "sand," your child says "box."

For variation, ask your child to say the first word of a compound word so that you can provide the second. Whether you play while driving to the supermarket or walking to the playground, keep the action quick in Compound Connection.

WORD BANK: butterfly, bathroom, bathtub, strawberry, classroom, gingerbread, afternoon, sandbox, baseball, beanbag, popcorn, clubhouse, sunshine, doghouse, gumdrop, sidewalk, football, basketball, sailboat, shoelace, rainbow, scarecrow, driveway, bedroom, snowman, snowflake, blueberry, downtown, railroad, horseshoe, dishwasher, pancake, airplane

REQUIRED:
• Your time

HOMONYM MATCHUP

SKILLS: Homonyms/Brainstorming

She *blew* out the *blue* candles on the cake! Homonyms are words that sound the same but are spelled differently and have different meanings. A favorite game, Concentration, is a great way to heighten awareness of homonyms.

Brainstorm a list of 21 pairs of homonyms. Write each pair on an index card, one on the left side of the card, the other on the right. Cut the cards in half and shuffle. Place the cards facedown in rows on the table. Alternate play, turning over two cards. If the words don't match, turn them facedown in the original position. If the words do match, pick them up, read them, use each in a sentence, and go again. The player with the most pairs at the end wins!

WORD BANK: sail-sale, tail-tale, pail-pale, right-write, no-know, new-knew, bare-bear, hair-hare, where-wear, eye-I, ate-eight, in-inn, night-knight, hear-here, for-four, flower-flour, our-hour, red-read, see-sea, read-reed, hole-whole, roll-role, root-route, we-wee, road-rode, led-lead, stair-stare, steak-stake

REQUIRED:
- Index cards
- Pencil/marker
- Safety scissors

SYNONYM SCRAMBLE

SKILLS: Synonyms/Expressive Language/Brainstorming

Little, small . . . big, tall . . . synonyms are fun for all! Enrich your child's vocabulary for speaking, writing, and reading. Enjoy a Synonym Scramble as you think of words that have the same meaning.

Ask your child, "Can you think of another word for 'great'?" Provide an example, using "great" in context, such as, "That movie was great!" Now do the Synonym Scramble by repeating the sentence, back and forth between you, each time replacing the word "great" with a synonym. "That movie was super!" "That movie was terrific!" "That movie was fantastic!" "That movie was amazing!" Keep going until you run out of words. Give your child the chance to begin the Synonym Scramble with an original sentence. Here are sample sentences to get you started.

SENTENCE BANK:
That medicine tastes awful, terrible, horrible, gross, disgusting, nasty!
Winter days are cold, icy, freezing, frosty, numbing!
The mountain is enormous, tremendous, large, huge, monumental, gigantic!
Field mice are little, small, teeny, tiny, minuscule, minute.
We drove down the street, avenue, road, highway, boulevard.
"I'm hungry," he shouted, called, cried, yelled, screamed.

REQUIRED:
- Your time

ANTONYM EGGS

SKILLS: Antonyms/Expressive Language/Brainstorming

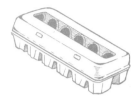

Refill an empty egg carton with new and old, hot and cold, shy and bold! Antonyms are words that are opposites. By using words in context, work together to generate opposites to enhance your child's speaking, reading, and writing vocabulary. For example, you say, "I open the door." Your child says, "I close the door." You say, "The jar is full." Your child says, "The jar is empty."

Cut index cards into four sections to make small word cards for all the antonyms you name. Fill an empty egg carton with antonym word cards. Put the word card "happy" in one egg section and the word card "sad" in the opposite egg section. Make a dozen antonym eggs and then a dozen more!

REQUIRED:
- Index cards
- Empty egg carton
- Marker
- Safety scissors

WORD BANK: high/low, above/below, in/out, up/down, black/white, near/far, big/little, ugly/pretty, sit/stand, walk/run, asleep/awake, noisy/quiet, happy/sad, over/under

SHORTCUT WORDS

SKILLS: Contractions/Vocabulary Development

When your tongue gets tired, put two words together to make one. Leave out one or more letters, slip in an apostrophe and you have a Shortcut Word!

Practice the contractions common to a first-grade vocabulary. Cut index cards in half. Make word cards for: "I will," "I'll," "you will," "you'll," "he will," "he'll," "she will," "she'll," "we will," "we'll," "they will," and "they'll." Put all the phrases in one paper bag labeled "Two Words." Put all the contractions in another bag labeled "Shortcut Words." Reach into the Two Words bag, pull out a card, read the words, and place the card faceup on the table. Ask your child to reach into the Shortcut Words bag, pull out one card, read the word, and decide whether it is the matching contraction. If it is a match, put the cards side by side. If not, place the contraction on the table. Alternate play until all matches have been made. Repeat the game using another group of contractions from the word bank provided.

REQUIRED:
- Index cards
- Marker
- Safety scissors
- Paper lunch bags

WORD BANK: he's, she's, it's, I'm, you're, we're, they're, can't, don't, doesn't, won't, isn't, wasn't, didn't, haven't, hasn't

S MAKES MORE

SKILLS: Plurals/Expressive Language/Cutting

For beginning readers, the several functions of the letter *s* can be confusing. To strengthen recognition of plural words, make an *S Makes More* book.

Work with your child to find and cut out pictures of items from magazines or catalogues. Look for pictures of, for example, cars, dogs, cats, trees, flowers, trucks, babies. Then fold several pieces of construction paper in half and place them one inside the other. Staple on the fold to make a book.

Label the cover, "*S Makes More.*" Open to the first interior facing pages. Glue, for example, one car to the left of the fold and a collection of two or more cars to the right of the fold. Write "car" on the singular side and "cars" on the plural side. Continue this process to complete your *S Makes More* book. Read the book together and add it to your child's personal library.

REQUIRED:
- Pencil
- Construction paper
- Magazines/catalogues
- Nontoxic glue
- Safety scissors
- Stapler

READING LOG

SKILLS: Literature Appreciation/Recording Data

Keep a running record of your child's reading by creating a personalized reading log. Use a notebook or journal. On the cover, print "Greg's Reading Log" or "Tanya's Reading Log," using your child's name. Open the notebook/journal so that the first two blank pages are facing you. Divide the left page into three columns headed "Title," "Author," "Date." Make the title and author columns wider than the date column. Divide the right page into two columns headed "Rating" and "Comment." Make the comment column wider than the rating column.

Establish a rating scale with your child. Use a four-star scale. Choose a rating word for a four-star book, such as *terrific;* for a three-star book, *very good;* for a two-star book, *good;* for a one-star book, *fair.* List these ratings in the top right-hand corner of the "Rating and Comment" page.

Each time your child completes a book, remind your young reader to record the title, author, date, rating, and a comment. Draw stars to show the rating or provide stickers or a star stamp. Encourage your child to share the reading log often.

REQUIRED:
- Notebook/journal
- Pencil

OPTIONAL:
- Star stickers/stamp

BOOK NOTE BOX

SKILLS: Literature Appreciation/Reading Comprehension/Written Expression

Put the shoes on the shelf and the book notes in the box! A shoe box can hold a rich record of your child's or your family's reading adventures. Cut a 3″ to 6″ slot in the center of the shoe box cover. Working independently or with family members, your child then decorates the shoe box using any available materials. Suggest that the decorations on the box follow a favorite book theme. When the decorations are complete, schedule a date and time for the family opening of the Book Note Box. From that day on, each member of the family completes a book note for each book read. The book note should include the title, author, illustrator, a comment, and a rating. The rating scale is up to you. For example, a three-point scale could include: 1—A must read!, 2—Good!, 3—Not recommended.

Family members can enjoy reading book notes at a set time or any time!

REQUIRED:
• Shoe box
• Safety scissors
• Nontoxic glue or tape
• Crayons/markers
• Construction paper
• Index cards
• Pencil

EYE ON THE AUTHOR

SKILLS: Literature Appreciation/Reading Comprehension/Drawing/Retelling/Making Comparisons

Leo Lionni? Tomie dePaola? Mem Fox? Kevin Henkes? Eric Carle? John Burningham? Focus your critical reading eye on these or any other author/illustrators of language-rich picture storybooks.

Choose a book by a favorite author, share it, then choose and read other books by the same author. Read each book aloud, looking for similarities or differences in the books. Engage your child in discussion of the stories. Directly ask, "What was the same about the books? What was different?" With an Eye on the Author, focus on the main characters, the settings, including where and when each story takes place, the wish or problem of the main character, and the solution to the problem or wish granted at the end.

Look closely at the illustrations, making note of the style of the illustrator and again making comparisons between books. Invite your child to draw a picture of a favorite character, scene, or event and to retell one of the stories. With an Eye on the Author, you'll be amazed by how much your child sees!

REQUIRED:
• Books by one author

OPTIONAL:
• Paper and pencil
• Crayons/markers
• Library/bookstore visit

LITERARY LUNCH

Invite your child to a literary lunch to foster a love of literature! In preparation for this fun-filled and yummy afternoon, you and your child each choose a favorite book to take along to lunch on a designated day at a local restaurant. At lunch, after placing your order, use the wait time to take turns telling each other about the book you have brought and what makes it a favorite. Encourage your child to talk about the five *W*'s—the who, what, where, when, and why of the story. You may decide to go first, in order to provide your child with a model critique of a book. Encourage other family members and friends to join the literary lunch.

REQUIRED:
- A favorite book for child
- A favorite book for parent(s)
- A favorite restaurant

OPTIONAL:
- Other family members or friends

FAMILY READ-IN

Cuddle up in front of a cozy fire or stretch out on a blanket under a shady tree! Whatever the season, wherever you are, a Family Read-In is a wonderful way to show your child that reading is special for all. Choose a time, on a snowy weekend afternoon or a summer blue-sky day. Designate the time as a Family Read-In. All family members gather, each with a chosen book, magazine, or newspaper. Have hot chocolate and cookies or lemonade and munchies as everyone gets comfy and reads.

REQUIRED:
- Books, magazines, newspapers
- A special place and time

OPTIONAL:
- Refreshments

PROMOTE-A-BOOK POSTER

SKILLS: Literature Appreciation/Reading Comprehension/Written Expression/Drawing & Painting/Cutting

Jump start your child's career in advertising. Encourage your first grader to make a poster to promote a favorite book. When your child completes the book, either independently or cooperatively, provide materials so that your child can write, draw, paint, color, cut, and paste a colorful and informative poster that includes the title, author, illustrator, main character, and setting. For example, to promote the book *Where the Wild Things Are*, by Maurice Sendak, your young ad executive could draw or paint the main characters Max and the Wild Things, and use colored tissue or construction paper to create the setting around them. Remind your child about the importance of writing in large letters so that the poster can be read from across the room. Display your poster in a place of prominence in your home.

REQUIRED:
- A favorite book
- Poster paper
- Crayons/markers/pencils

OPTIONAL:
- Tissue paper
- Tape or nontoxic glue
- Safety scissors
- Other recyclable materials
- Library/bookstore visit

STRAWS OR STICKS

SKILLS: Reading Comprehension/Characterization/Expressive Language/Drawing/Cutting

Drinking-straw or Popsicle-stick puppets of the main characters in a favorite book provide opportunities for your child to enhance expressive language skills while building literal and inferential comprehension skills. Choose a favorite book from your child's collection or from your school or local library. Read the book together, focusing on the dialogue. Select two characters from the story who hold a conversation. Using the illustrations as a guide, draw the characters on white paper. Color the drawings. Cut them out and attach them with nontoxic glue, tape, or staples to the upper half of a drinking straw, Popsicle or lollipop stick, or pencil.

Now you are ready to cast your puppet show. Act out an existing scene from the story or go beyond the text by taking the point of view of the character and creating a new scene or conversation.

Books that lend themselves well to this activity include *The Runaway Bunny* by Margaret Wise Brown, *Harry and the Terrible Whatzit* by Dick Gackenbach, and *Ira Sleeps Over* by Bernard Waber.

REQUIRED:
- A favorite book
- Paper and pencil
- Safety scissors
- Tape, stapler, or nontoxic glue
- Drinking straws, Popsicle or lollipop sticks
- Marker

OPTIONAL:
- Library/bookstore visit

IMAGINE THAT . . . ◆ ◆

SKILLS: Reading Comprehension/Characterization/Imaginative Thinking/Drawing

We learn about a character in a book from what the character says and does and from what others say about the character. Illustrations and descriptions also show how the character looks and acts. Sometimes a character is described and we are left to imagine how that character appears. For example, in Kevin Henkes's *Owen*, we read about the Blanket Fairy but never see the Blanket Fairy. The reader is left to wonder how the Blanket Fairy looks and acts.

Imagine That . . . with any book you read. Imagine that there really are blanket fairies, wild things, whatzits, two-headed giants, and trolls. Talk about the characters met in books read, how they look and act! Then, draw them!

REQUIRED:
- A book
- Paper
- Crayons/markers

OPTIONAL:
- Library/bookstore visit

CHARACTER WHEELS

SKILLS: Reading Comprehension/Characterization/Adjectives/Drawing/
Recording Data/Making Comparisons

How does a character look? How does a character act? Make Character Wheels to record the words your child uses to tell about a book character. Draw a large circle on a piece of paper. Draw a small circle in the center of the large one. Then draw six lines or spokes from the inner circle to the outer circle. Read a book together. In the small circle, write the main character's name and/or draw a picture of the character. Then engage in lively conversation about the main character. Talk about how the character looks and acts. For example, read *Cyrus the Unsinkable Sea Serpent* by Bill Peet. Make one character wheel to record the adjectives your child uses to tell how Cyrus looks—huge, long, wavy—and one character wheel to tell how Cyrus acts—brave, angry, helpful. Use the wheels to compare and contrast characters met in books by the same author or different authors. Your first grader's "wheels" will spin as awareness of characterization grows.

REQUIRED:
- A favorite book
- Paper and pencil
- Markers/crayons

OPTIONAL:
- Library/ bookstore visit

SETTING IN A SHOE BOX

SKILLS: Reading Comprehension/Setting/Imaginative Thinking/Cutting/Drawing

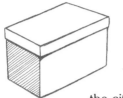

Capture the where and the when of a story by creating the setting of a book in a box. Choose a favorite book from your child's collection or the local library. Read the book together, focusing on the setting. Using the text and illustrations as a guide, engage your child in conversation about the where and when of the story. "Does the story take place inside or outside? In the city or the country? On a rocket bound for Saturn or on a magical island? Is it morning, noon, or night? Spring, summer, autumn, or winter? Past, present, or future?"

Decide on a specific scene to draw or build in the box. With the opening facing you, use materials to recreate a castle, meadow, forest, farm, village, pirate ship, mountain top, or the ocean floor.

Make use of all interior surfaces of the box and exterior surfaces as well.

Be creative! Use blue cellophane for lakes and rivers, pipe cleaners for vines and trees, silver foil for stars, clay for furnishings, cardboard cut-outs for characters. Make the setting come to life using multimedia materials.

REQUIRED:
- A book
- Shoe box
- Safety scissors
- Nontoxic glue
- Construction paper
- Markers/crayons
- Cardboard
- Pipe cleaners, foil, cellophane

OPTIONAL:
- Library/bookstore visit

CUT APART COMICS

SKILLS: Reading Comprehension/Expressive Language/Story Sequence/Cutting

No matter what the length, every story has a beginning, a middle and an end. As oral language develops, first graders need to play with language, working to organize the order in which they tell or write a story. They also need to recognize sequence in the stories they read. One way to build your child's awareness of sequence is to share newspaper or bubble gum wrapper comics. Look at a three- to five-frame comic sequence together. Ask your child to tell the story based upon the cartoons. Encourage your first grader to imagine what the characters are saying. Guide the process by saying, "What happened first?" Move on, when ready, to, "What happened second?" "What happened next?" "What happened last?" Then read the comic together.

Now try Cut Apart Comics. Choose a comic to cut apart. Challenge your child to arrange the comic in correct story sequence, telling the tale while completing the task.

REQUIRED:
- Comics
- Safety scissors

A+ ACTIVITIES FOR FIRST GRADE

DRAW A STORY

SKILLS: Reading Comprehension/Listening Comprehension/Story Sequence/Story Form/Drawing/Retelling

As children read, write, or listen to stories, they learn that all stories have a beginning, a middle, and an end. In the beginning, an author introduces the main character(s), the setting, and the wish, problem, or dilemma. In the middle, the main character(s) works to make the wish come true or solve the problem or dilemma. At the end, if all goes well, the wish is granted or the problem is solved.

Share a book with your child, discussing the parts of the story as you read. Encourage your first grader to draw the story after reading or listening to the book. Fold a piece of construction paper into three equal sections, accordion style. Label the left section "Beginning," the middle section "Middle," and the right section "End." Ask your child to draw pictures to show what happened at the beginning, in the middle, and at the end. When the pictures are complete, ask your child to retell the story from beginning to end.

REQUIRED:
- A book
- Construction paper
- Pencil/markers/crayons

OPTIONAL:
- Library/bookstore visit

JUST THE FACTS

SKILLS: Reading Comprehension/Literal Recall

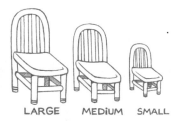

LARGE   MEDIUM   SMALL

Facts are bits and pieces of information that we know to be true. Next time you read a story with your child, focus on the facts. While reading, talk about the who, what, where, and when, asking questions to build your child's awareness of factual information. Make statements that are both true and false about the story, to check whether your child focuses on the facts and recalls details.

Start with a familiar book, one that your child has previously heard or read. After reading, say, "It's a fact that Goldilocks went to the house of four bears." Your child will catch on quickly and respond, "No, it's not a fact! There were three bears." Continue with, "It's a fact that Goldilocks sat on three chairs." Give your child time to respond, "Yes!" Now say, "It's a fact that Goldilocks ate the bears' ice cream." Let your child correct you. "No, she ate their porridge!"

Try Just the Facts again, using a book your child doesn't know. Follow the same procedure to build skill in comprehension and literal recall of facts and details.

REQUIRED:
- A book

OPTIONAL:
- Library/bookstore visit

THE MOUNTAINTOP IDEA

SKILLS: Reading Comprehension/Listening Comprehension/Main Idea/Supportive Details

The main idea of a story is the Mountaintop Idea. That is, like a mountaintop, the main idea covers all the details below it and tells about the whole story.

Demonstrate this concept concretely. Make a main idea mountaintop to accompany any book you share. Draw a big mountain on construction paper. After reading a book, discuss what the story is mostly about and write the main idea inside the mountain at the top. For example, read *Stellaluna* by Janell Cannon. Write in the mountaintop, "Stellaluna the fruit bat is separated from her mother and raised by birds." Below the mountaintop, write four details, pieces of information that support or tell about the main idea.

1. When mother bat was chased by an owl, she dropped Stellaluna.
2. Stellaluna landed in a nest of young birds.
3. The mother bird fed Stellaluna.
4. The young birds played with Stellaluna.

> **REQUIRED:**
> • A book
> • Construction paper
> • Marker
>
> **OPTIONAL:**
> • Index cards
> • Library/bookstore visi

Each time your child reads or listens to a book, write the main idea on a mountaintop. A mountaintop on an index card, tucked into the book, acts as a great line marker and bookmark, too!

HOW DO YOU THINK . . .?

SKILLS: Reading Comprehension/Inferential Thinking/Characterization

How do you think Chrysanthemum of Kevin Henkes's book *Chrysanthemum* feels when children in class make fun of her name? How do you think Koala Lou of Mem Fox's book *Koala Lou* feels when she learns that she won second place in the gum tree climbing contest? How do you think Big Bad Bruce feels in Bill Peet's *Big Bad Bruce* when he discovers he is the size of a chipmunk?

By asking your first grader how he or she thinks any character feels in a certain situation, you are reinforcing the ability to make an inference based upon what your child has read or already knows.

Choose a story to read together. Be sure to ask, "How do you think . . .?

> **REQUIRED:**
> • A book
>
> **OPTIONAL:**
> • Library/bookstore visit

M&M READING

SKILLS: Reading Comprehension/Literal Recall/Inferential Thinking

Have you ever read a page in a book and wondered, "What was that all about?" Because beginning readers put huge energy into recognizing and decoding words, they, too, often get to the end of a page without having recall of what they have read. M&M Reading will make a difference. It demonstrates concretely the importance of actively engaging with text.

Tell your child that the best way to enjoy M&M's is to eat them one at a time. If you pour a handful into your mouth, chew once, and swallow, it is as if you never had them at all! You have to eat a second handful to ensure appreciation! The same is true with reading aloud or silently. Treat each sentence as an M&M. Read a sentence, letting one M&M melt in your mouth. Before moving to the next sentence, stop to think about or talk about the sentence. Take a second M&M and move to sentence two. Repeat the process. When you reach the bottom of the page, you'll know what you have read and you'll enjoy what you have eaten!

REQUIRED:
• A book
• M&M's

OPTIONAL:
• Library/bookstore visit

WHAT DO YOU KNOW ABOUT THAT?!

SKILLS: Brainstorming/Recording Data/Reading Comprehension/Literal Recall/Inferential Thinking

Prior to reading any piece of nonfiction writing, children benefit from being given the opportunity to tell what they *K*now or believe to be true about the topic, what they *W*ant to know about the topic, and, after reading, what they *L*earned about the topic. The acronym KWL is one in common use across the grades and the curriculum. By activating prior knowledge, you provide added incentive to the beginning reader who approaches reading about the subject with purpose and enthusiasm.

The next time you and your child pick up a book to read about bears, tornadoes, presidents, or dinosaurs, put KWL to work. Before reading, talk about what you know or believe to be true about the subject. Record this information in the first column of a three-column KWL chart. Discuss and record in column two what you want to know. Read the book together, looking for information to confirm what you knew or believed to be true. Look for information that answers your questions. After reading, discuss new learning and record in column three. Using the *K*now, *W*ant to know, *L*earn plan is an effective way to heighten understanding of new material.

REQUIRED:
• Nonfiction reading material
• Paper and pencil

OPTIONAL:
• Library/bookstore visit

FROGGY GETS WHAT?!

Can a frog get dressed to go out and play in the snow? Can a girl grow antlers? Use literature to show your first grader the difference between fantasy and reality.

Choose a book such as *Froggy Gets Dressed* by Jonathan London or *Imogene's Antlers* by David Small. Look at the cover illustration first. Ask your child to find three things that show the story is make believe. Enjoy the conversation, having fun with the idea that, for example, a frog lives in a house and wears pajamas. Talk about where a real frog lives in the summer and winter.

Read the story together. Discuss the things that couldn't happen in the real world and the things that could. As a follow-up activity, ask your child to tell a story, draw a picture, or write a story modeling the book just shared. For example, Imogene woke up one morning to discover she had grown antlers. Tell your child to imagine waking up one morning with an animal body part—a beak, wings, horns, a tail! What would it be and what will happen? The difference between fantasy and reality will be clear!

REQUIRED:
• A book

OPTIONAL:
• Paper and pencil
• Crayons/markers
• Library/bookstore visit

DON'T TURN THE PAGE

SKILLS: Reading Comprehension/Predicting Outcomes/Recording Data

You don't need a crystal ball to predict what might happen next! You need story clues and what you already know! Read a story together, but don't turn the page until you make a prediction of what will happen next.

A perfect book for predicting the outcome is *Who Sank the Boat?* by Pamela Allen. Before you begin this story, write down your prediction of which animal will sink the boat—the cow, the donkey, the sheep, the pig, or the mouse. Use what you know about the animals to support your prediction. Throughout the book, the author asks, "Who sank the boat?" as she introduces each character. Don't Turn the Page until you've answered the question by predicting. Both you and your child will be excited to learn whether your prediction was true for this book or any book you choose to read!

REQUIRED:
• A book

OPTIONAL:
• Library/bookstore visit

CONCRETE CONCLUSIONS

SKILLS: Reading Comprehension/Drawing Conclusions

Stories don't always tell all we need to know. First graders can draw conclusions by moving from the concrete to the abstract.

Put M&M's on the table. Eat only yellow ones. Ask your child, "What do you know about me and the M&M's?" Your child responds, "You like the yellow ones."

Put an apple, orange, and pear on the table. Take the pear. Ask your child to draw a conclusion or tell what is true about you and the fruit.

Put paper circles, squares, and triangles on the table. Take only triangles. Ask your child to draw a conclusion.

Now use books or make up short anecdotes. Ask, "What is probably true?" Try this one:

Sue and Jack ran home from school. When they arrived, they were dripping wet. Mom was at the door with towels. Sue and Jack changed into dry clothes and then ate hot soup.

Ask your child to draw conclusions about Sue and Jack. The story doesn't say, but Sue and Jack probably didn't have umbrellas or raincoats. It was probably sunny when they left for school. They were cold when they got home.

The conclusion you'll draw is that your first grader understands!

REQUIRED:
- M&M's
- Fruit
- Paper shapes
- A book

OPTIONAL:
- Library/bookstore visit

I'M HUNGRY, SO . . .

SKILLS: Reading Comprehension/Cause & Effect

I'm hungry, so I eat a snack. The baby is sleepy, so she takes a nap. The flower needs light, so it turns toward the window. An essential component of reading comprehension, listening, and analytical thinking is to understand causal relationships. First graders enjoy giving the possible effect of a cause and then recognizing this same relationship in the books and materials they read or hear in all subject areas.

Over breakfast or while driving to the market or a Little League game, engage your child in a quick and easy cause–and–effect activity. Simply say, "Finish my sentence any way you can so that it makes sense."

Sample starters include: He hit a home run, so . . .

It began to rain, so . . .

She ran so fast that . . .

The boy forgot to tie his shoe, so . . .

REQUIRED:
- Your time

Now ask your child to start the sentence. No matter who starts the process, invite everyone at the table or in the car to provide a possible effect.

Transfer this same kind of thinking to reading. Next time you share a book, fiction or nonfiction, look for and discuss cause and effect!

THE ANIMAL BOOKS GO HERE

SKILLS: Reading Comprehension/Classification

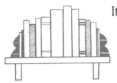

It is important for first graders to see that things can be put into groups. A great way to demonstrate this concept is by classifying the books in your child's personal library. Make the categories simple so that sorting can occur by title and cover. Possible category groupings include:

1. Short Books	Medium Books	Long Books
2. Farm Animals	Jungle Animals	Forest Animals
3. Water Animals	Land Animals	Sky Animals
4. Books About People	Books About Animals	Books About Things
5. Real People	Make Believe People	
6. Real Animals	Make Believe Animals	
7. Male Authors	Female Authors	
8. Hardcover Books	Paperback Books	

REQUIRED:
• Books

The possibilities are as wide as your child's imagination. Before long, your first grader will make categories independently and have the most organized library in the house!

UPPERCASE ONLY

SKILLS: Capitalization/Recording Data

The first word of a sentence needs an uppercase letter and so do the names of people (Zachary, Mrs. Wong), places (Michigan), months (June), and days of the week (Saturday). Present your first grader with the chance to do an Uppercase Only search. Select a favorite book from your child's personal library. Read the book together, pointing out that each sentence begins with an uppercase letter. Note that the names of people, places, months, and days also begin with uppercase letters.

Next make a four-column chart. Label the first column "First Words," the second column "Names of People," the third column "Names of Places," and the fourth column "Months and Days." Choose a page from the book to review. Work together to find the words that begin with an uppercase letter. Print the words in the appropriate column on the chart. Select a second page and repeat the process. Be sure to discuss the words listed. Talk about what made each of the words Uppercase Only.

REQUIRED:
• A book
• Paper and pencil

OPTIONAL:
• Library/bookstore visit

STOP SIGN SENTENCES

SKILLS: Punctuation/End Marks

First graders learn that a sentence is a group of words that tells a complete thought. To help your first grader remember that a sentence must be followed by a period (.), question mark (?), or exclamation point (!), tell your child that a sentence is like a car. When it comes to a stop sign, a car must stop. Otherwise the car might bump into another car. In the same way, a sentence needs to stop at a stop sign. Otherwise it bumps into another sentence.

The stop signs used for sentences are the period, question mark, and exclamation point. Use a period when the sentence tells something. Use a question mark when the sentence asks something. Use an exclamation point when the sentence tells something exciting. On a piece of paper, write a series of three sentences without "stop signs." Read the sentences and ask your child to write the correct stop sign at the end of each one. Start out with the sample sentences below. Then do Stop Sign Sentences any day!

SAMPLE SENTENCES:

Mom read a book(.)
Did you like the book(?)
It was great(!)

I went for a swim(.)
Was the water cold(?)
The water was freezing(!)

REQUIRED:
• Paper and pencil

A SENTENCE A DAY

SKILLS: Punctuation/Capitalization/Following Directions

For practice in applying rules of capitalization and end-mark punctuation, give your child a Sentence a Day. Omit the uppercase letter at the beginning and leave out the period at the end. Forget to include an uppercase letter at the start of a person's name and o mit an exclamation point. Write the name of a place with a lowercase letter and leave out a question mark.

Now put your child to work as the editor. Ask your first grader to circle any word that is missing an uppercase letter and to write the period, question mark, or exclamation point if it is missing at the end. Check completed work together. Then thank your first grader for helping you edit your sentences!

SAMPLE SENTENCES:

did you see frank	Did you see Frank?
mrs. pollock is the teacher	Mrs. Pollock is the teacher.
texas is huge	Texas is huge!
is the moon made of cheese	Is the moon made of cheese?
bobby won the race	Bobby won the race!
karen likes to run	Karen likes to run.
did dorothy go to ohio	Did Dorothy go to Ohio?
evan hit a homerun	Evan hit a homerun!
joan baked cookies on monday	Joan baked cookies on Monday.

REQUIRED:
• Paper and pencil

SANDWICH BAG SENTENCES

SKILL: Sentence Structure

First graders need to know how to build complete sentences. Help your child become more familiar with correct sentence structure by making Sandwich Bag Sentences. To prepare for this activity, cut six index cards into four sections to make 24 word cards. Copy each word of the sentence, "The brown dog ran," onto word cards, one word per card. Be sure to use an uppercase letter on "The" and include a period on the card with "ran." Put these cards into a sandwich bag. Repeat the process for the sample sentences below, one sentence per bag.

A boy went to school.
My dad ate lunch.
Two happy girls play ball.
The yellow bird made her nest.

REQUIRED:
• Index cards
• Sandwich bags
• Safety scissors
• Marker

Now you are ready to invite your child to build Sandwich Bag Sentences. Give your child one bag. Remove the cards from the bag. Place them on the table and arrange the cards so that they make a complete sentence. Remind your child to use the uppercase letter and the end mark as clues. Ask your first grader to read the completed sentence. Repeat the process for all Sandwich Bag Sentences.

FOLLOW THE STEPS

SKILLS: Brainstorming/Recording Data/Written Expression/Revising/Proofreading/ Editing/Drawing

Even as early as first grade, writers follow the steps that are part of the writing process for pieces they would like to publish. You can guide your child through these steps whenever you write together at home.

Preparation: This step, also called prewriting, can take on many forms. Brainstorm ideas orally. Write them down. Complete a graphic organizer such as a story map, story web, or story star.

First Draft: Weave the ideas into a series of sentences.

Revision: Change ideas, add details, remove information.

Proofread/Edit: Check mechanics, including spelling, capitalization, and punctuation.

REQUIRED:
• Paper and pencil

OPTIONAL:
• Book-making supplies
• Crayons/markers

Publish: Display the finished story in any format. Your child may wish to recopy the story in book form, adding illustrations.

Add the published story to your child's library after your young writer reads the story aloud to the family.

WRITE ABOUT CHART

SKILLS: Brainstorming/Written Expression/Preparation/Recording Data/Categorizing

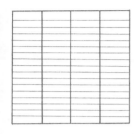

Post a Write About Chart in your child's room so that your young writer will always have an idea of something to write about. Head the chart, "Things I Want to Write About." Then divide the chart into columns or boxes by topic, selecting those topics with your child. Possible categories include "Favorite Things" (my truck, my Legos, my Beanie Babies), "Favorite Places" (Grandma's house, the beach, the science museum), "Favorite Hobbies" (baseball card collecting, stamp collecting), "Favorite Activities" (baking, painting, reading), "Sports" (baseball, skating, swimming), "Things I Want to Learn About" (insects, seeds, clouds), "Magic Places" (a giant's castle, a dragon's cave). Add ideas under categories whenever they arise and check off ideas when stories are written.

REQUIRED:
• Construction paper
• Pencil

STORY MAP

SKILLS: Brainstorming/Recording Data/Written Expression/Story Sequence

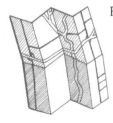

Follow a road map to get from place to place. Follow a Story Map to get from beginning to end! Graphic organizers are helpful tools for all writers, especially those beginning to write in first grade.

Hold a piece of paper horizontally. Fold the paper evenly into three columns. Write "Story Map" across the top. Label the left column "Beginning." Beneath the label, near the margin, write "Main Character(s): _____." Next, write "Setting: Where _____ When_____." Near the bottom of the column, write "Problem or Wish: _____." Label the center column "Middle," and the right column "End." Prior to writing a story, brainstorm with your child. Fill in the Story Map with the ideas generated. Encourage your child to follow the map while writing the story. Weave the ideas together from beginning to end.

For variation, set the map up as a Story Web. Write the name of the main character in a center bubble with setting, problem, events, and solution in bubbles all around. No matter what the form, a graphic organizer is a simple, concrete, and usable tool!

REQUIRED:
• Paper and pencil

STORY IN A STAR

SKILLS: Written Expression/Story Form/Recording Data

Good things can happen when you wish upon a star, or when you write upon a star! By using a five-point star as a story map or graphic organizer, you can help your child plan a story to include the five *W*'s: *Who, What, Where, When,* and *Why.*

Draw a large five-point star on a piece of paper. Label each of the five points with one of the *W*'s. Engage your child in a lively conversation about the work in progress. Ask, "Who is the story about?" Record the response inside the "Who" point. Ask, "Where did the story take place?" Again, record the response in the appropriate point.

Continue in this fashion until brief information is recorded in all five points. Then work together to weave the ideas into the story. While your child is writing or dictating, ask, for example, "When did you say the story takes place?" Refer to the star organizer for information. The combination of your questions and the recorded ideas will enhance the organization with which your child tells the tale.

REQUIRED:
• Paper and pencil

JUMP START WRITE

SKILLS: Written Expression/Imaginative Thinking

Picture storybooks are a rich resource for generating ideas for writing. Imaginations are sparked with the enthusiasm that comes from enjoying a good tale!

Choose a book to read and talk about together. Then capture your ideas by modeling the tale in your own story. Imagine what would happen if you had a magic pot just like the one that makes pasta in Tomie DePaola's *Strega Nona*. What words would you use to make your pot start and stop and what food would your pot make? Imagine the life of an invisible possum in Mem Fox's *Possum Magic*. Try your hand at writing about the day Grandma Poss used her bush magic to make you invisible. Delight in the fantasy of Raymond Briggs's wordless book *The Snowman*. Then write a story about the day your snow person comes to life!

Pick a book to Jump Start Write!

REQUIRED:
• Picture storybook
• Paper and pencil

OPTIONAL:
• Library/bookstore visit

CIRCLE STORY

SKILLS: Written Expression/Story Sequence/Predicting Outcomes/Drawing

One thing leads to another in the delightful Laura Numeroff books, *If You Give a Mouse a Cookie, If You Give a Moose a Muffin,* and *If You Give a Pig a Pancake.* On your next visit to the library or bookstore, read one or more of these stories together. Talk about the events as they happen, focusing on how one event leads to the next. Before turning pages, ask your child to predict what may happen.

Now set aside time to coauthor a Circle Story. Follow the pattern of the Numeroff books. Decide upon a main character. Perhaps you'll give a bear a banana or give a monkey a marshmallow. Create a sequence of three to five events with the final one returning to the beginning. Write each event on a separate sheet of paper. Then invite your child to draw a picture to accompany each event. Make a cover page with the title, author, and illustrator. Bind the book with staples or paper fasteners. As an option, punch a hole in the top left-hand corner. Tie the book together, read, and add to your child's library.

> **REQUIRED:**
> - Library/bookstore visit
> - Paper and pencil
> - Markers/crayons
> - Stapler/paper fasteners
>
> **OPTIONAL:**
> - Hole punch
> - Ribbon/yarn/string

JUST WRITE!

SKILLS: Written Expression/Imaginative Thinking

Every story doesn't need to be published. Imagine a late afternoon when your child has just finished piano lessons, soccer practice, and homework. It isn't time for dinner yet, nothing is on television, an older sibling is using the computer, and Mom and Dad are busy doing other things. Take a moment out for Just Write!

The topic is up to you and/or your child. The only rule, make it fun! Imagine that your pencil starts to talk! Your cookie ran away! You ate an apple and turned into a tree! You watched a butterfly and suddenly found yourself flying beside it! You shrank! You grew!

Anything goes! Take a pencil, paper, five minutes and write. When you have both finished your stories, read and compare your work. Notice the variations that occur even though you wrote on the same subject.

No preparation activity, no drafting, no revising, no proofing, editing, or publishing. Just Write!

> **REQUIRED:**
> - Paper and pencil

WITHOUT A WORD

SKILLS: Expressive Language/Written Expression/Predicting Outcomes/Fantasy versus Reality/Story Sequence

Wordless picture books provide wonderful opportunities for your first grader to enhance expressive and written language skills. Enjoy a book such as *Good Dog, Carl* by Alexandra Day or *Pancakes for Breakfast* by Tomie DePaola. While "reading," tell the story from the illustrations. Work collaboratively to predict what will happen next, before you turn the page. Talk about the setting, discussing the where and when. Ask questions to focus your child on the character. From *Good Dog, Carl* ask, "Why is Carl a good dog?" "What is one thing Carl does that a real dog could do?" "What is one thing Carl does that a real dog couldn't do?" From *Pancakes for Breakfast* ask, "How do you think the little lady feels when she discovers that she has no eggs?" "Do you think the little lady is a hard worker?" "Why?" From start to finish, add words to the tale.

On a reread, put your words to paper, asking your child to write or dictate the story in sequence. Finally, read your child's completed story while looking at the wordless book.

REQUIRED:
- Wordless book
- Paper and pencil
- Markers/crayons

OPTIONAL:
- Library/bookstore visit

DEAR TOAD . . . ◆

SKILLS: Reading Comprehension/Written Expression/Imaginative Thinking

Bring literature to life! After reading a book, imagine that the main character is real. Discuss the events of the story and the actions as the main character worked to solve a problem or make a wish come true.

Encourage your child to write a friendly letter to the main character, sharing opinions, questions, or advice. Your first grader may even want to invite the book character to come for a visit. The content of the letter is determined by the nature of the book. For example, in "The Letter," from *Frog and Toad Are Friends* by Arnold Lobel, Toad is very sad because no one ever sends him a letter. Then one day, Toad receives a letter from Frog. The letter makes Toad very happy. Your child can make Toad happy, too, by writing Toad a letter.

As an option, delight your child by taking on the persona of Toad to respond to your child's letter.

REQUIRED:
- Favorite book
- Writing paper or stationery
- Pencils

OPTIONAL:
- Envelope
- Library/bookstore visit

TOP-TO-BOTTOM POETRY

SKILLS: Written Expression/Poetry/Characterization/Brainstorming

Describe a book character and write a poem, too! An acrostic is a poem in which each line begins with the letters, in sequence, of the person, place, or thing you want to describe.

Ask your child to choose a person, place, or thing from any story read or heard. For example, if your child reads *Julius, The Baby of the World,* by Kevin Henkes, choose the name "Julius" or the word "baby." Brainstorm ideas for each letter of the word before your young poet writes or dictates the acrostic. Highlight the first letter of each line so that the connection between the word and the description is shown.

Repeat this activity, adding each new poem to your child's personal book of poetry. Staple pages together or punch a hole in the upper left-hand corner of each page. Tie with yarn, ribbon, or string. An example follows. Can you guess whom it describes?

REQUIRED:
- Favorite book
- Paper and pencil

OPTIONAL:
- Stapler
- Hole punch
- Yarn/ribbon/string
- Library/bookstore visit

Babbles and gurgles,
As he plays in his crib,
Blowing bubbles and making
You kiss and admire!

CARDS BY ME

SKILLS: Brainstorming/Imaginative Thinking/Written Expression/Drawing

Happy Birthday, Happy Anniversary, and Get Well, too! There is no card more special than the one personally designed and written by a child. One fold in a piece of paper and your first grader can write wishes for any special celebration or holiday. Just provide the materials and spend a little time talking about the message that fits the event. Suggest a two-line rhyme or simply a sentence or two to make the greeting just right.

REQUIRED:
- Construction paper
- Pencil
- Crayons/markers

OPTIONAL:
- Nontoxic glue
- Safety scissors
- Ribbon
- Doilies
- Glitter

Encourage your card designer to decorate the cover and inside pages with drawings for the occasion. Have colored tissue, doilies, ribbon, and glitter available, too! Finally, a logo such as Cards by Me, substituting your child's name for *Me,* that is, "Cards by Liz" or "Cards by Jeff," with the date, adds the finishing touch on the back cover.

FOLD A BOOK

SKILLS: Written Expression/Imaginative Thinking/Drawing

Turn a single piece of paper into a four-page book to give your first grader pride of authorship. Fold a piece of paper into four equal sections. Place the fold on the left to form a front cover, two interior facing pages, and a back cover. With this simple design, your child can regularly add to a library of personal works.

Consider a 26-volume alphabet collection, for example. On the front cover, print uppercase "A" and your first-grade author's name. On the left interior page, draw or paste a picture of something that begins with *a*, an ant, perhaps. Write the word that identifies the picture on the right interior page. Print lowercase "a" on the back cover. Repeat the process for each letter of the alphabet.

Make a favorite food book, a seed to plant book, a seasons book, or a shapes book. Write a story about two-headed giants, a tale of talking tigers or a magic carpet ride. Whatever the topic, real or fantasy, Fold a Book provides structure and incentive for young writers.

REQUIRED:
- Paper and pencil
- Markers/crayons

OPTIONAL:
- Magazines
- Safety scissors
- Nontoxic glue

COLOR SPLASH

SKILLS: Brainstorming/Observation/Written Expression/Recording Data/Drawing/Cutting

Splash color across the page to create a favorite-color book. Generate a list of things that are, for example, green. Start at home, listing things both inside and out. Continue by observing things in your neighborhood. Choose five to ten items to include in your "Book of Green."

Make a construction paper cover, the bigger the better. Print the title and authors in bold letters. Decorate the cover using green. Then, for each item on the green list, make one page. Encourage your child to draw the green item or use a magazine picture. Above or beneath the picture, identify the item, writing, "Green is broccoli" (page one), "and grass" (page two). "Green is a leaf" (page three), "and a ball" (page four). "A scarf is green" (page five), "and a car is green" (page six).

Continue in this way until all items have been included in your "Book of Green." Punch three holes along the left margin and tie the book together with green ribbon or yarn. Make this book the first of several for your child's Color Splash library.

REQUIRED:
- Construction paper
- Hole punch
- Pencils/markers/crayons
- Yarn/ribbon

OPTIONAL:
- Magazines
- Safety scissors
- Nontoxic glue

HAVE JOURNAL WILL TRAVEL

SKILLS: Written Expression/Drawing

Never go off on a trip without a travel journal at the ready! Illustrate and date each page as the journal is developed. Set aside a few moments each day to write. As one option, keep individual journals so that you can share ideas among family members. A second option is to create a family travel journal. Your first grader writes about the first day, a brother or sister records the second day, and Mom or Dad does the third day. Continue the sequence throughout the trip. A third option is to have your child illustrate the daily adventures and dictate the text to another family member. Your journal is a collective cooperative keepsake to treasure.

REQUIRED:
• Journal/notepad
• Pencil
• Crayons/markers

ERRAND DAY WRITE

SKILLS: Written Expression/Recording Data/Story Sequence/Drawing

In the delightful picture storybook, *The Big Green Pocketbook* by Candice Ransom, a young girl spends a morning doing errands with her mom. The story sequentially tells about each place visited and each errand done, from the bank, to the dry cleaners, to the drugstore.

When you and your child go out to do a few errands, try an "Errand Day Write" when you get home. Work together to make a story map that lists, in order, each errand you did. Encourage your child to include the who, what, where, and when. For example, to start the story, ask, "Who went out to do errands?" Your child answers and writes, "My mom/dad and I went out to do errands . . ." Ask, while your child is writing, "When?" Your child continues, ". . . this morning." Then ask, "Where?" Your child writes, "We went to the mall." Then ask, "What did we do first?" Your child continues, "First we went to . . ." At the end, ask your child to write one closing sentence to tell about the morning. For example, "We got everything done and had fun, too!" Illustrate the story if you wish.

REQUIRED:
• Errand run
• Paper and pencil

OPTIONAL:
• Crayons/markers
• Library/bookstore visit

FAMILY PHOTO WRITE

SKILLS: Written Expression/Story Sequence

Pictures say a thousand words, especially when you use them as writing prompts for your child. Pull out some of those photo envelopes piling up in a drawer! Let your first grader choose a picture to write about from a birthday party, family trip, or Saturday picnic in the park or backyard. Talk about who is in the picture, when and where it was taken, and what is happening. Then ask your child to write the story of the picture. If you wish, mount the picture on construction paper or poster board along with the caption your child has written.

As an option, encourage your child to choose a series of three or four pictures to use as a visual organizer for writing a sequential story. Follow the same procedure, perhaps placing the finished work in a photo album or journal.

REQUIRED:
- Family photos
- Paper and pencil

OPTIONAL:
- Construction paper or poster board
- Nontoxic glue
- Photo album or journal

FAMILY WRITE-ALONG

SKILLS: Written Expression/Drawing

Everyone is a writer! The more your child sees you write, the more eager your child will be to write!

Have a supply of writing materials in the center of the kitchen or dining room table. Gather the family around the table after an outing, vacation, holiday celebration, or get-together. Talk about the experience just shared. Then, distribute materials and write! During writing time, answer any questions your child might ask and provide encouragement as needed. If your child is not yet writing independently, feel free to take dictation or ask your child to draw a picture to tell about the family event.

When everyone has completed a piece, enjoy drinks and a snack as each writer takes the author's chair to share individual work. Be sure each author takes a bow to a rousing round of applause!

REQUIRED:
- Paper and pencils
- Markers/crayons

OPTIONAL:
- Refreshments

SOUND SPELL

When your child is just beginning to write, encourage sound spelling! Sound spelling or invented spelling is an effective way to build confidence in the developing writer. Ask your child to say a word slowly and listen for its sounds. Assist in the process by asking, "What sound do you hear at the beginning? What is the name of the letter that makes that sound? Write the letter. What sound do you hear in the middle? What is the name of the letter that makes that sound? Write the letter. What sound do you hear at the end? What is the name of the letter that makes that sound? Write the letter."

If your child is unsure, provide the letter name or tell your first grader to write a dash in place of the unknown letter. Combine this process with use of your child's personal spelling dictionary (see Spellbound). In this way, your child doesn't become dependent on either method but uses a range of strategies as spelling skills develop.

REQUIRED:
• Paper and pencil

SPELLBOUND

When your first grader is writing, you can write unknown words on Post-it® notes and stick them on a bulletin board or wall. You can also help your child make a personal spelling dictionary or handbook of frequently used words. Whether the words are on the wall or in a bound book, your child will have ready access to a growing vocabulary of high frequency words for writing.

Use a notebook as a spelling dictionary. On the cover, print, for example, "Debbie's Spelling Dictionary." Make a two-sided page for each letter of the alphabet, printing the letter in uppercase and lowercase at the top of both sides of the page. When your child asks how to spell, "again," "my," "once," or "where," turn to the appropriate page in the spelling dictionary. Write the word for your child or dictate the word, letter by letter, to your child so that your beginning speller can make the entry. As the dictionary fills with words, your first grader will take pride in being able to spell words independently by using this helpful tool.

REQUIRED:
• Notebook
• Pencil/marker
• Post-it® notes

SPELL CHECKER

SKILLS: Spelling/Visual Discrimination/Visual Memory

brd
bird
FLuw
FLew
ovr
over

You don't need a computer to be a "Spell Checker"! As first graders begin to write, they often rely upon their awareness of letter sounds to "sound spell" unfamiliar words. Encourage your son or daughter to do so! When your first grader writes, "A rd brd fluw ovr mi hd" for "A red bird flew over my head," praise the effort and celebrate the successful attempt at sound spelling. Then give your child the important job of spell checker. Provide a pencil and ask your first grader to check each word to make sure it includes at least one of the "superstar letters," the vowels *a, e, i, o,* or *u.* Tell your Spell Checker to circle the words that are missing a superstar letter. Then, use a children's dictionary if available, or simply a piece of paper and a pencil, to show your child how the word looks in a book. Finally, write the book spelling just above the sound spelling to reinforce the visual memory of standard book spelling.

REQUIRED:
• Paper and pencil

OPTIONAL:
• Dictionary

MULTISENSORY SPELL

SKILLS: Spelling/Visual Discrimination/Visual Memory/Auditory Discrimination/
Kinesthetic Motor

SPELLING LIST

1. Apple –
2. Board –
3. Captain –
4. Desk –
5. Eagle –
6. Friend –

Use sight, sound, and touch to reinforce your first grader's developing skill in spelling. When your child brings home the weekly spelling list from school, join the practice that occurs over the week. Encourage your child to look at a word as you read it or say it aloud. Have your child repeat the word. Spell the word as you point to each letter. Ask your child to spell the word while pointing to each letter. Now each of you should write the word on paper, naming each letter as you write. Say the word again when it is written. Repeat the process for each word on the list.

For added practice, take the word to the sky. Use the index finger and middle finger of your writing hand to "skywrite" the word. Next, put the word on the table, using the same two fingers to "write" the word on the surface. Encourage your child to "write" the word on your back so that you can guess it! Practice "writing" the word in any dry ingredient—flour, salt, sugar, or gelatin powder—spread in a flat container. Use your senses to spell!

REQUIRED:
• Weekly spelling list
• Paper and pencil
• Granular substance
• Flat plastic container
  with cover

SPELL DOWN

SKILLS: Spelling/Visual Discrimination/Visual Memory/Auditory Discrimination/Making Comparisons

cat, fat,
hat, mat,
rat, sat

Start at the top with a word such as *cat.* Spell all the way down until you've written *rat!* There are patterns in groups of words that enhance reading and writing vocabulary.

Keep a Spell Down notebook. On each page of the notebook, write a single word, one that your child can read. Be aware of the pattern or spelling rule focused on at school so that you can match home activity with classroom instruction. When your child is working on words with short *a,* for example, do Spell Down with a short *a* starter word. Write *pan* at the top of the page and say, "Go." Your child then writes a list of words beneath *pan* by changing the initial letter. *Pan* generates *ban, bran, can, clan, Dan, fan, Fran, man, Nan, ran, tan,* and *van.*

To vary the activity, join your child in Spell Down. Write a word at the top of the page in your child's notebook and on a piece of paper for yourself. Say, "Go," complete the list, and compare the results by reading the words each of you has spelled down!

REQUIRED:
• Notebook or paper
• Pencils

AIRPLANE ANAGRAM

SKILLS: Spelling/Visual Discrimination/Visual Memory/Recording Data/Making Comparisons

Are we there yet? Make air travel easy and build spelling skills and visual discrimination skills by playing Airplane Anagram.

Once airborne or when sitting and waiting for a delayed flight, write *airplane* across the top of a sheet of paper. Fold the paper into four equal columns. Label the columns "2," "3," "4," and "5." Say, "Go!" Using the letters of *airplane,* make as many words as you can by reordering the letters in *airplane.* Write the two-letter words in the "2" column, three-letter words in the "3" column, four-letter words in the "4" column, and five-letter words in the "5" column. Your child can work independently or in collaboration with you.

When two or more people play, make an *airplane* sheet for each. Set a time limit for finding and recording words. Then compare word lists. Receive one point for each word you have written that no other player has made. Play to an agreed-upon score. Continue play, using trip-related words such as the name of the place of departure or the name of the destination.

Sample words made from *airplane* include: 2—an, in; 3—nap, pin; 4—near, leap; and 5—plane, ripen

REQUIRED:
• Paper and pencils

GROCERY ASSISTANT

SKILLS: Spelling/Dictation

Even though trips to the grocery store are often rushed, squeezed between carpools and other commitments, take time every so often to make your visit to the market an educational experience for your child.

To start, dictate all or a portion of the grocery list to your child. Encourage sound spelling but write in the standard spelling above each word. Once at the grocery store, let your assistant help you find the items by reading the list, the store aisle signs, the labels of the items, and the prices.

Although your shopping may take a little longer than usual, you'll bring home more than groceries!

REQUIRED:
- Grocery story visit
- Paper and pencil

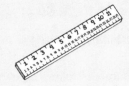 # MATH

Children enter first grade with a working knowledge of math concepts. They have engaged in five years of concrete exploration both at home and at school. They are now ready to continue their discovery and exploration of the methods of mathematics.

During the first grade year, children are immersed in math. They are surrounded by number lines, shapes, patterns, and concrete materials, including counters, attribute blocks, pattern blocks, dominoes, and dice. They are provided with authentic tools, including rulers, tape measures, calculators, money, calendars, thermometers, and clocks. When first graders investigate and validate their ideas through exploration and manipulation, they thrive.

First grade is a time when children make amazing discoveries in math. They attach meaning to numbers and symbols. They move from concrete thinking to abstract thinking, from rote counting to problem solving. Young mathematicians begin to recognize that math is everywhere, both inside and outside the classroom.

Celebrate the discoveries your child makes in math exploration. Marvel at visual patterns in a painting or the symmetry of a butterfly. Predict what exit number will come next on the highway, or estimate the number of beans in a bag. Explore number patterns in your neighborhood or use recycled materials to construct three-dimensional structures. Add numbers on an Addition Ball or travel the Math Path gameboard to practice subtraction facts. Delight in math as your child develops a strong foundation for the development of lifelong skills.

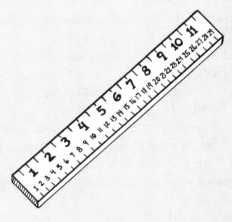

NUMBERS ALL AROUND

SKILLS: Number Awareness/Number Recognition/Brainstorming/Drawing

Invite your child to be a number detective! Math and numbers follow us everywhere from supermarkets and magazine ads to road signs and menus.

To help your child see that numbers are everywhere, create a collage entitled "Numbers All Around." Provide your child with magazines, maps, ticket stubs, receipts, television/movie listings, food containers, newspapers, and anything else that can be recycled. In addition to the materials provided, remind your child to think of items that can't be cut up—road signs, team jerseys, license plates—but can be drawn to add to the collage.

Provide your child with an appropriate work space and time to complete the number search. You may want to join in the fun as your child cuts, draws, arranges, and pastes number selections onto a piece of construction paper. Demonstrate that a collage of numbers can be designed as your child chooses. Display the completed collage in a special place in your home so that your number detective can revisit the work of art and add to it at any time.

REQUIRED:
- Construction paper/ poster board
- Safety scissors
- Tape or nontoxic glue
- Recyclable print materials
- Crayons/markers/ colored pencils
- Drawing paper

ARITHMEQUILT

SKILLS: Number Awareness/Connecting Math & Literature/Brainstorming/Drawing

Numbers are part of all aspects of our day. They literally make the world tick! How would we bake cookies without temperature settings for the oven? How would we get to appointments on time without clocks? How would we find favorite television or radio programs without channel and station numbers? How would we find a friend's house without street numbers? How would we stay within the speed limit, know what day it is, or check our weight? How would we buy anything?

Integrate number awareness with literature and art by making an Arithmequilt. For background information, visit your school library, local library, or bookstore. Enjoy reading *The Josefina Story Quilt* by Eleanor Coerr, *The Patchwork Quilt* by Valerie Flournoy, and *The Keeping Quilt* by Patricia Polacco. In each, appreciate the value and purpose of a special quilt.

Create an Arithmequilt at home, making your special quilt by dividing a large piece of poster board into patches. Brainstorm all the jobs of numbers. Then, in each patch, draw a picture and label each item that has found a place on your Arithmequilt. Encourage every member of the family to contribute to the design.

REQUIRED:
- Library/bookstore visit
- Poster board
- Markers/crayons

HOUSEHOLD MATH SURVEY

SKILLS: Number Awareness/Surveying/Recording Data

Numbers are essential in the operation of household items. Take a household math survey to see the important role numbers play in our lives at home. With pad and pencil in hand, start the survey in the kitchen. List the items as you point out and talk about the use of the timer and settings on the microwave, stove, refrigerator, mixer, dishwasher, and toaster. How do the numbers help us operate these appliances? Encourage your child to continue the survey independently in other rooms. Look for numbers on the washer, dryer, television, video cassette recorder, stereo, radio, remote control, and clock. When your child returns from the household math survey, ask where numbers were found. Your child will be amazed at how many items depend on numbers to work properly.

REQUIRED:
• Pencil and paper

HIGHWAY MATH

SKILLS: Number Awareness/Number Recognition/Counting/Skip Counting/Addition

Whether you're driving to the market or to a different state, make the drive go by faster by engaging your child in a game of Highway Math. License plates, exit signs, mile markers, billboards, and cars all contain numbers that provide loads of fun and practice in a variety of math skills.

If you are driving on the highway, ask your child to notice whether the exit numbers are going up or down. If you pass Exit 19, ask your child what exit will come next. What exit will come in five exits? Point out the mile markers. If you pass Mile Marker 54, ask what mile marker came before it. How many mile markers have we passed since Mile Marker 47? Count the number of blue cars and the number of red cars.

If you are driving in your neighborhood, point out numbers on houses. Ask your child to look for a pattern in the numbers. Does the pattern go by twos, fives, odds, or evens? When stopped at a traffic light, add the digits of a license plate. Count the number of traffic lights you pass in one minute.

Play Highway Math and your travel time will be fun and educational!

REQUIRED:
• Your time

THE NUMBER RHYME

SKILLS: Number Awareness/Rhyme

"One is fun, one sun, one is a yummy cinnamon bun!" No matter where you are, no matter what the time, you can engage your child in the Number Rhyme!

Ask your child, "Can you think of a word that rhymes with *one?*" Provide an example, leaving out a word for your child to provide. "Two is blue, two is true, two is a monkey in the _____ (zoo)." Do the Number Rhyme back and forth between you, each time changing the rhyming word. Keep going until you run out of rhymes. Then try a rhyme with *three.* Give your child the chance to begin the Number Rhyme by choosing the number and saying the first rhyme.

RHYME BANK:

Three a bee, three a tree, three happy starfish in the sea!

Four a door, four the floor, four little puppies in the store!

Five alive, five dive, five buzzing bees in a hive!

Six mix, six bricks, six big horses doing tricks!

Seven eleven, seven is heaven!

Eight great, eight date, eight hippos are late!

Nine fine, nine mine, nine yellow lollipops in a line!

Ten men, ten in the den, ten white eggs and a fat brown hen!

REQUIRED:
• Your time

MATH LITERATURE

SKILLS: Number Awareness/Connecting Math & Literature

First graders are exposed to rich children's literature that takes them to faraway places and introduces them to unusual characters. When reading, children often feel what the character feels. Just imagine how the children in Pat Hutchins's *The Doorbell Rang* felt as they tried to figure out how they could equally share twelve cookies with unannounced guests and visitors.

Many wonderful pieces of children's literature provide a backdrop for rich discussion about math and numbers. Visit your school or local library to choose math literature.

Help Penny measure in Loreen Leedy's *Measuring Penny.* Enjoy an afternoon with the inchworm from *Inch by Inch* by Leo Lionni. Spend a day with pigs while reading about time and money in Amy Axelrod's *Pigs on a Blanket* and *Pigs Will Be Pigs.*

Other math stories to share and discuss with your child are: *Bears Odd Bears Even* by Harriet Ziefert, *A Remainder of One* and *One Hundred Hungry Ants* by Elinor J. Pinczes, *Sea Sums* by Joy N. Hulme, *One Hole in the Road* by W. Lisa-Nikola, *Jellybeans for Sale* by Bruce McMillan, *One Carton of Oops!* by Judy Bradbury, and *Bunches and Bunches of Bunnies* by Louise Mathews.

REQUIRED:
• Math stories
OPTIONAL:
• Library/bookstore visit

RIDDLE TIME

SKILLS: Number Awareness/Counting/Addition

There is something about a riddle that tickles the fancy of young children. Whether they know the answer or not, children like to hear a riddle again and again and like to tell the riddle repeatedly. Tell riddles to build your child's counting skills, number awareness, thinking skills, and language skills.

Ask,

"What has two wings, one beak, and hoots?"   "An owl!"

"What has four wings, two beaks, and hoots?"   "Two owls!"

"What has four legs, one shell, and moves slowly?"   "A turtle!"

"What has eight legs, two shells, and moves slowly?"   "Two turtles!"

"What has two hands, one face, twelve numbers, and ticks?"   "A clock!"

"What has two arms and four legs?"   "A chair!"

Give your child the opportunity to make up riddles to ask you.

REQUIRED:
• Your time

TELEPHONE

SKILLS: Number Awareness/Number Recognition/Number Writing

Telephones and phone numbers provide opportunities to use numbers in real-world contexts. Help your child memorize your telephone number in several ways.

First, show your child the number on the face of your telephone. Clearly print the telephone number on an index card or Post-it® note. Ask your child to read the number aloud. Post the number on the refrigerator. Ask your child to look at the telephone number and read it often.

Over the next few weeks, ask your child to copy the number onto other index cards or Post-it® notes. Post the cards in several easy-to-see places, on a mirror in the bedroom, on a night stand, or in the family room or playroom.

Finally, ask your child to recite the telephone number. Remember, the more your child sees, writes, and says the number, the easier it will be to memorize.

REQUIRED:
• Telephone
• Index cards or Post-it® notes
• Pen and pencil

CATERPILLAR COUNTERS

SKILLS: Number Awareness/Number Recognition/Ordinal Numbers/Drawing/
Number Writing/Counting/Skip Counting

Make counting loads of fun with a Caterpillar Counter! Cut a 6″ circle from construction paper. Ask your child to draw a cute caterpillar face on the circle. Cut two 3″ antennae to attach with nontoxic glue to the head. Next, for the body of the caterpillar, cut a supply of 3″ circles from construction paper. Connect a circle to the head with nontoxic glue or tape. Add circles one at a time until the body is ten circles long. Finally, ask your child to write the number "1" in the center of the first circle, "2" in the center of the second circle, and "3" in the center of the third circle. Continue to ten. Pointing to each segment of the caterpillar, count from one to ten or reverse and count from ten to one. Add to the caterpillar, making it up to one hundred circles long. Tape it to a wall and use it as an aid for counting in sequence or skip counting by twos, fives, or tens.

REQUIRED:
- Construction paper
- Safety scissors
- Nontoxic glue or tape
- Pencil/marker/crayon

CELEBRITY NUMBER

SKILLS: Number Recognition/Counting/Measuring/Drawing/Constructing/Addition

The numbers 0 through 9 deserve celebrity status! These characters are responsible for forming all other numbers we know. Give extra attention to each number during Celebrity Number Week. Choose a number of focus. Write the number clearly on a piece of paper. Post the paper in a place of prominence and introduce your child to the week's Celebrity Number.

During the course of the week, focus on the Celebrity Number. For example, during "6" week, eat six bananas and decorate cookies with six of anything. Read the words and enjoy the pictures on page six of six different books. Find things that measure six inches, centimeters, or feet. Roll a die and see how many sixes you can roll in six throws. Eat dinner at 6:00. Draw pictures of things in groups of six. Make a structure out of six empty paper towel rolls. Figure out how old you will be in six years. The possibilities are endless!

Select a different Celebrity Number each week in random or sequential order. Give the Celebrity Number the recognition it deserves!

REQUIRED:
- Time and imagination

A+ ACTIVITIES FOR FIRST GRADE

MERRY-GO-ROUND MATH

SKILLS: Number Awareness/Measuring/Shape Recognition/Money/Time

Turn on a little music and ride the merry-go-round of math! Encourage your child and all members of the family to fill the merry-go-round with knowledge of numbers, measures, shapes, money, and time.

Set up five stations on the merry-go-round by placing five large sheets of construction paper and markers on the floor in five different locations *around* the room. Label one "Numbers," the second "Shapes," the third "Money," the fourth "Time," and the last "Measures." Assign a starting station for each family member. Then set a timer to three minutes and say,

"Go!" While at each station, the player writes or draws anything related to the category of the station until time is up. Then, in a clockwise direction, each player moves to the next station. Set the timer again and begin, reading over what is already written and making sure to provide new information. Continue play until all players have visited all five stations. At the end of the merry-go-round ride, share all the information collected. Keep the completed sheets accessible so that your child can add information at any time.

REQUIRED:
- Five sheets of construction paper
- Five markers

OPTIONAL:
- Background music

BOOK OF ONE

SKILLS: Number Recognition/Number Writing/Drawing/Number Words

Turn a sheet of paper into a Book of One . . . Two, Three, Four, Five, Six, Seven, Eight, Nine, Ten!

Fold an 8½″ × 11″ sheet of white paper into four equal sections. Place the fold on the left and presto! You have a front cover, two interior facing pages, and a back cover. Follow these simple instructions as your child creates a collection of number books.

On the front cover, ask your child to write the number "1." On the left interior page, draw or paste a picture of one thing. On the right interior page, write "1" and the word that identifies the picture. For example, paste or draw a picture of a dog on the left page. Write "1 Dog" on the right page. Finally, write the word *One* on the back cover. Repeat the process for each number through ten.

REQUIRED:
- 8½″ × 11″ paper
- Pencils/markers/crayons

OPTIONAL:
- Library/bookstore visit
- Magazines
- Safety scissors
- Nontoxic glue

Read your child's number books together, along with other counting books such as *Ten Black Dots* by Donald Crews or *The M&M Counting Book* by Barbara Barbieri McGrath.

DRIZZLE AND GRIDDLE

SKILLS: Number Recognition/Number Writing/Number Formation

Recognize numbers and eat them, too! Have a pancake breakfast that is sure to be a hit with every member of the family. Prepare your usual pancake recipe. Pour the batter from mixing bowl to spouted measuring cup or pitcher. Then supervise the fun as you drizzle the batter onto the griddle in the shape of numbers. Griddle the number of people in the family. Griddle the age of your child. Griddle the date. Griddle a lucky number. Note the way numbers reverse when you flip the pancakes. Then flip them again to demonstrate correct directionality on the plate. Serve with butter, maple syrup, and a whole lot of fun!

REQUIRED:
- Pancake batter
- A spouted measuring cup or pitcher

OPTIONAL:
- Butter
- Maple syrup

TEN TO ONE FIND

SKILL: Number Recognition

First graders need to become as familiar with numbers as they are with cookies and milk! The more exposure to numbers, the better! Send your child on a Ten to One Find each time you read the morning news.

Open a newspaper or magazine on the table or floor, preferably to a page with advertisements. Ask your child to search for the numbers "10" to "1." Either call the numbers one by one and work as a team, or have your child work independently on one page while you work on another. Circle all the numbers found. Review your findings to determine whether all ten were found. Note those missing. Turn to another page and continue the exploration until the Ten to One Find is complete.

Add more numbers to the find over time. Ten to one, you'll both have fun!

REQUIRED:
- Newspaper or magazine
- Pen/pencil/marker

NUMBER DOT MATCH

SKILLS: Number Recognition/One-to-One Correspondence

Play Number Dot Match to help your child recognize and attach meaning to numbers. You need 20 index cards and a marker. Clearly write, one number per card, the numbers 1 to 10. On the remaining 10 cards, make bold dots to represent each number, one to ten. For example, put one dot on one card, two on another, three on another. Continue until you have used all cards.

Divide your playing surface into two areas, one for cards with numbers, the other for cards with dots. Spread the cards facedown in their respective areas. Now you're ready for action!

Your child picks up one card from the number-card area and names it. Your first grader then chooses a card from the dot-card area. Is it a match? If the number corresponds with the dots, it's a match and that player keeps those cards. If a match isn't made, the player returns the cards facedown to their original position. Alternate turns. Play until no cards remain on the playing surface. The player with the most pairs at the end is the winner.

REQUIRED:
- 20 index cards
- Marker

PUTTIN' ON THE GLITZ

SKILLS: Number Recognition/Number Formation/Number Sequence/One-to-One Correspondence/Drawing/Cutting

Use glitter and glue to make a number book to help your child sequence, form, and match objects to numbers. Working on a 6″ × 9″ sheet of construction paper, help your child write the number "1" in glue. Sprinkle glitter over the wet glue and place on a flat surface to dry. Continue this process until you have a page for each number, one through ten.

When each page is dry, shake excess glitter into a container for reuse. Now encourage your child to either cut or draw objects to match the number on each page. For example, cut or draw one star for the "1" page, cut or draw two mushrooms for the "2" page, and cut or draw three dogs to add to the "3" page. Add objects to each page through 10.

Make a cover that includes the title and author of the number book. Punch a hole in the top left corner and bind with a piece of yarn or ribbon. Add the book to your child's library and share often.

REQUIRED:
- 11 sheets 6″ × 9″ construction paper
- Glitter
- Nontoxic glue
- Safety scissors
- Additional sheets construction paper
- Markers/crayons
- Yarn/ribbon
- Hole punch

ROLL 'EM AND TAKE 'EM

SKILLS: One-to-One Correspondence/Number Recognition/Counting/Addition/Subtraction

Grab a die and a handful of pennies and attach meaning to numbers! Sit facing your child with a bank of 50 pennies between you. Alternate rolling the die and taking pennies from the bank. For example, when a player rolls a six, that player takes six pennies from the bank. Play until the bank is empty.

Ask questions such as, "How many pennies do you have?" "How many pennies do I have?" "How many pennies would you have if I gave you five from my pile?" "How many pennies would I have left if you took seven from my pile?"

To add extra challenge, use two dice or increase the number of pennies in the bank.

REQUIRED:
• 50 pennies
• One die

OPTIONAL:
• Extra pennies
• Extra die

SIXES AND SEVENS

SKILLS: Number Recognition/Number Awareness/Counting/Cutting

From September to June, first graders celebrate a sixth or seventh birthday. This year, when it is time to prepare your child's birthday celebration, choose six or seven as the theme of the day.

If you plan a party, consider the idea of inviting six friends for a sixth birthday or seven friends for a seventh. Greet your child in the morning with six or seven hugs and a birthday story such as *Clifford's Birthday Party* by Norman Bridwell or *Some Birthday* by Patricia Polacco. Throughout the day, celebrate six or seven in all you do! Together make a six or seven badge for the birthday child! Cut sixes or sevens from construction paper for decorations. Cluster six or seven candles on the cake, keeping the one for good luck to the side. Open six or seven gifts. Play games that focus on six or seven such as "Pin the Star on the Six" or "Drop the Seven Clothespins in the Bottle." Have partygoers make words using the first six or seven letters of the alphabet. Use glitter glue to decorate goodie bags with sixes or sevens. The six or seven celebration is sure to be special!

REQUIRED:
• Party supplies
• Safety scissors
• Construction paper

PROGRESSION COLLECTION

SKILLS: One-to-One Correspondence/Number Sequence/Counting

One spoon, two forks, three bananas, four cups, five cans, six cookies, seven pretzels, eight jellybeans, nine crayons, ten tea bags and you've got a Progression Collection. Create one of your own and attach meaning to numbers.

Ask your child to get one fork and bring it to the table. Now tell your collector to bring two spoons to the table to place to the right of the fork. Then ask for three bananas, four cups . . . all the way to ten. When finished, review the Progression Collection by asking your child to count and name the items in each set or group moving from left to right. Vary the activity by completing an outdoor Progression Collection.

> **REQUIRED:**
> • Miscellaneous household items
>
> **OPTIONAL:**
> • An outdoor walk

A NUMBER ON MY BACK

SKILLS: Number Writing/Number Recognition/Number Formation

Use the sense of touch to strengthen number formation and number recognition. Practice number writing without a pencil and paper! All you need is a finger for a pencil and a back to serve as paper.

Stand with your child directly behind you. Tell your child to "write" a number on your back with the index finger of his or her writing hand.

Say, "Please write your age." Ask your child to say the number and, using his or her index finger, "write" the number, moving from top to bottom and left to right. Repeat, several times, requesting different numbers such as the number of people in the family, the age of a sibling, the number of chairs at the kitchen table.

Now write a number on your child's back. Ask your first grader to guess the number after you write it. Alternate roles as you continue to write and guess numbers.

> **REQUIRED:**
> • Your time

THE NUMBER JUMBLE

SKILLS: Number Sequence/Number Recognition

Recognize and put numbers in sequential order by playing the Number Jumble. Sit beside your child at a table. Place the numbers 0 to 10 before you in sequential order. Use homemade number cards or, if available, plastic or rubber numbers. Call out, "Number Jumble," and join your child in jumbling the order of the numbers. Then ask your child to put the numbers back in order. Upon completion, read the numbers together, pointing to each number as it is named. Repeat the process, including numbers to 15. Work with a goal of sequencing more numbers each time you play. To speed up the fun, set a timer to a minute and beat the clock!

REQUIRED:
- Number cards

OPTIONAL:
- Plastic, rubber numbers
- Timer

LOST AND FOUND

SKILLS: Number Sequence/Number Recognition

Find missing numbers in a sequence by playing Lost and Found. Sit beside your child at a table. Place the numbers 0 to 10 before you in sequential order. Use homemade number cards or, if available, plastic or rubber numbers. Ask your child to read the numbers.

Now play Lost and Found. Tell your child not to peek as you remove two numbers from the sequence. Quickly hide the cards in the room in safe and accessible places. When you return, ask your child to look at the cards on the table, read them, and determine which numbers are lost. Then your child begins the room search for the lost numbers. When the numbers are found, return to the table and put the numbers where they belong in the sequence.

Vary the activity by using a timer. See how long it takes for your first grader to find and sequence the numbers.

REQUIRED:
- Number cards

OPTIONAL:
- Plastic or rubber numbers
- Timer

JUMBO NUMBO

SKILLS: Number Recognition/Counting/Skip Counting/Addition/Subtraction

You don't need to push the furniture aside to make room for your Jumbo Numbo number line. All you need to do is find a little floor space! Have fun using gross motor skills to enhance your child's counting skills.

On 20 8½″ × 11″ sheets of paper, write the numbers 1 through 20, one number per sheet. Tape the right edge of the "1" sheet to the left edge of the "2" sheet, the right edge of the "2" sheet to the left edge of the "3" sheet. Continue to "20," folding accordion style to facilitate the process.

Unfold your Jumbo Numbo number line on the floor. Secure corners with tape. Ask your child to remove shoes and stand on "10." Begin Jumbo Numbo with a request such as, "Stand on the number that is two less than ten." With your child now on "8," say, "Move to the number that is six more than eight." Your child moves six steps to "14." Now tell your child to move to "20." Ask, "How many steps did you take to get from '14' to '20'?" Continue in this manner, taking turns on the Jumbo Numbo number line. Fold accordion style for easy storage.

REQUIRED:
- Paper
- Marker
- Tape

SMART CHART

SKILLS: Number Writing/Number Recognition/Number Sequence/Counting/Skip Counting/Number Patterns

Make and use a counting chart to practice a range of counting skills!

Cut one hundred 2″ squares. While your child writes the numbers 1 through 50, one per square, you write 51 through 100. At the top of a sheet of large poster board, ask your child to arrange the numbers 1 through 10, left to right in a row. Check to see that the numbers are in sequence. Work together to glue the squares, in order, on the paper. Repeat, using the rest of the squares. Arrange the squares so your counting chart has ten numbers per row, ten numbers per column all aligned.

Use your chart to practice an array of skills with your young mathematician. Ask your child to cover the odd or even numbers using pasta shells. Discuss the pattern seen. Tell your child to cover numbers ending with 0 or 5. Ask your first grader to notice a pattern. Tell your child to cover the number that is one less than 37 or one more than 83. Use the counting chart to practice counting by twos, threes, sixes, or twenties.

Skills will grow with a Smart Chart.

REQUIRED:
- Poster board
- Construction paper
- Safety scissors
- Nontoxic glue
- Markers
- Pasta shells

COUNT, COUNT, COUNT

SKILLS: Counting/One-to-One Correspondence

In school, first graders are expected to count, count, and count some more! Encourage your child to do the same at home.

Count doors, windows, and sinks. Count buttons, zippers, and pairs of socks in closets and drawers. Count fruits and vegetables in the refrigerator, cookies in the jar, cans in the cabinets.

Outside, count the trees on your block, the number of cars that go by in two minutes, and the mailboxes in your neighborhood.

Wherever, and whenever, encourage your child to count, count, count!

REQUIRED:
• Your time

PHYSICOUNT

SKILL: Counting

Take advantage of both fine motor skills and gross motor skills to enhance counting ability. Tap a foot to music and count the taps. Clap your hands to a rhyme and count the claps. Jump on a pogo stick and count the jumps. Pedal a bicycle and count the rotations to get from one place to another. Spin a hula hoop around your waist and count the revolutions before it drops to the floor. Play jump rope and count the jumps and the turns of the rope. Play hopscotch and count the hops. Count the stairs as you go up and the stairs as you come down. Count the steps from one side of the room to the other. Count jumping jacks and tosses of a ball. Count the number of pretzels or kernels of popcorn you take from the bowl. Count the chews before you swallow. Count the number of finger taps on the keyboard. Count the number of strokes to print a letter or word. If it moves, do Physicount!

REQUIRED:
• Your time

SIMON SAYS . . . COUNT

SKILLS: Counting/Addition/Subtraction/Skip Counting/Number Patterns

Simon says, "Clap six times." Simon says, "Take two steps forward." Simon says, "Blink 1 plus 4 times." "Blink 6 minus 5 times." Gotcha!

Visit the old favorite Simon Says, but for this version, include numbers and counting in all commands. Remind your child that players complete the command only when Simon Says! After a round or two, invite your child to be Simon. Simon says, "Use the commands below to get started!"

Simon Says:

Tap your knees three times.
Wiggle eight fingers.
Take nine steps backward.
Turn around one time.
Bend to the right seven times.
Count by twos to 20.
Finish the pattern 1, 3, 5, . . . 19

Hop 2 plus 5 times.
Wave two arms.
Jump 8 minus 4 times.
Tap your foot five times.
Touch your toes six times.
Count down from 20 to 0.
Count by tens to 100.

REQUIRED:
• Your time

THE WOW NUMBER

SKILLS: Number Awareness/Number Recognition/Counting/Measuring

One hundred is the Wow Number to first graders. It is the number that packs a wallop! A first grade perception of 100 is that it is *huge, enormous, gigantic, powerful!* Build your child's awareness of 100 with hands-on activities.

Walk 100 steps. Build a jigsaw puzzle with 100 pieces. Make a design with 100 toothpicks. Locate page 100 in a book. Count 100 words on a page. Run a 100-yard race. Build a 100-link paper chain. Eat 100 Cheerios. Measure 100 inches. Group 100 pennies. Hop 100 times. Skip 100 skips. Jump rope 100 jumps.

Draw a line 100 centimeters long. Count from 0 to 100 and 100 back to 0. Count 100 days beginning on January first. Clap 100 times. Time 100 seconds. Time 100 minutes. Be aware of 100, the Wow Number.

REQUIRED:
• Your time and creativity

GATHER 100

Give meaning to 100 by gathering a collection of 100 small items! Together, decide upon the items to gather. Place each collection of 100 in a plastic bag. Items to collect include buttons, beads, chocolate chips, jellybeans, raisins, noodles, toothpicks, paper clips, shells, pebbles, acorns, Legos, Cheerios, coins. The possibilities are endless.

When the collections are complete, encourage your child to explore the nature of each one. Remove the items from one bag and spread them on the table or work surface. Manipulate the items by grouping them into sets of ten and counting by tens to 100. Repeat the process with sets of five and sets of two. Return the items to the bag and try the same procedure with another collection.

Compare collections. Talk about similarities and differences in terms of weight, volume, and appearance. Through this kind of exploration, your child is sure to develop awareness of 100.

For extra exposure to 100, visit your library or bookstore to read *The 100th Day of School* by Angela Shelf Medearis or *One Hundred Hungry Ants* by Elinor J. Pinczes.

> **REQUIRED:**
> • Collections of 100 items
> • Plastic bags
>
> **OPTIONAL:**
> • Library/bookstore visit

FIVE LITTLE ♦ ♦ ♦ BOOK

You don't need to wait for a shuttle launch to count down from five to one. Make a counting-down book instead.

To get ideas going, visit your local library or bookstore to share a counting-down book such as *Five Little Monkeys Sitting in a Tree* by Eileen Christelow or *Five Little Ducks* illustrated by Ian Beck. Ask your child to predict the number of animals that remain from one page to the next as you read the story.

Now encourage your child to write another Five Little . . . Book. Fold three sheets of paper, one inside the other, in half. Staple at the fold to make a book. Decide upon an animal, and write on the cover, "Five Little Penguins" by Jordan, for example. Then begin the story. "Five little penguins, sitting on an iceberg, one slid in. Four little penguins . . ." Use the first two facing pages for five penguins, the next two facing pages for four, and so on to one. Illustrate the story and provide time for your young author to read the Five Little . . . Book to the family.

> **REQUIRED:**
> • Library/bookstore visit
> • Three sheets of paper
> • Stapler
> • Crayons/markers/pencil

HIDE-AND-SEEK COUNTDOWN

SKILLS: Counting/Skip Counting/Following Directions

When was the last time you had a good old-fashioned game of hide-and-seek? Now is the time!

Designate an area of the house or yard for hiding and seeking. Take turns being hider and seeker. As the seeker, count down from one hundred to zero by ones, twos, fives, or tens as the hiders find hiding places. At the end of the countdown, the seeker calls, "Ready or not, here I come!" Allow three minutes for the seeker to find the hider. Have a stopwatch handy as an option for timing the seeker. Call out clues to assist the seeker when the time expires.

For a variation of hide-and-seek, prepare quick seek directions before playing. While the seeker counts, place the directions in plain view so that the seeker can follow the step-by-step directions to find you. An example is: "Take three giant steps from beside the kitchen telephone into the dining room. Turn right and walk twelve tiny steps into the living room." No matter what the format, a game of hide-and-seek enriches counting-down ability and following multistep directions, too!

REQUIRED:
• Your time
OPTIONAL:
• Paper and pencil
• Timer

COUNT IT DOWN

SKILLS: Counting/Addition/Subtraction/One-to-One Correspondence

Notice how a group of items gets smaller when we take items away. Count It Down is a game you win when you have nothing left!

Sit facing your child. Distribute 40 pennies to each player as a personal bank. The first player rolls a die, says the number, takes that number of pennies from the personal bank and places them in the middle of the playing surface. Alternate turns. Continue play until one player has an empty bank. You must roll an exact number to empty the bank. For example, if four pennies remain, the player must roll a 4 to win.

To add extra challenge, play with two dice and add more pennies to each player's personal bank.

REQUIRED:
• 80 pennies
• One die
OPTIONAL:
• Two dice

HIGH COUNT

SKILL: Skip Counting

What a wonderful feeling we get when we accomplish something we have never done before! Challenge your child to reach new heights, counting by twos, fives, and tens!

Ask your first grader to count by twos, starting at zero. When your child reaches a personal limit, record the date and the number reached on a paper labeled "Counting by twos." Repeat the process, counting by fives and then by tens. Record the date and the number reached on sheets of paper labeled "Counting by fives" and "Counting by tens." Store your record sheets in a safe place.

Every few weeks, take out the record sheets and challenge your child to beat the high count. Each time you do this, record the date and number your child reaches. Whenever your child counts to a higher number, your skip counter is a high-count record breaker!

REQUIRED:
• Paper
• Pen/pencil

NOSES AND TOES

SKILLS: Counting/Skip Counting

How many noses in a family of five? How many toes in a family of four? Ask your child to count noses and toes in the family. For extra counting practice, count mouths, eyes, ears, and fingers.

Have fun counting by ones as you count mouths and noses. Enjoy counting by twos with eyes and ears. Count by fives with fingers and toes. Count by tens by counting all fingers and toes.

Encourage your child to find and count other things that come in twos, fives, and tens.

REQUIRED:
• Your time

BACK-AND-FORTH COUNT

SKILL: Skip Counting

Anytime is counting time! No matter where you are, this fast-paced counting activity can help your child master counting by numbers other than one.

Say to your child, "Let's count by twos. I'll start. Two!" Your child says, "Four!" You say, "Six!" Your child says, "Eight!" "Ten!" "Twelve!" "Fourteen!" "Sixteen!" Keep alternating and go as high as you can counting by twos.

Follow the same method counting by fives, tens, and hundreds. Be sure to give your child a chance to start a Back-and-Forth Count.

For an exciting twist, count by twos again . . . this time backward from any number.

REQUIRED:
• Your time

PRESS AND READ

SKILLS: Skip Counting/Calculator

A calculator serves as a great teaching tool when counting by any number! With a calculator, your child sees each number said with the press of a button.

Check the calculator to be sure zero is showing in the display. Ask your child to press the [2] key, then the [+] key, then the [2] key. Now tell your child to look at the calculator display and read the number seen, 2. Press the [=] key. Read 4. Press the [=] key. Read 6. Continue counting by twos as you press the [=] key. Press the key and read the number simultaneously to enhance your child's ability to count by twos.

Practice counting by any number. Press the [5] key, then the [+] key, then the [5] key and the [=] key to count by fives. Press the [10] key, then the [+] key, then the [10] key and the [=] key to count by tens. Use Press and Read to count by any number.

REQUIRED:
• Calculator

THREE-BAG TOSS

SKILLS: Skip Counting/Addition

Ready! Aim! Toss! Play Three-Bag Toss anytime, inside or out! This game of skill will challenge your child physically and provide practice counting by twos, fives, and tens.

On a 12″ × 18″ sheet of construction paper, clearly write a large 2. On a 6″ × 9″ sheet, write a large 5. On a 4″ × 6″ sheet, write a 10. Place these sheets of paper on the ground three to five feet in front of you. Supply your child with three beanbags.

Tell your child to toss each beanbag, one at a time, so each lands on one of the number sheets. After three tosses, your child retrieves the beanbags and counts the score. For example, if three beanbags land on the "5" sheet, your child counts, "5, 10, 15." If two beanbags land on the "2" sheet and one lands on the "10" sheet, your child counts, "2, 4, 14." If a tossed beanbag misses the sheets, the player tosses again. Alternate turns, tossing three beanbags at a time. The player with the high score wins the round.

As your child's skills develop, play Three-Bag Toss with 25s, 50s, and 100s.

REQUIRED:
- Construction paper
- Three beanbags
- Marker

FUN = 41

SKILLS: Calculator/Addition/Recording Data

Strengthen your child's addition and calculator skills by assigning numerical values to the letters of the alphabet. Then determine the "value" of everyday household items from vegetables to pets. Use the point system provided.

a=1, b=2, c=3, d=4, e=5, f=6, g=7, h=8, i=9, j=10, k=11, l=12, m=13, n=14, o=15, p=16, q=17, r=18, s=19, t=20, u=21, v=22, w=23, x=24, y=25, z=26

For example, list the values assigned to c, a, t. Record these values on a sheet of paper.

c = 3
a = 1
t = 20

Use a calculator to find the total value, 24, for *cat*. Talk about the use of the [+] key and the [=] key. Play several rounds using individual words. Then move on to contests between two words. For example, *sink* versus *oven*.

s =	19		o =	15
i =	9		v =	22
n =	14		e =	5
k =	11		n =	14
	53			56

In a close contest, *oven* wins 56 to 53!

REQUIRED:
- Household items
- Paper and pencil
- Calculator

A⁺ ACTIVITIES FOR FIRST GRADE

WORDULATOR

SKILLS: Calculator/Number Recognition

Did you know you can enter certain numbers into a calculator and change them into letters by turning the calculator upside down? Turn your calculator into a Wordulator and help your child sharpen calculator skills.

Say numbers as your child enters them into the calculator. For example, you say, "Seven"; your child enters 7. You say, "Seven"; your child enters another 7. Say, "One"; your child enters 1. Say, "Four"; your child enters 4. The calculator display should now show 7714. To be sure the correct numbers were entered, ask your child to read the numbers back to you.

Now turn the calculator so that the display window is at the bottom. Believe it not, even though the letters are mixed uppercase and lowercase, 7714 on an upside-down calculator spells "hill." After reading the word, ask your child to clear the calculator using the appropriate key. Use your Wordulator to make other words from upside-down numbers. Use the samples below to get you started.

77345 = shell		317	= lie
7738 = bell		5537	= less
7108 = boil		710	= oil
345 = she		7105	= soil

REQUIRED:
• Calculator

PAWS AND TAILS

SKILLS: Counting/Sorting/One-to-One Correspondence/Recording Data

Line up stuffed animals, pick a body part, and count! How many eyes are in the stuffed animal collection? How many paws, tails, wings, whiskers, mouths? Chart the results simply by listing the body parts and the total number of each counted.

Sort the stuffed animals by habitat and count! How many live in the woods? How many live in the ocean? How many live in the desert, the jungle, or the mountains? How many live on a farm or in your yard? Chart the results by listing the habitats and the total number of animals that live in each.

Sort the stuffed animals by land or water and count! How many live on land? How many live in water? Chart the results of the survey by listing the animals that live on land and the animals that live in the water.

No matter how you sort them, no matter what the task, stuffed animals provide hours of mathematical fun!

REQUIRED:
• Stuffed animals
• Paper and pencil

SCHOOL DAYS

SKILLS: Place Value/Counting

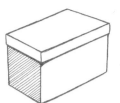

Count along with the number of days in school and help your child understand the relationship between ones, tens, and hundreds.

Use three empty shoe boxes or coffee cans. Label one container "100s," one container "10s," and one container "1s." Place these containers, in that order, from the left to right, in a place accessible to your child.

Choose a day, and before leaving for school, ask your child to drop a drinking straw in the container labeled "1s" to represent day number one. If you don't start on the first day of school, be certain to record the day you start keeping track. Drop a straw in the "1s" container, each day, until day number ten. On that day, bundle the ten "1s" with a rubber band and drop them in the "10s" container. Continue, remembering to bundle ten "1s" to drop into the "10s" container every ten days until the hundredth day. On that day, bundle the ten "10s" with a rubber band. Drop them into the "100s" container.

Talk about the relationship between ones, tens, and hundreds. Continue until the last day of school. If your child would like, start again on the first day of second grade!

REQUIRED:
• Three empty containers
• Drinking straws
• Rubber bands

SWITCH-A-ROO

SKILL: Place Value

Switch-a-Roo is a fun-filled, fast-paced number game that requires the switching of numbers in the ones place and the tens place.

Say a two-digit number. Ask your child to switch the order of the digits in the number to make a new number. For example, say, "47!" Your child responds, "Switch-a-Roo, 74!" You say, "42!" Your child responds, "Switch-a-Roo, 24!" Note that a move from the tens place to the ones place and the ones place to the tens place changes the number.

Now give your first grader the chance to say a number for you to "Switch-a-Roo." Your child says, "17!" You respond, "Switch-a-Roo, 71!" Your child says, "65!" You respond, "Switch-a-Roo, 56!"

Play Switch-a-Roo anytime and better acquaint your child with place value.

REQUIRED:
• Your time

BIGGEST SMALLEST

SKILLS: Place Value/Number Recognition

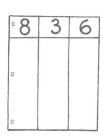

Building three-digit numbers helps your child understand place value! On index cards, clearly write, one number per card, the numbers 1 to 9. Sit next to your child and shuffle the number cards. Place the cards in a pile before you. Tell your child to take three cards off the top of the deck. Challenge your first grader to make the biggest number possible using the digits on the three cards. For example, your child selects digits 2, 6, and 7 and manipulates the digits to make 762. Ask your child to read the number.

Now, tell your child to move the digits around to make the smallest number from 2, 6, and 7. Your first grader works with the digits to make 267 and reads the number.

Play often, noting that by moving digits from place to place, different numbers are made.

REQUIRED:
• Nine index cards
• Marker

836 MIX

SKILLS: Place Value/Number Recognition/Number Writing

A quick and easy activity for building place value skills is 836 Mix! All you need is paper and a pencil and you're ready for a number anagram challenge. Write "836" across the top of a sheet of paper. Fold the paper into three equal columns. Label the columns "One Digit," "Two Digit," and "Three Digit." Say, "Go!" Using the digits of 836, make as many numbers as you can by reordering the digits. Write the one-digit numbers in the One-Digit column, two-digit numbers in the Two-Digit column, and the three-digit numbers in the Three-Digit column. Your child can work independently or in collaboration with you. When two or more people play, make an "836" sheet for each. Set a time limit for finding and recording numbers. Then compare number lists. Receive one point for each number you have written that no other player has made. Play to an agreed-upon score. Continue play, using any three-digit number you choose.

Number Bank for 836 Mix: 3, 6, 8, 36, 38, 63, 68, 83, 86, 368, 386, 638, 683, 863

REQUIRED:
• Paper
• Pencils

ADDRESS SURVEY

Investigate odd and even numbers in your neighborhood. Take a survey of address numbers from houses and buildings on your street.

Draw a line down the center of a sheet of paper. Label the left column "Left Side of the Street." Label the right column "Right Side of the Street." Take a pencil with you and go for a walk on your street.

Read and record the numbers on the houses and buildings on the left side of the street. Ask your child to look for a number pattern on the record sheet. Read and record the numbers from the right side of the street. Again, ask your child to look for a number pattern.

Point out that the numbers on one side of the street are even—0, 2, 4, 6, 8—and the numbers on the other side are odd—1, 3, 5, 7, 9. Discuss that numbers that end with 0, 2, 4, 6, and 8 are even, and numbers that end with 1, 3, 5, 7, and 9 are odd.

To further support awareness of odds and evens, read *Even Steven, Odd Todd* by Kathryn Cristaldi.

REQUIRED:
- Paper and pencil
- Neighborhood walk

OPTIONAL:
- Library/bookstore visit

PENNY PARTNERS

Penny Partners will help your first grader label numbers odd or even.

On five index cards, print the word "Odd." On another five, print "Even." Gather 55 pennies and arrange them in 10 piles on the table. Working left to right, make a one-penny pile, a two-penny pile, a three-penny pile . . . all the way to a ten-penny pile.

Count the pennies in the one-penny pile. Point out that the penny is all alone. It doesn't have a partner. Tell your child that one is an odd number because, just like the penny, it doesn't have a partner. Your child places an Odd card below the one-penny pile. Now count the two-penny pile. Show your child that the two pennies are partners. That makes two an even number. Your child places an Even card below the two-penny pile.

Continue through the ten-penny pile as your child manipulates pennies to check whether each has a partner. Discuss the odd/even number pattern and the fact that numbers ending in 0, 2, 4, 6, and 8 are even, and the numbers ending in 1, 3, 5, 7, and 9 are odd.

REQUIRED:
- 55 pennies
- 10 index cards
- Marker

PULL DOWN THE ODDS

SKILLS: Odds & Evens/Number Patterns/Skip Counting/Number Formation/Visual Patterns

Glue a 1 to build recognition of odds and evens! Use nontoxic craft glue to form a 1 on construction paper. While the glue is wet, cover it with yarn, string, or ribbon. Dry on a flat surface. On another sheet of construction paper of the *same* color, repeat the process with 3, covering the glue with the *same* medium. Continue with the odd numbers through 9. Then, line up the odds and skip count 1, 3, 5, 7, 9. Let your child use his or her index finger to trace the numbers while saying them. Note the color of the paper and the material from which the odds were formed.

Repeat the process for the even numbers, 2 through 10. Use a different color construction paper and a different medium to form the numbers.

Finally, line up the odds and evens, 1 through 10. Use the color of the paper as well as the ribbon, yarn, or string as visual aids for recognizing odd and even. Ask your child to pull down the odds while counting. Line up the numbers again. This time ask your child to pull down the evens.

REQUIRED:
• Construction paper
• Nontoxic glue
• String, ribbon, or yarn

ONE IS 1

SKILLS: Number Words/Number Recognition/Number Sequence/Counting

Match number words with numbers to build awareness that "one" is the same as "1." Print the number words *zero* through *ten* on index cards, one word per card. Beneath each word, draw the equivalent number of stars. Write the numbers 0 through 10 on index cards, again one number per card. Put the number word cards in a bag labeled "Words," and the number cards in another bag, labeled "Numbers." Invite your child to reach into the Word bag, choose and read a card, then lay it on the table. Next reach into the Number bag and do the same. Ask, "Is it a match?" If the word and number match, place them beside each other on the table. If not, leave each faceup on the table. Follow your child's example as you draw from the bags. Alternate turns and continue play until all words and numbers are matched. Then, work together to place the word and number card pairs in sequential order. Count from zero to ten as you return word and number cards to the appropriate bags. Over time, include the numbers 11 through 20.

REQUIRED:
• Index cards
• Marker
• Two paper lunch bags

MATH ACTIVITIES

FRACTIONS ABOUND

SKILLS: Fractions/Recording Data/Drawing

Encourage your child to keep an eye out for objects with fractional parts.

Around the house, notice an egg carton sectioned into twelve equal parts, or twelfths. Look at the panes in a window. A six-pane window has six equal parts, or sixths. Check the notations on measuring cups—$\frac{1}{8}$, $\frac{1}{4}$, $\frac{1}{3}$, $\frac{1}{2}$.

Take a walk in your neighborhood. Bring paper and a pencil. Point out other things that have equal parts. Give your child a chance to study and draw the equal parts of the object. A traffic light, for example, is sectioned into three equal parts, or thirds. A street is often split into two lanes, or halves. Keep an ongoing record of anything your child finds that is created from equal fractional parts.

REQUIRED:
• Paper and pencil

FOOD FRACTIONS

SKILL: Fractions

A fraction is an equal part of a whole. If a cookie is broken into two equal parts, each is one-half of the whole cookie. If it were broken into four equal parts, each is one-fourth of the whole cookie. Use food to give your first grader concrete experience with fractions.

Graham crackers break easily into four equal sections. Point out these sections and tell your child that each is one-fourth of the whole cracker. Ask your child to break the cracker into fourths and eat one-fourth. Ask, "How many fourths are left?"

Peel an orange and break it into equal sections. Lay them on a plate. If there are 12 equal sections, then each section is one-twelfth of the whole orange. Ask your child to eat seven-twelfths of the orange and give five-twelfths to you.

Order a pizza and focus on the slices as equal parts of the whole pizza.

Encourage your child to be on the lookout for other foods that break into equal parts.

REQUIRED:
• Graham cracker

OPTIONAL:
• Orange
• Pizza

FRACTION ACTION

SKILLS: Fractions/Cutting

Create new shapes from the equal parts that make up circles, squares, and rectangles to expose your child to how fractions are written.

From a large sheet of construction paper, cut a 6″ to 8″ circle. Ask your child to fold the circle in half and open it. Point out the fold that splits the circle in half. Now, turn the circle so the fold is horizontal. Tell your child to fold the circle again to make four equal parts. Label each part "¼." Then cut the circle along the folds and notice that each part is the same size. Ask your child to reassemble the parts to make a circle. Encourage your child to arrange the parts into a different shape. Glue this shape onto another sheet of construction paper for display. Repeat the process using squares and rectangles.

REQUIRED:
- Construction paper
- Safety scissors
- Nontoxic glue
- Marker

HIGHER OR LOWER?

SKILL: Number Relations

This guessing game provides great entertainment whether you are stuck in traffic or waiting for a bus. Say to your child, "I am thinking of a number between six and ten." Your child responds with a guess such as, "Seven." You respond by saying either "higher" or "lower," depending on your child's guess. Continue in this manner until the number is guessed. Alternate turns so that your child has the opportunity to ask you whether a number is higher or lower.

As you continue play, select larger numbers and greater ranges.

REQUIRED:
- Your time

MATH ACTIVITIES

CARD COMPARE

SKILLS: Number Relations/Number Recognition

Remember the card game War? This version, Card Compare, will help your child see number relationships in terms of "greater than," "less than," and "equal to."

Remove jacks, queens, kings, aces, and jokers from the deck. Sit opposite your child. Shuffle the cards and deal an equal number, facedown, to each player. Each player takes the top card from his or her pile and places it faceup on the playing surface. Ask your first grader to look at the cards. If your child plays a 7 and you, a 4, your child says, "Seven is greater than four." Your child keeps those cards and adds them to the bottom of his or her pile. If your child plays a 6 and you, a 10, your child says, "Six is less than ten." Since your child's number is less than yours, add those cards to the bottom of your pile. Play until one player has no cards left.

Occasionally, players may play numbers that are equal. If you both play a 3, your child says, "Three is equal to three." When this occurs, turn over cards until someone wins the round.

REQUIRED:
• Playing cards

ALL ROADS LEAD TO EIGHT

SKILLS: Equivalent Names/Addition/Subtraction

Just as there is more than one road to get to where we want to go, there are many ways to arrive at a number. All Roads Lead to Eight challenges you and your child to discover all the different ways to arrive at a number between one and nine.

On a sheet of paper, write "8." Work together to write as many ways as you can think of to show eight. Start by writing "7 + 1" on the paper. Then ask your child to write another way to show eight. Your first grader may write "1 + 7," "8 + 0," "5 + 3," or "4 + 4." Encourage your child to add to the "8" list as new ways to show eight are discovered. Play often, changing the activity to, for example, All Roads Lead to Five.

Variation: Ask your child to use addition *and* subtraction to show a number. The possibilities for challenge and enrichment are great.

REQUIRED:
• Paper and pencil

ADDITION ARTIST

SKILLS: Addition/Drawing/Number Writing

Help your Addition Artist draw his or her way to a basic understanding of addition. Hold a sheet of construction paper horizontally. Draw two lines from the top to the bottom, creating three equal sections. At the top of the left section, clearly print, "First There Were"; the middle section, "Along Came"; and the right section, "Now There Are."

Tell your child to draw four insects in the "First There Were" section. Now, ask your child to draw two insects in the "Along Came" section. Ask your child to count the total number of insects. Draw six insects in the "Now There Are" section. Finally, your child writes the number that corresponds with the insects in each section. Write "4" in the left, "2" in the middle, and "6" in the right.

Ask your child to tell the insect addition story, using the writing and pictures as clues. Your child's story will sound something like, "First there were four insects. Along came two more insects. Now there are six insects altogether."

Variation: Act as the Addition Artist as your child tells the addition story.

REQUIRED:
- Construction paper
- Markers/crayons

ADDITION BALL

SKILL: Addition

Spend time playing catch, and help your child learn addition facts at the same time!

Blow up a beach ball. Use a permanent marker to print numbers, 0 through 9, on the ball. Use the entire surface, printing the numbers in random order. Now, you and your child are ready for a game of catch with an added element.

Stand face to face, no more than four feet apart. Tell your child to use two hands to catch the ball when you toss it. If a player's hand doesn't land on a number, use the number closest to that hand. For example, one hand lands on "4," the other lands on "3." The player adds the numbers together and shouts the sum, "Seven!" The player tosses the ball back. Continue playing Addition Ball and help your child work toward mastery of addition facts.

REQUIRED:
- Beach ball
- Permanent marker

FIND A SUM

SKILL: Addition

When we add numbers, the total is called the sum. Help your child become more adept at adding two one-digit numbers by playing Find a Sum. Clearly write the numbers "0" through "18" on nineteen index cards, one number per card. Depending on the weather and time of year, hide the cards throughout your home or yard in safe and accessible places. Start with five to eight cards. Challenge your child to find the sum of each addition problem you say. For example, say, "Four plus six." Your child must find and return the "10" card. Say, "Five plus eight." Your child must find and return the "13" card.

Variation: Ask your child to challenge you by hiding the cards and asking you to find them. Follow the same procedure. Play again, increasing the number of sum cards hidden.

REQUIRED:
- Nineteen index cards
- Marker

ADDITION WHEEL

SKILL: Addition

Make addition wheels to practice addition facts with sums to eighteen. Fasten a small paper plate to the center of a large paper plate with a paper fastener. If paper plates aren't available, cut two circles out of oak tag or cardboard. Write "1 +" to the right of the fastener on the small plate. Print the numbers 0 through 9 equally spaced all around the edge of the large plate.

Turn the large plate so that your child can add 1 + 0, 1 + 1, 1 + 2, 1 + 3 . . . all around the wheel to 1 + 9.

Follow the same procedure to practice all the addition facts. Make a small number wheel for each of the numbers 2 through 9, including the "+" sign to the right of each number. Attach a different small wheel to the large wheel each time you wish to practice another set of addition facts.

REQUIRED:
- Large and small paper plates
- Marker
- Paper fasteners

OPTIONAL:
- Oak tag or cardboard
- Safety scissors

DOMINO DROP—ADDITION

SKILLS: Addition/Counting

Drop a handful of dominoes on the tabletop and add! First look at the dominoes as they've landed and count the dots on each one in play. Then, using one or two dominoes at a time, create addition problems for your child to solve. For example, drop four dominoes. One lands with four dots and two dots showing. Ask, "What is four plus two?" and/or "What is two plus four?" Your child should count the dots to verify response. The second domino shows six dots and three dots. Ask, "What is six plus three?" and/or "What is three plus six?" Continue in the same manner with the third and fourth domino. Then try combinations. The third domino has two dots and five dots. The fourth domino has one dot and zero dots. Ask, while moving the dominos one beside the other, "What will I get if I add this domino (seven dots) with that domino (one dot)?" For variation, invite your child to ask you the domino addition questions. The domino effect is sure to be a positive one when you play Domino Drop.

REQUIRED:
• Dominoes

LUCKY NUMBER

SKILLS: Addition/Recording Data/Number Writing

Many of us have numbers we consider lucky. Your child can make a lucky number by adding a few "personal" numbers together.

Help your child gather "personal" numbers. On a sheet of paper, ask your child to write the number of letters in his or her first name. Then ask your child to write his or her current grade level and total number of brothers and sisters. Next, write the numbers that represent your child's month and day of birth. Do not include the year. Add the numbers to make the lucky number. Follow the example below.

Jaime	5
Grade one	1
Brothers/sisters	4
Day of month	2
November	<u>11</u>
	23

Jaime's lucky number is 23!

Variation: Use a calculator and counters as your child works out his or her personal lucky number. Give your child the opportunity to find personal lucky numbers for all family members.

REQUIRED:
• Paper and pencil

OPTIONAL:
• Counting chips
• Calculator

SUBTRACTION ARTIST

SKILLS: Subtraction/Drawing/Number Writing

Draw your way to the difference as a Subtraction Artist.

Hold a sheet of construction paper horizontally. Draw two lines from the top to the bottom, creating three equal sections. At the top of the left section, clearly print, "First There Were"; the middle section, "Went Away"; and the right section, "Are Left."

Tell your child to draw six cats in the "First There Were" section. Now, ask your child to draw one cat in the "Went Away" section. Ask your child to determine the number of cats remaining after one went away. Then, he or she draws five cats in the "Are Left" section. Finally, your child writes the number that corresponds with the cats in each section: "6" in the left, "1" in the middle, "5" in the right.

Ask your child to tell the cat subtraction story, using the writing and pictures as clues. Your child's story will sound something like, "First there were six cats. One cat went away. Now, five cats are left."

Variation: Act as the Subtraction Artist as your child tells the subtraction story.

REQUIRED:
• Construction paper
• Markers/crayons

SUBTRACTION BALL

SKILL: Subtraction

Double the fun of practicing subtraction facts by playing Subtraction Ball!

Blow up a beach ball. Use a permanent marker to write the numbers 0 through 9 on the ball. Use the entire surface, printing the numbers in random order. Note: If you have played Addition Ball, use the same ball. Now, you are ready to play.

Stand face to face, no more than four feet apart. Tell your child to use two hands to catch the ball when you toss it. If a player's hand doesn't land on a number, use the number closest to that hand. If one hand lands on "8" and the other lands on "5," the player subtracts the "5" from the "8" and shouts the difference, "3!" Remind your child to start with the bigger number when subtracting. The player tosses the ball back. Continue playing Subtraction Ball to strengthen subtraction skills.

REQUIRED:
• Beach ball
• Permanent marker

FIND A DIFFERENCE

SKILL: Subtraction

When we subtract one number from another, we find the difference. To help your child practice subtraction facts play Find a Difference. Clearly write the numbers 0 through 9 on ten index cards, one number per card. Depending on the weather and time of year, hide the cards throughout your house or yard in safe and accessible places. Start with four to six cards. Challenge your child to find the difference of each subtraction problem you say. For example, say, "Seven minus two." Your child must find and return the "5" card. Say, "Three minus one." Your child must find and return the "2" card. Encourage your first grader to use fingers to find each difference.

Variation: Ask your child to challenge you by hiding the cards and asking you to find them. Follow the same procedure. Play again, increasing the number of difference cards hidden.

REQUIRED:
- 10 index cards
- Marker

DOMINO DROP— SUBTRACTION

SKILLS: Subtraction/Addition/Counting

Subtract the dots you see when you drop a bunch of dominoes! Look at the dominoes as they've landed and count the dots on the facing side of each one. Then use one domino to create subtraction problems for your child to solve. For example, drop four dominoes. One lands with five dots on the left and two dots on the right. Ask, "What is five dots minus two dots?" Another domino lands with four dots and three dots showing. Ask, "What is four dots minus three dots?" Continue in the same manner with the third and fourth domino.

Challenge your child by using two dominoes for each problem. The two-step problem requires that your child first add the dots on each domino. For example, one domino has four dots and five dots or nine dots all together. Another domino has six dots and one dot or seven dots all together. Now ask your child to subtract the smaller number, "7," from the larger, "9." Variation: Take turns asking the domino subtraction questions.

REQUIRED:
- Dominoes

SUBTRACTION IS MY BAG!

SKILLS: Subtraction/Number Recognition

Start with the bigger number and subtract in this hands-on activity! Clearly write the numbers 0 through 9 on ten index cards, one number per card. Place the cards in a paper bag. Clearly write a minus sign (–) in the center of an index card and place it on the table. Now play Subtraction Is My Bag!

Reach in, pull out one number card, say the number, and place it faceup on the table. Reach in again, pull out another card, say the number, and place this one faceup on the table. Ask your child to identify the larger number and move it to the left of the minus sign. Tell your child to say the name of the smaller number and place it to the right of the minus sign. Then, ask your child to subtract, encouraging use of fingers, toes, noodles, or any other manipulative to aid in finding the difference. You can be sure your child will say, Subtraction Is My Bag!

REQUIRED:
- 11 index cards
- Marker
- Paper bag
- Manipulatives

MATH PATH

SKILLS: Addition/Subtraction

Follow Math Path to practice addition *and* subtraction facts! Open a file folder horizontally. In the upper left-hand corner, draw a 1″ square. Label it "Start." Do the same in the lower right-hand corner. Label this square "Finish." Build a winding Math Path by drawing 20 to 30 connecting squares between Start and Finish. Next, cut 10 index cards in half. Print "+" on 10 cards and "-" on 10 cards. Mix the cards and place them in a pile. Use two dice and buttons or coins as game pieces.

To start, player one rolls the dice, adds the numbers, and moves that number of spaces on the board. The second player does the same. From then on, a player draws the top card from the pile and rolls the dice. That player adds or subtracts the two numbers depending on the "+, -" card chosen. For addition, the player moves ahead that number of spaces. For subtraction, the player moves back that number of spaces. Alternate turns. The first to reach Finish wins. Fold game for storage.

For addition only, use the "+" cards.

REQUIRED:
- File folder
- Crayons/markers
- Index cards
- Safety scissors
- Buttons or coins
- Dice

FIVE-LOOP FACTS

SKILLS: Addition/Subtraction/Number Writing

Paper chain your way to addition and subtraction practice with Five-Loop Facts!

Prepare strips of colored construction paper approximately 8″ × 2″. Then make a five-loop paper chain for any addition fact. For example, to practice 3 + 4 = 7, write "3" on the first strip, "+" on the second strip, "4" on the third strip, "=" on the fourth strip, and "7" on the fifth strip. With the "3" showing on the outside of the first strip, join the two ends with glue or tape to make a loop. With the writing visible, insert and connect the "+," "4," "=," and "7" to make the Five-Loop Fact. Then ask your child to read "3 + 4 = 7." Follow the same procedure for each addition fact practiced.

Make Five-Loop Facts for subtraction, too. Again, sequentially connect five loops left to right, this time using the minus sign as in "9 – 4 = 5." Practicing the facts was never this much fun!

> **REQUIRED:**
> - Construction paper
> - Safety scissors
> - Nontoxic glue or tape
> - Marker

ROUND THE TABLE FUN

SKILLS: Addition/Subtraction

B	i	N	G	O

9	5	1
8	3	4
6	2	7

Everyone knows the thrill of calling out, "Bingo!" Give your child the chance to get three in a row—across, up and down, or diagonal—while building knowledge of addition and subtraction facts.

Make a bingo card for each member of the family so that everyone can participate in the fun. Write "Bingo" across the top of the cards and divide each into nine equal sections, three rows across and three rows down. Clearly write the numbers 1 through 9, one per section, in random order on each card.

Distribute a card to each player, including the caller. Place a supply of paper or plastic game pieces in the center of the playing area. Then, pull up chairs around the table and begin.

The designated caller for the first game announces a "Plus" or "Minus" Round. For a "Plus" round, call out addition facts, "Five plus two," for example. Everyone covers "7." For a "Minus" round, call out subtraction facts, "Eight minus five," for example. Everyone covers "3." Continue until one player gets three in a row and calls, "Bingo!"

Variation: Challenge players to cover sections to make an *X, L,* or border for "Bingo!"

> **REQUIRED:**
> - Construction paper
> - Marker
> - Paper or plastic game pieces

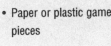

A SIX STORY

SKILLS: Addition/Subtraction

The next time you're waiting in line at a restaurant, market, or post office, ask your child to tell you a Six Story.

A Six Story is a three-sentence story that involves the number six and focuses on either addition or subtraction. First tell an addition Six Story. "*Six* dogs were playing in the park. Two more dogs came to play. Now there are eight dogs in all."

Try a subtraction Six Story. "*Six* birds were building a nest. Two birds flew away. Now there are four birds left." Challenge your child to tell you a Six Story.

Remember that the storyteller gives all the data.

Variation: The listener can solve the problem by completing the third sentence.

Wherever you are, try a seven, eight, nine, ten, twenty, or any number story!

REQUIRED:
• Your time

RABBIT EARS

SKILLS: Problem Solving/Brainstorming/Counting

Get into Rabbit Ears thinking by sharing a rabbit book such as *The Runaway Bunny* by Margaret Wise Brown. Enjoy the engaging story and then count ears!

Present your child with a Rabbit Ears problem. Give your child the opportunity to think of strategies to solve the problem, "What is the total number of ears on six rabbits?" Provide crayons and paper so that your child can draw six rabbits and count the ears. Provide clay and cotton so that your child can create six three-dimensional rabbits. Provide a pencil and paper and see what strategies your child discovers by dividing the paper into six sections. Discuss the strategy your child implemented. Ask what other strategies could be used. Explore possibilities together. Extend the activity by asking your child to determine the total number of ears on three rabbits or ten rabbits! Working with Rabbit Ears will show your child that the process is important when problem solving.

REQUIRED:
• Paper
• Crayons/pencils

OPTIONAL:
• Clay
• Cotton
• Library/bookstore visit

SPIDER LEGS

SKILLS: Problem Solving/Brainstorming/Counting

The Itsy Bitsy Spider has been around for a long time. Children have sung about it and can read about it in *The Itsy Bitsy Spider,* illustrated by Iza Trapani. If possible, share *The Itsy Bitsy Spider, The Very Busy Spider* by Eric Carle, or any book about spiders. Note that spiders have eight legs.

With its eight legs, a spider facilitates problem solving. Give your child the opportunity to think of strategies to solve the problem, "What is the total number of legs on four spiders?" Provide crayons and paper so that your child can draw four spiders and count the legs. Provide clay so that your child can make four spiders. Provide a pencil and paper. See whether your child discovers that by dividing the paper into four sections, he or she can make a tally. Discuss the strategy your child used. Ask what other strategies could be used. Explore possibilities together. Extend the activity by asking your child to determine the total number of legs on six or nine spiders! Working with spider legs will clearly demonstrate that there are more ways than one to solve a problem.

REQUIRED:
- Paper
- Crayons/pencils

OPTIONAL:
- Library/bookstore visit
- Clay
- Any hands-on materials

TRIKES AND BIKES

SKILLS: Problem Solving/Brainstorming/Counting

Many first graders are already riding bicycles while younger brothers and sisters are enjoying time on tricycles.

View bicycles and tricycles in your home or neighborhood or in magazines or books. Point out that a bicycle has two wheels, and a tricycle, three.

Now challenge your child to determine the total number of wheels on four bicycles and five tricycles. Provide crayons and paper so that your child can draw four bicycles and five tricycles and count the total number of wheels. Provide Popsicle or lollipop sticks and checkers or small disks so that your child can build bicycle and tricycle frames and wheels. Give your child a pencil and paper so that your child can try other strategies. Discuss these strategies and ask what other strategies can be used. Together, explore possibilities. Extend the activity by asking your child to determine the total number of wheels on six bicycles and seven tricycles! Working with Bikes and Trikes gives your child the opportunity to solve the same problem using several strategies.

REQUIRED:
- Paper
- Crayons/pencils

OPTIONAL:
- Popsicle/lollipop sticks
- Checkers or small disks
- Magazines or books

MATH ACTIVITIES

GRADE ONE IS FIRST

SKILLS: Ordinal Numbers/Number Sequence

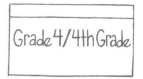

First grade, first base, first prize, and first in line! Help your child become even more familiar with the ordinal numbers by playing Grade One Is First. Clearly print "Grade 1, 1st Grade" on an index card. Then make another index card for "Grade 2, 2nd Grade." Continue in this manner through "Grade 10, 10th Grade."

Sit opposite your first grader. Fan the cards and ask your child to choose one. Read the card together. If the card says, for example, "Grade 4, 4th Grade," exclaim, "You are in 4th grade!" Place the card on the table. Choose another and repeat the process. When the 10 cards have been selected, work together to place the cards in sequence on the table.

Ask your child to put "Grade 1" first, "Grade 2" second, "Grade 3" third, and so on to "Grade 10" tenth.

For added exposure to ordinal numbers, visit your library or bookstore and read *Me First* by Helen Lester, the story of a young pig who always wants to be first, and *Koala Lou* by Mem Fox, the story of a young koala who hopes to win first prize but comes in second.

REQUIRED:
- Index cards
- Marker

OPTIONAL:
- Library/bookstore visit

MAKE-A-CLOCK

SKILLS: Time/Number Writing/Cutting

What time is it when the big hand is on the 12 and the little hand is on the 3? Your child can make a clock using everyday household items. Set up a work area so that your child can view an analog clock as a model. A wall clock or wristwatch will do. Using a paper plate as a clock face, your child writes in the hours, starting at 12 and moving clockwise to 11. Help your child cut an hour hand from construction paper. Attach it to the center of the clock face with a paper fastener.

Now work with the clock. First, set the hour hand and ask your child to tell you the approximate time. For example, place the hour hand directly on 5 or place it halfway between 9 and 10. Next, ask your child to set the time for you to read, moving the hour hand in a clockwise direction. When your child seems comfortable with the hour hand, add a minute hand to the clock. Use the completed clock to display bedtimes, mealtimes, and other significant times in the daily routine.

REQUIRED:
- Paper plate
- Markers/crayons
- Paper fastener
- Colored construction paper
- Safety scissors

REMINDER CLOCKS

SKILLS: Time/Number Writing/Making Comparisons

Make your child more independent at bedtime! Create reminder clocks to show important times in your first grader's daily routine.

Use a paper plate as a clock face. Help your child write in the hours, starting at 12 and moving clockwise to 11. When the numbers are complete, draw the hour hand and the minute hand to show a particular time. For example, if you are making a bedtime clock, and your child's bedtime is 7:30, draw the hands on the clock to show 7:30. Label the clock "Bedtime." If you are making a dinnertime clock, and you eat dinner at 6:15, draw the hands on the clock to show 6:15. Label the clock "Dinnertime." Choose whatever times are important to you and your child.

Post these clocks in a place where your first grader can compare them to a household clock. When your child sees that the bedtime reminder clock matches the time on the household clock, you won't need to remind your time teller that it is time to get ready for bed.

REQUIRED:
- Paper plates
- Marker/Crayon

TIME TO . . .

SKILLS: Time/Brainstorming/Written Expression/Drawing

Time to get up! Time to make your bed! Time to eat breakfast! Time to brush your teeth! Time to go to school! Time to do your homework! Time to eat dinner! Time to take a bath! Time to go to bed!

During the course of the day, children hear "Time to . . ." often enough to know daily routines. Put this information to work by making a "Time To . . ." book in the same way that author/photographer Bruce McMillan did in his book, *Time To* . . . Fold one sheet of paper into another until you have a booklet of ten to twelve pages. Staple the booklet along the fold. Then, holding the booklet with the fold to the left, label the cover, for example, Jared's Time-To Book. Brainstorm a series of daily events. Then, open the booklet. On the left facing page, draw a clock with hands indicating seven o'clock. Beneath it write, "7:00 a.m." On the right facing page, write, "Time to get up." Draw a picture. Continue through the day to complete the book. Read together and add to your child's personal library.

REQUIRED:
- Construction paper
- Pencil
- Crayons/markers
- Stapler

OPTIONAL:
- Library/bookstore visit

IN A MINUTE

SKILLS: Elapsed Time/Counting/Recording Data

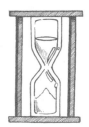

In our fast-paced world, all of us have used the phrase, "Wait a minute!" and all of us have been asked to "Wait a minute." You have probably said, "In a minute," to your first grader, and your first grader has most likely said, "In a minute," to you.

Demonstrate the duration of a minute in a concrete way with the In a Minute games. Invite everyone in the family to participate. Take turns acting as the event caller and timer. Keep a supply of pencils, paper, and munchies handy. Time each event to a minute. Designate the gold, silver, and bronze medalist at the end of each event.

As caller, announce, for example, "The Pretzel-Stick-Eat Event, ready, set, go!" Time each contestant for one minute. Count the pretzels consumed as each participant eats pretzel sticks, one at a time, for one minute. At the end of the minute, call, "Stop!" and record results.

Select from the event bank below or construct activities of your choosing. Let the games begin!

EVENT BANK:		
First-Name Print	One-Foot Hop	Two-Foot Jump
Circle Draw	Star Draw	Munchie Eat
Hand Clap	Touch Your Toes	Jumping Jacks

REQUIRED:
- Paper and pencils
- Munchies
- Timer

DIZZY DAYS

SKILLS: Calendar/Days of the Week/Predicting/Sequencing

Use literature and Dizzy Days to help your child learn to recognize and sequence the names of the days of the week. Visit your school or local library or bookstore to enjoy *Today Is Monday* by Eric Carle or *Cookie's Week* by Cindy Ward. Each story is a delightful romp, day by day, through the week. While reading a first, second, and even third time, ask your child to predict which day comes next.

Then, at home, play Dizzy Days. Write the days of the week on index cards, one day per card. Place the cards in sequence on the table and read them together, reminding your child to look at the uppercase letter in each day's name as a sound helper to remember the name of the day. Now, "dizzy" the days and try to put them back in the correct sequence. Work collaboratively until your child is ready to complete the sequence independently.

REQUIRED:
- Index cards
- Markers

OPTIONAL:
- Library/bookstore visit

SEVEN-DAY STORY

SKILLS: Calendar/Days of the Week/Written Expression/Drawing/Sequencing

What better way to organize the days of the week than to write a personal Seven-Day Story. Make an accordion book from four folders or folded sheets of paper or index cards. Tape the right edge of the first folded paper to the left edge of the second, the second to the third, and the third to the fourth. Fold accordion style, front to back.

Ask your child to print, "Seven-Day Story by Gina," for example, on the cover. Open the accordion book, page by page, saying the names of the days of the week, Monday through Sunday, as you do so.

Begin writing on a Monday afternoon or evening. Discuss your child's day. Choose one special event from the day. Write on the first interior page with text as simple as, "Monday, Ice Cream Day" or as complex as, "On Monday we went to get ice cream cones after school." Encourage your child to draw a picture on the same page to accompany the text. Follow the same procedure for each successive day of the week. On Sunday night, enjoy an accordion story of a wonderful week while practicing the sequence of days!

> **REQUIRED:**
> • Four folders, index cards, or sheets of paper
> • Tape
> • Markers

SCRAMBLED MONTHS

SKILLS: Calendar/Months of the Year/Dictation/Drawing/Sequencing

It can be challenging for first graders to name the months of the year in sequence. Let your child do the writing, one month per index card, as you dictate and spell the names of the months January through December. Add a drawing to each card as a visual reminder of the month. For example, draw a snowman for January, a heart for February, a kite for March, an umbrella for April, a flower for May, a baseball bat for June, an American flag for July, a beach ball for August, a book for September, a pumpkin for October, a turkey for November, and a holiday drawing for December.

Place the cards in sequence on the table and read them together, reminding your child to look at the uppercase letter in each month's name as a sound helper, and the picture for each month as a visual helper, to remember the name of the month. Now, scramble the months and try to put them back in correct sequence. Work collaboratively until your child is ready to complete the sequence independently.

Enjoy extra practice by following twin mice through a year in Leo Lionni's book, *A Busy Year*.

> **REQUIRED:**
> • Index cards
> • Markers/crayons
>
> **OPTIONAL:**
> • Library/bookstore visit

CALENDAR CREATORS

SKILLS: Calendar/Number Writing/Number Sequencing/Drawing

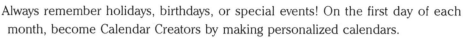

Always remember holidays, birthdays, or special events! On the first day of each month, become Calendar Creators by making personalized calendars.

Hold a brightly colored sheet of 12″ × 18″ construction paper vertically. Fold the paper in half from top to bottom. Open the sheet of paper and place it in front of you. Three inches below the crease, make five rows of seven 1½″ squares, creating a grid of a calendar month. Label each column, at the top, with the appropriate day of the week starting with Sunday. Using a premade calendar as a guide, add the dates in the top right corner of each square. When the days and dates are complete, work together to fill in birthdays, holidays, and events that are important to your child and/or family.

Use the top half of the paper to print the month in bold letters and to illustrate a scene particular to the month.

> **REQUIRED:**
> • 12″ × 18″ sheet construction paper
> • Ruler
> • Markers/Crayons
>
> **OPTIONAL:**
> • Premade calendar

HANDS AND FEET

SKILLS: Nonstandard Linear Measure/Counting

Your first grader can measure length using hands and feet! Nonstandard units of measure provide a concrete demonstration of the need for standard units of measure: inches, feet, and yards.

To measure the length of a countertop using your hands, place one hand over the other from one edge of the counter to the other. Simultaneously, count the number of hand lengths you use. When you reach the end, report that the countertop is 11 "Mom hands" long. Now ask your child to measure the length of the countertop in the same manner and report the results. For example, the countertop is 17 "Keith hands" long. Why did each of you get a different result?

Next, measure the length of a room using your feet. Walk heel to toe from one side to the other. Simultaneously, count the number of feet lengths required. When you finish, tell your child that the room is 21 "Mom feet" long. Your child then measures the room in the same way and reports that the room is 27 "Keith feet" long. Again, ask your child why each of you got a different result.

> **REQUIRED:**
> • Objects to measure

MEASURING ME

SKILLS: Standard Linear Measure/Metric Linear Measure/Recording Data

How long is it from your elbow to your fingertips? Use a tape measure to determine length and to explore inches and feet. Note that 12 inches is equivalent to one foot. Measure your child from knee to floor. On a sheet of paper record: "knee to floor = 13 inches or one foot, one inch." Ask your child to measure and record, on another sheet of paper, the length from your knee to the floor. Continue with the following suggestions, writing the results on your record sheets.

- waist to floor
- shoulder to fingertips
- top of head to chin
- top of head to toes
- elbow to wrist

REQUIRED:
- Paper and pencil
- Tape measure

When complete, save the record sheets. Repeat this activity often, noting growth.
Variation: Measure in centimeters and meters.

HEIGHT CHART

SKILLS: Standard Linear Measure/Recording Data

All living things grow at different rates. Measure your child's height with a tape measure and record it on a height chart.

While you can buy a height chart at most toy/educational stores, making one is simple! Choose a doorway. Ask your child to stand against it with a straight back. Place a small piece of masking tape on the wall to show your child's height. Now use a tape measure to determine your child's height, measuring from the floor to the tape.

On the tape, clearly print the date of the measurement and your child's height in feet and inches. Measure your child once a month for a year.

Review the data periodically. Talk with your child about months in which the most growth occurred. At the end of the year, determine how many inches your child has grown.

REQUIRED:
- Tape measure
- Marker
- Masking tape

OPTIONAL:
- Store-bought height chart

RULER OR YARDSTICK?

SKILL: Standard Linear Measure

What tool do you use to measure a crayon, a Ruler or Yardstick? Have fun as you explore the use of these measuring tools.

Begin by asking questions such as, "What do you use to measure a pencil, a ruler or yardstick?" "What do you use to measure a bed, a ruler or yardstick?" Engage your first grader in discussion of each response. Ask, "Why did you choose a ruler to measure the pencil?" "Why did you choose a yardstick to measure the bed?"

Now let your child put theory to practice by measuring these objects. Extend your explorations to measure the television screen, the toaster oven, a shoe, an area rug, a floor tile, a mirror, a cabinet door, a windowpane, a front-porch step, a section of the sidewalk, a swing seat, a park bench. Provide a 12″ ruler and a yardstick and measure away!

REQUIRED:
- 12″ ruler
- Yardstick
- Objects to measure

CENTIMETER SENSE

SKILLS: Metric Linear Measure/Recording Data

Make sense of centimeters in a quick and easy way! Show your child a ruler marked with centimeters and inches. Observe that a centimeter is smaller than an inch. Explain that we can measure small objects in centimeters as well as in inches.

Divide a piece of paper into two columns, one labeled "Object," the other labeled "Measurement." Now put the ruler to work! Select a range of objects and measure them in centimeters. Record the data as it is collected. Be sure to label measurements "cm." For example, measure a finger. Write "finger" in the "Object" column. Write "3 cm" in the "Measurement" column. Your child is sure to have Centimeter Sense after measuring items in and around your home.

Provide more exposure to the metric system by measuring objects in millimeters and meters, following the same procedure.

REQUIRED:
- Ruler marked with inches and centimeters
- Objects to measure
- Paper and pencil
- Meter stick

A+ ACTIVITIES FOR FIRST GRADE

WEIGHT WORK

SKILLS: Standard Measure/Predicting/Estimating/Making Comparisons

Use a bath scale to explore weight. Place the scale on the floor. Ask your child to step on the scale. Read the weight displayed. Explain that the scale's job is to let you know how heavy something is in pounds. Next, tell your child to push down on the scale with two hands. Work together to get an accurate reading. Now tell your child to push down with one hand. Will the scale show a higher weight or a lower weight? Discuss the results.

Continue explorations with the scale. How many pounds do four books weigh? Six books? How many books does it take to get 10 pounds? Twenty pounds? Estimate the weight of a favorite toy. Place it on the scale. Was your estimation close? Weigh a bag of potatoes or onions, a bunch of bananas, or a loaf of bread. Weigh members of the family. Who is the heaviest? The lightest? Weigh anything that fits on a bath scale!

For extra Weight Work, use the scales in the produce department of the grocery store to weigh fruits and vegetables. At the checkout, point out the electronic scales used by the cashier.

REQUIRED:
- Bath scale
- Objects to weigh

OPTIONAL:
- Supermarket visit

MIX AND MEASURE

SKILL: Standard Measures

Children love to Mix and Measure. For exposure to standard measures, invite your first grader to participate in the routine procedures that occur in the kitchen. Provide concrete experiences for application and cook up loads of fun together.

Whenever you are baking or cooking, expose your child to the use of measuring cups, measuring spoons, temperature settings on the oven, and kitchen timers.

Pancakes and waffles require the measuring and mixing of ingredients. Allow your child to help prepare breakfast. Baking cookies, brownies, cakes, and pies requires measuring, mixing, and setting oven temperatures and timers. Invite your first-grade baker to help in all steps of the process.

Prepare marinades for chicken, meat, or fish; create sauces for casseroles; mix oil, vinegar, and spices for salad dressings; measure ingredients for soup, rice, chili, or tacos. No matter what the recipe, your child and you will have a great time in the kitchen!

REQUIRED:
- Time in the kitchen
- Recipes and ingredients
- Measuring cups and spoons
- Kitchen timer

THERMOMETER READER

Appoint your child official Thermometer Reader! Establish an ongoing outdoor temperature routine and keep a record of the daily temperature in your area.

Discuss outdoor temperature. Talk about the two thermometer scales, Fahrenheit and Celsius. Ask questions such as, "Does the temperature change with the seasons?" "What type of clothing should I wear if it is 28°F?" "85°F?"

Show your child how to read an outdoor thermometer. Focus on either Fahrenheit or Celsius. Specify a time for your child to read the thermometer each day. Provide a sheet of paper for your child to record the temperature and the date. If you do not have an outdoor thermometer, show your child how to find the daily temperature in the newspaper. Work with either the high or low temperature reported each day.

Encourage your child to observe temperature trends, looking for warm or cold spells. Point out the coldest day and the warmest day. When your child feels confident in this role, ask your Thermometer Reader to record the temperature in both Fahrenheit and Celsius.

REQUIRED:
- Outdoor thermometer
- Paper and pencil

OPTIONAL:
- Daily newspaper

IN THE KNOW

SKILL: Standard Measures

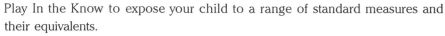

Play In the Know to expose your child to a range of standard measures and their equivalents.

Make a playing card for each of the following measures: one foot, one yard, one minute, one hour, one day, one week, one month, one year, one dozen. Set these cards aside.

Make a playing card for each of the following: 12 inches, 3 feet, 60 seconds, 60 minutes, 24 hours, 7 days, 4 weeks, 12 months, 12 items.

Make a set of nine index cards, each with an equal sign (=) written in the center.

Sit beside your child. Place the first set of cards, face up, in a column to the left. Shuffle the second set of cards and place face up, in a column to the right. Place the set of equal sign index cards down the center, between the two columns.

Now work with your child to match the two columns, discussing the equivalent amounts as you do so. Practice together until your child is able to match the cards independently to be In the Know.

REQUIRED:
- Index Cards
- Marker

HEADS OR TAILS?

SKILLS: Predicting/Recording Data/Making Comparisons

Call it in the air! Practice your coin-flipping skills and have fun making predictions, too. Fold a piece of paper in half. Label one side "Heads" and the other "Tails." Use a quarter to explore the differences between heads and tails. Tell your child you will flip the coin 20 times. Ask your first grader to predict how many flips will land on heads and how many will land on tails. Record the predictions at the top of each column and start flipping! Each time the coin lands on heads, make a tally mark in the "Heads" column. When the coin lands on tails, make a tally mark in the "Tails" column. Take turns so that your child has a chance to flip the coin.

When you have made 20 flips, examine the data. Ask, "Was your prediction correct? Was it too high? Was it too low? What is the difference between your prediction and the actual result?"

After discussing the results, try again with 50, 100, or 200 flips!

REQUIRED:
• Quarter
• Paper and pencil

BEANS IN A BAG

SKILLS: Estimating/Counting/One-to-One Correspondence/Recording Data/Making Comparisons

Children love to guess how many of anything are inside a bag or jar. Through trial and error, first graders gradually develop the ability to make reasonable estimates. Let your child use visual and tactile clues with each estimation task you provide.

Write the heading "Estimation Log" on a piece of paper. Fold the paper into three columns labeled, "Item in the Bag," "My Estimation," "Actual Number." Give your first grader a plastic sandwich bag filled with jellybeans. Be sure the bag is securely fastened. Let your child hold the bag, manipulate the jellybeans inside, observe the configuration of jellybeans, and then estimate the number of jellybeans in the bag. On the log, write "jellybeans" in the first column and your child's estimate in the second column. Now, open the bag and invite your child to count the jellybeans. Record the actual number in the third column.

Repeat the process with pretzels, beans, buttons, or raisins. Compare the estimated number to the actual number of each item.

REQUIRED:
• Any small countable items
• Plastic sandwich bags
• Paper and pencil

INSIDE SURPRISE

By using tactile clues, your child can solve the mystery of the Inside Surprise. Manipulate unseen items for size, shape, and weight to enhance estimation skills.

Divide a piece of paper into four columns labeled "Bag #," "Estimation," "Actual Number," and "Brown Bag Contents." Write "Bag #1," "Bag #2," and so on through "Bag #5" down column one and on five brown paper lunch bags. Select collections for each bag. Vary your choices so that the items exhibit different characteristics. Seal each bag with tape. Give your child Bag #1. Let your child hold the bag, manipulate the contents, and consider size, shape, and weight. Ask, "How many objects do you think are in Bag #1?" Record the results. Continue until an estimate is provided for each bag. Then, invite your child to open Bag #1, empty the contents, and count. Record the actual number and the name of the item. Discuss the characteristics your child used to make an estimate. Compare the estimated number to the actual number. Repeat the process for each bag.

REQUIRED:
- Any small countable items
- Five brown lunch bags
- Paper and pencil

ITEM BANK: five stones, a handful of chocolate chips, six paper clips, two dry sponges, four paper napkins

ESTIMATION STATION

How many tablespoons of sugar will it take to fill a cup? Your first grader will enjoy estimating at the Estimation Station.

Cover your work surface with wax paper, foil, or plastic wrap. Place a bag or canister of sugar, a tablespoon, and a cup on the work surface. Ask your child to examine the size of the tablespoon and cup. Now ask your child to estimate the number of tablespoons of sugar needed to reach the top of the cup. Record the estimate. Now tell your child to fill the cup with sugar, counting each tablespoon used. When the sugar reaches the top of the cup, compare the estimated number with the actual number of tablespoons required to fill the cup.

REQUIRED:
- Tablespoon
- Cup
- Sugar
- Wax paper, foil, or plastic wrap

Keep the Estimation Station open so that your child can explore estimating with a variety of containers and other measuring cups and spoons.

TALLEST TO SHORTEST

SKILLS: Ordering/Ordinal Numbers/Measuring/Recording Data/Drawing/Making Comparisons

Practice ordering with members of the family. Invite your first grader to arrange members of the family in order of height, tallest to shortest, with the tallest to the left. Remind your child to join the line!

On a piece of paper, record from left to right, the results of the lineup. For example, write, "Dad, Mom, Melissa, Kelli, Russell, and Me." Above the names, ask your child to draw the people.

Now, ask questions that focus on the ordering part of the activity. For example, "Who is the tallest person in our family?" "Who is the shortest person in our family?" "Who is second tallest?"

Save the portrait. In another few months, do another Tallest to Shortest family portrait to see if the order has changed.

REQUIRED:
• Construction paper
• Markers/crayons

OPTIONAL:
• Tape measure

WHAT'S FOR DINNER?

SKILLS: Recording Data/Counting/Number Writing

Mon	Tues	Wed
2	3	4
9	10	11
16	17	18

Chicken or fish? Red meat, pasta, or vegetables? Make a table to record the number of times you serve a particular food for dinner over the course of a month.

Hold a 12″ × 18″ sheet of construction paper vertically. Write the heading "Dinner" across the top of the paper, and just below it, draw a horizontal line from the left edge of the paper to the right. Now draw two lines down the paper, making three equal columns. Label the left column "Meal," the middle column, "Tally," and the right column, "Total." Draw five horizontal lines, an equal distance apart, to the bottom of the paper. In the "Meal" column, print, for example, "Chicken" in the first row, "Fish" in the second, "Red Meat" in the third, "Pasta" in the fourth, and "Vegetables" in the fifth.

Keep track of family dinners for one month. Each time fish is part of the meal, your child puts a tally mark in the "Tally" column next to "Fish." At the end of the month, count the tally marks for each item and enter the number in the "Total" column. Discuss the findings from the What's for Dinner? survey as you plan your menu for the coming month.

REQUIRED:
• Construction paper
• Marker
• Ruler

SHOES AND SOCKS

SKILLS: Recording Data/Making Comparisons/Counting

Expose your child to graphing and straighten out the closet and drawer at the same time! Draw two columns, 10″ × 1″, on a sheet of paper. Divide each column into equal segments, ½″ to 1″ wide. Write "Shoes" at the base of one column and "Socks" at the base of the other. Open the closet and begin! For each pair of shoes or sneakers found, your child colors one segment on the "Shoes" column. Open the drawer and inventory the socks. For each pair found, your child colors one segment of the "Socks" column. If necessary, extend the columns to a second sheet of paper taped to the top of the first. When the graph is complete, compare the results by counting the colored segments in each column. Ask questions such as, "How many pairs of shoes do you have?" "How many pairs of socks do you have?" "Do you have more socks than shoes?" "Do you have fewer shoes than socks?"

Variation: Increase the challenge with a three- or four-column graph. Count shoes and socks by color, then move on to T-shirts and sweaters, long-sleeved and short!

REQUIRED:
- Construction paper
- Crayon or marker
- Shoes and socks

TOOTH TABLE

SKILL: Recording Data

Losing a tooth is an exciting experience for a first grader! Build your child's knowledge of tables and graphs by making a Tooth Table.

Hold a 12″ × 18″ sheet of construction paper vertically. Write the heading "Tooth Table" across the top of the paper, and just below it, draw a horizontal line from the left edge of the paper to the right. Now draw a line down the center of the paper. Label the left column "Date Lost." Label the right column "New Tooth." Draw horizontal lines, approximately ¾″ apart, to the bottom of the paper.

Hang the tooth table in an accessible place. Each time your child loses a tooth, write the date in the left column. When your child notices a new tooth starting to grow, write the date in the right column. Important milestones are noted as your child takes charge of recording the information.

REQUIRED:
- One sheet 12″ × 18″ construction paper
- Marker
- Ruler

COIN HANDBOOK

SKILLS: Coin Recognition/Coin Value/Money Notation

1¢
$.01

Make a Coin Handbook from five index cards. Your child can refer to the handbook for help in recognizing coins and recalling their values.

Staple the index cards along the left edge and cover with tape for binding. Label the front cover, "Coin Handbook by Colin," for example. Open the booklet to the first right-facing page, tape a penny to the center of the page, and write "Penny, 1¢, $.01." Open to the next page, tape a nickel to the center of the page, and write "Nickel, 5¢, $.05."

Use the same procedure for "Dime" and "Quarter" on pages three and four. Your child can carry the Coin Handbook anywhere for easy reference.

Variation: Tape two of each coin in the handbook, one showing heads, the other, tails. Or, make an individual handbook for each coin by folding one index card in half. Write "Penny" on the front cover; write "1¢" on the left interior page; tape two pennies to the right facing page, one showing heads, the other, tails; and write "$.01" on the back cover.

REQUIRED:
- Index cards
- Marker
- Stapler/Tape
- Coins

COIN SORT

SKILLS: Coin Recognition/Sorting/Coin Value/Addition

Do you ever wonder how much money you have in that big jar of change sitting on a shelf or in a corner? Let your first grader help you find out!

Use four paper cups as sorting bins. Tape a penny to the outside of the first cup, a nickel to the outside of the second cup, a dime to the third, and a quarter to the fourth. Supply your child with a handful of loose change including pennies, nickels, dimes, and quarters. Ask your child to sort the coins by putting pennies in the penny cup, nickels in the nickel cup, dimes in the dime cup, and quarters in the quarter cup.

Variation: For extra challenge, label the cups with the coin value. Ask your child to sort the coins, find the value of the coins in each cup, and find the total value of all the coins.

REQUIRED:
- Four paper cups
- Pennies, nickels, dimes, and quarters
- Tape

OPTIONAL:
- Marker

WOULD YOU RATHER?

SKILL: Coin Value

Does a dime have the same value as ten pennies? Are five nickels equal to a quarter? Help your child understand the value of different coin combinations by asking questions that start with the phrase, "Would you rather . . ." "Would you rather have seven pennies or a dime?" "Would you rather have four nickels and four pennies or a quarter?" "Would you rather have two pennies, three nickels, and a dime or 50 cents?" "Would you rather have 10 dimes or a dollar?" Alternate asking and answering the "Would you rather . . ." questions. To add to the fun, provide a working bank of pennies, nickels, dimes, and quarters.

REQUIRED:
• Your time

OPTIONAL:
• Pennies, nickels, dimes, and quarters

LOOSE CHANGE

SKILLS: Coin Recognition/Sorting/Coin Value/Recording Data/Making Comparisons/Counting/Addition

What do you do with the Loose Change you find in the bottom of a handbag, briefcase, or pocket? Is it collecting in a jar, piggy bank, or bureau drawer? When was the last time you counted all those dusty pennies, nickels, dimes, and quarters? Put your first grader to work on the Loose Change.

Next time you come home from a workday, running errands, or an evening out, put the loose change in a jar, vase, or piggy bank labeled "Loose Change." After a week, dump the container and sort and total the value of the coins with your child. Record the date and the amount of money collected. Then, put the coins back into the container. Each day, encourage all family members to contribute to the Loose Change bank. Each week, on the designated day, dump, sort, and count the coins. Record the results for week two and compare the total to that of week one. Return the coins to the container. Keep a supply of coin rolls handy for sets of 100 pennies, 40 nickels, 50 dimes, and 40 quarters. At the end of the month, visit the bank together to deposit the loose change to your child's account.

REQUIRED:
• Loose change
• Paper coin rolls
• Marker
• Paper and pencil

OPTIONAL:
• Bank visit

A+ ACTIVITIES FOR FIRST GRADE

COIN SWAP

SKILLS: Coin Recognition/Coin Value/Place Value/Counting

Crack open the piggy bank for an exciting interactive game that your child will want to play repeatedly. Prior to the start of the game, gather 40 pennies and eight nickels to serve as the bank. Place these coins between the players. Players take turns rolling a die and collecting pennies from the bank. For example, if a player rolls a three, that player takes three pennies. When a player acquires five or more pennies, the player says, "Swap" and exchanges five pennies for a nickel. The game ends when all nickels have been claimed. The player with the most nickels is the winner. When your child gets the hang of Coin Swap, you may want to add more coins to the bank or play with two dice. Variation: Add four dimes to the bank.

REQUIRED:
- One die
- Eight nickels
- 40 pennies

OPTIONAL:
- One additional die
- Four dimes
- Additional coins

MONEY SPIN

SKILLS: Coin Recognition/Coin Value/Addition

How much money do you have if you are holding three dimes? How about two quarters and a penny? Play Money Spin and practice totaling the value of coin combinations.

Cut an 8″ square from a piece of cardboard. Draw a diagonal line from the top left-hand corner to the bottom right-hand corner. Do the same from the top right-hand corner to the bottom left-hand corner.

Place different coin combinations in each of the four areas of the gameboard. For example, place a nickel and a penny in one area and two nickels and a dime in another. In another area, place two dimes and six pennies. Place a quarter, a nickel, and two pennies in the remaining area.

Hold a paper clip at the center of the board with a pencil. A player spins the paper clip by flicking it with a finger. Wherever the clip stops, the player counts the total value of the coins. If correct, the player takes the coins. If incorrect, the coins stay on the board. Alternate turns until no coins remain on the board. The player with the highest total wins.

Play often, changing the combination of coins in each area.

REQUIRED:
- Cardboard
- Coins
- Pencil
- Paper clip
- Safety scissors

SHOPPER

SKILLS: Coin Recognition/Coin Value/Addition

Help your child learn to spend wisely! Your child plays the role of shopper, you play the role of storekeeper, and household items double as inventory.

Place a pencil, paper clip, eraser, sponge, and sheets of paper on a table. Place an index card next to each. Write on each card the cost of each item. Label the pencil "18¢," the paper clip "7¢," the eraser "10¢," the sponge "25¢," and the paper "5¢ per sheet."

Provide your child with a supply of pennies, nickels, dimes, and quarters.

Invite your child to shop. Give your child enough time to decide on purchases. As the storekeeper, make change for your shopper as needed. Ask questions such as, "What item is most expensive?" "Least expensive?" "What two items can you buy with 17¢?" "If one sheet of paper costs 5¢, what do three sheets cost?" Discuss the various coin combinations that make 25¢ to pay for the sponge. Assist your shopper as appropriate.

Variation: Increase the cost of each item and bring dollars into the store.

> **REQUIRED:**
> - Five small household items
> - Pennies, nickels, dimes, and quarters
> - Index cards
> - Marker
>
> **OPTIONAL:**
> - Dollars

STOREKEEPER

SKILLS: Coin Recognition/Making Change/Coin Value/Counting

Making change can be difficult for children and adults, so difficult, in fact, that most modern cash registers do the work for us, calculating and displaying the change due a customer. Still, it is important for your child to have opportunities to make change by "counting up."

Set up a household store. Your child plays the storekeeper and you play the shopper. Place a pot, spoon, cup, dishtowel, and rubberbands on a table. Write the cost of an item on an index card and place it next to the item. Label the pot "18¢," the spoon "7¢," the cup "12¢," the dishtowel "36¢," and the rubberbands "6¢ each."

As the shopper, be sure you have a supply of coins. Provide your child with pennies only to make change.

Ask the storekeeper, "How much is one spoon?" Your child answers, "7¢." Ask to buy one spoon. Pay for it with a dime. Your child, using pennies, says "7," the price, then counts out change, "8, 9, 10 cents," while giving you three pennies.

Role-play other transactions as your storekeeper practices counting up to make change.

> **REQUIRED:**
> - Five small household items
> - Pennies, nickels, dimes, and quarters
> - Index cards
> - Marker

DESIGN A DOLLAR

SKILLS: Dollar Recognition/Observation/Number Recognition/Brainstorming/Imaginative Thinking/Drawing

Dollars go in cash registers, wallets, and bank drawers, circulating from one to the next without anyone stopping to look at anything other than the number in each of the four corners. Ones, fives, tens, twenties, fifties, and hundreds rarely get much notice! Take a few minutes to do some dollar detecting with your first grader. Study a one dollar bill. Talk about the portrait of George Washington, first president of the United States. Look for and read familiar words. Ask your child to find and count all the 9s or 7s or 4s on the bill. Focus on the serial number. Search for the year the bill was made. Look for the tiny key. Find the eagle. Find the word "one" as many times as you can. Talk about the value of the bill in relation to coins. Ask what you might be able to buy for one dollar. Follow the same procedure for other bills available.

Then, invite your child to Design a Dollar. Draw a rectangle the size of a dollar bill. Ask your child to fill in the rest. The dollar amount, a self-portrait perhaps, and notations of any kind are in the hands of the designer.

REQUIRED:
• Paper currency
• Paper and pencil
• Markers/crayons

PATTERNWEAR

SKILLS: Visual Patterns/Observation/Counting

The clothing we wear is often covered with patterns! Whether the pattern is a checked shirt, a floral skirt, or a striped sneaker, clothing gives first graders many patterns to see and discuss.

Encourage your child to take an inventory of patterns on clothing. Ask questions to get started. How many pairs of your pants have a pattern? Are there any sweatshirts or sweaters in the closet that have a pattern? What are these patterns? Are they patterns of colors, shapes, or lines?

Tell your child to be on the lookout for patterns on the clothing of other family members. For fun, designate a day "Pattern Day," when all family members wear at least one thing with a pattern.

REQUIRED:
• Your time

POTATO PATTERNS

SKILL: Visual Patterns

Potatoes can be used in a variety of ways. Turn two potatoes into four design stamps. Your child can decide on a design for each and then use the stamps to make potato pattern posters.

Cut a potato widthwise. Each half serves as a stamp. Show your child the flat end of each stamp. Using a plastic knife, work together to carve a different design into the flat end of each potato half. Choose a checkerboard, spiral, star, or diamond. The possibilities are enormous! Repeat the process with another potato, giving you four stamps in all.

Now, provide your child with construction paper and a shallow dish of tempera paint. Make a potato pattern poster by dipping the design end of a stamp into the paint. Press the potato onto the paper to make a print. Encourage your child to make potato pattern posters using anywhere from two stamps to four. Dry flat and display!

REQUIRED:
- Two potatoes
- Plastic knife
- Construction paper
- Dish
- Nontoxic paint

PATTERN NECKLACES

SKILL: Visual Patterns

Patterns are all around us! We see them in the clothes we wear, the flowers we grow, and the wallpaper we hang. Help your child recognize and manipulate patterns by making pattern jewelry.

Cut a 24″ length of plastic lacing (gimp), available at most craft stores. Tie a double knot at one end of the plastic lacing and tape that end to the table. Provide your child with a supply of plastic beads. As an alternative to beads, use vegetable food coloring to dye any shape of pasta with holes. Whether you use beads or pasta, include four colors. Ask your child to choose a color pattern for the necklace. For example, if your child selects a red, white, blue, and green pattern, begin by sliding a red bead on the lacing, followed by white, blue, and green. Continue the pattern until the pattern necklace is complete.

Make sure enough slack remains for safe placement of the necklace on your child. A pattern bracelet will complete the ensemble!

REQUIRED:
- Plastic beads in four colors
- Plastic lacing/gimp
- Tape
- Ruler
- Safety scissors

OPTIONAL:
- Pasta
- Food coloring/paint

A+ ACTIVITIES FOR FIRST GRADE

JUICY FRUITY

SKILLS: Visual Patterns/Observation

The colors and textures of fruit provide Juicy Fruity pattern work to enhance your child's visual discrimination and fine motor skills while offering a tasty dessert at the same time!

Plan a Juicy Fruity fruit stick dessert that you and your child construct together. Cut fruits such as cantaloupe, honeydew, watermelon, and pineapple into small cubes or balls. Have a supply of grapes, strawberries, and blueberries available as well. Then, using small wooden skewers, make Juicy Fruity fruit sticks. Simply skewer the fruit in whatever order strikes your creative fancy. Encourage your child to do the same. Then, place your finished skewers on the work surface. Talk about the patterns themselves as you admire the order of fruits and colors. Ask your child to copy your pattern on a second skewer while you copy the pattern created by your child on your second skewer. Now, working independently, move on to new patterns. Again, upon completion, copy each other. Continue until you've created enough fruit sticks to satisfy the appetites of everyone in the family. Then enjoy your Juicy Fruity fruit stick pattern dessert.

REQUIRED:
- Fruit
- Knife
- 6" wooden skewers

SHAPE SEARCH

SKILLS: Shape Recognition/Observation/Recording Data/Drawing

How many different shapes can you find in a five-minute walk outside? Equipped with a notepad or clipboard, with paper and a pencil, become shape detectives in your neighborhood. Look for the rectangle in a traffic light or the circle of the light itself. Find a square on a signpost or an oval on a streetlight. See the circle of the sewer cover and the square of a drain grate. Notice the triangle of a fir tree or the rectangle of a doorway. Record your observations, writing words and drawing shapes. Once at home, make a list, by shape, of all the things you found.

REQUIRED:
- Notepad or clipboard with paper
- Pencil
- Neighborhood walk

MATH ACTIVITIES

SWINGING SHAPES

SKILLS: Shape Recognition/Measuring/Visual Patterns/Drawing/Cutting

Circles and squares twist and twirl on a Swinging Shapes mobile! Provide an $8\frac{1}{2}'' \times 11''$ piece of paper and a pencil when you ask your child to name and draw shapes. Give assistance as needed to draw a circle, square, rectangle, triangle, oval, and diamond. Then ask your child to draw a large circle on a bright sheet of construction paper. Print "Circle" in the center. Cut out the circle. Choose a different color for each shape and repeat the process.

When all shapes are ready, place a wire hanger on the work surface. Arrange the shapes on the work surface until you decide on a pattern for your mobile. For example, from left to right, begin with the circle placed 2" below the base of the hanger. Next set the square to the right of the circle, 10" below the base. Put the rectangle next at 5" below the base. Continue in this manner until all shapes have been placed. Then cut lengths of string to attach to the top of each shape and tie to the hanger. Hang the completed mobile for all to admire.

REQUIRED:
- $8\frac{1}{2}'' \times 11''$ paper
- Pencil/marker
- Construction paper
- String/yarn
- Wire hanger
- Safety scissors

JIGGLE SHAPES

SKILL: Shape Recognition

The next time Jell-O® is on your dessert menu, make shapes that wiggle and jiggle! Follow the directions for Jigglers on the Jell-O® box. Pour the liquid into a 13" × 9" pan and refrigerate until firm, approximately three hours. Before lunch or dinner, supervise your child as you work together to cut the Jell-O® into Jiggle Shapes. Use a butter knife or plastic knife to ensure safety. Encourage your child to cut triangles, squares, rectangles, diamonds, pentagons, hexagons, and circles. Help your child remove each shape from the pan. Identify the shapes before you eat them!

Variation: Cut Jiggle Letters and Jiggle Numbers, too!

REQUIRED:
- Jell-O®
- 13" × 9" pan
- Butter knife/plastic knife

ILLUSHAPE

SKILLS: Shape Recognition/Manipulating Shapes/Drawing/Cutting

Have you ever heard your first grader say, "I don't know how to make a giraffe!"? Have you ever heard your first grader say, "I don't know how to make a flower!"? Young children don't automatically recognize that by making and combining shapes they know, they can make or draw just about anything!

Work with your child to draw and cut shapes to make a giraffe. Cut a small oval for the head and a large oval for the body. Cut five long, thin rectangles for the neck and legs. Cut three short, thin rectangles for the two horns and the tail. Finally, cut circles for the eyes, a circle for the nose, and several circles for spots.

Use a sheet of 12″ × 18″ construction paper for the background. Manipulate the shapes, arranging them as you would puzzle pieces to make the giraffe. Glue the shapes to the background paper and display.

Anytime your child says, "I don't know how to make a . . . ," respond, "Of course you do! Use shapes!"

REQUIRED:
• Construction paper
• Safety scissors
• Nontoxic glue

MARSHMALLOW SCULPTURES

SKILLS: Making Three-Dimensional Objects/Imaginative Thinking

Help your child gain an understanding of three-dimensional objects by creating Marshmallow Sculptures.

Provide an ample supply of toothpicks and mini-marshmallows. Cover the working surface with a piece of cardboard so that completed sculptures can be moved. Demonstrate that by sticking the toothpicks into marshmallows and connecting them, you form three-dimensional shapes. Connect eight marshmallows with twelve toothpicks to make a cube.

Connect four marshmallows with six toothpicks to make a pyramid. Encourage your child to be creative while building more three-dimensional sculptures. Explore and have fun!

REQUIRED:
• Mini-marshmallows
• Toothpicks

POLY-STRAWS

SKILLS: Recognizing Polygons/Making Polygons/Observation

Construct your own polygons! Polygons are closed, two-dimensional figures made from line segments (sides) that join three or more points. A triangle is a three-sided polygon, a rectangle is a four-sided polygon, and an octagon is an eight-sided polygon.

Use straws and twist-ties and work with your child to understand how polygons are formed. Start with a triangle with equal sides. Slide one end of a twist-tie into one end of a straw. Then slide the other end of the twist-tie into another straw until the ends of the two straws meet. The meeting point forms one angle of the triangle. Repeat the process with a third straw to form the other two corners. The ends of the twist-ties may need to be pinched a bit to slide into the straws.

Observe the triangle. How many sides and angles are there? Are the sides the same length? How many straws and twist-ties were needed to make the triangle?

Encourage your child to make other polygons. Create regular polygons by joining straws of the same length, or irregular polygons by joining straws of different lengths.

REQUIRED:
• Straws
• Twist-ties

OPTIONAL:
• Safety scissors

SYMMETRICAL LETTERS

SKILLS: Symmetry/Brainstorming/Observation

Symmetrical objects have the same characteristics on both sides of a center dividing line. Together, brainstorm things that are symmetrical. A butterfly, window panes, and a design on a tablecloth can be symmetrical. A circle, square, and diamond are symmetrical, too! Now ask your child whether any uppercase letters might be symmetrical. On an index card, clearly print the letter, "A." Ask your child to draw a dotted line from the top of the A to the bottom. Next, examine the A and the dividing line to determine whether A is symmetrical. Repeat the process with the remaining letters of the alphabet. Use the list below as a guide to recognize symmetrical letters and numbers.

Symmetrical Letters: A, H, I, M, O, T, U, V, W, X, and Y
Symmetrical Numbers: 0, 8

REQUIRED:
• Index cards
• Marker

BEAUTIFUL BUTTERFLY

SKILLS: Symmetry/Observation/Drawing/Painting

A beautiful butterfly is a great example of natural symmetry. On your next visit to the library or bookstore, notice the symmetrical pattern on the butterfly that emerges from the cocoon in Eric Carle's *The Very Hungry Caterpillar*.

Create your own symmetrical and beautiful butterfly. Hold a piece of white construction paper horizontally and fold it in half. Use a pencil as you work together to draw the outline of half a butterfly to the left of the fold. You'll need to include, from the crease over, half a small oval for the head, one antenna, one eye, and half a nose and mouth. Just beneath the small oval and connected to it, draw half a large elongated oval for the body. Draw two legs at the base of the body and one near the top. Draw a full wing attached to the body.

Use tempera paint to create your butterfly. Encourage your child to paint carefully over the outline drawn. Then, paint a design on the butterfly wing. While the paint is wet, fold carefully at the crease and gently press down. Open the paper to reveal your symmetrical Beautiful Butterfly.

REQUIRED:
• Construction paper
• Pencil
• Tempera paint/ paintbrush

OPTIONAL:
• Library/bookstore visit

FAMILY MATH LOG

SKILLS: Math Awareness/Math Appreciation

Keep a running record of your family's math experiences by creating a personalized Family Math Log. Use a notebook or journal. On the cover, print "Family Math Log by Julia, Adam, Mom, Dad," for example. Encourage each family member to contribute to the Family Math Log at least once a week. What follows is a sample of a typical week in the Family Math Log.

On Monday, Julia draws a picture of a garden she saw with a pattern of yellow and red tulips. On Tuesday, Adam writes about Monday night's football game, including total number of points and touchdowns scored by each team. On Wednesday, Mom writes a note to Julia and Adam to tell them that their allowance will increase by $.75 to $1.50. On Thursday, Dad pastes a grocery receipt into the journal. On Friday, Julia writes that she learned how to use a ruler in school, and Adam reports that he worked with fractions. On Saturday, Mom and Dad write a math riddle for Julia and Adam to solve. On Sunday, everyone in the family takes a few moments to view the log and comment on the different ways we use math every day.

REQUIRED:
• Notebook/journal
• Pencil/pen/crayons

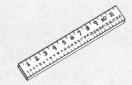

SCIENCE

Imagine the look of awe in your child's eyes when you catch sight of a rainbow after a storm. Think about the shouts of excitement when you notice the first snowflakes of winter or the first sprout of a spring flower. Real-life experiences spark the curiosity and wonder of scientific investigation.

The science activities that follow invite, encourage, and stimulate interest. Across a range of topics, you and your child brainstorm, ask ques tions, and investigate the natural world through observation, making comparisons, predicting, experimenting, and drawing conclusions. You'll have the opportunity to blaze trails with inventors, bring the five senses to life, design fingerprint characters, use x-ray eyes, research animals from ant to elephant, forecast the weather as family meteorologist, sink a ship, dance with a shadow, make a rainbow, celebrate the seasons, sprout popcorn kernels and beans, thank a tree, and care for the earth.

We have provided you with basic factual information to enhance discussions and discoveries. Keep your explanations simple, providing your young scientist with information that matches a first grader's level of understanding. Above all, celebrate the wonder of the world around you!

TRAILBLAZERS

SKILLS: Brainstorming/Written Expression

Where would we be without the curiosity, determination, perseverance, and courage of inventors and scientists, past and present?

Talk to your child about trailblazers, those people who have made a difference in our world because of their scientific explorations. Talk about Alexander Graham Bell, who invented and patented the telephone in 1876. Discuss Thomas Alva Edison, who in 1880 invented the electric light bulb. Marvel at George Washington Carver, who, during his lifetime from the 1860s to 1943, discovered more than three hundred ways to use peanuts. Mention Wilbur and Orville Wright, the brothers who in 1903 made the first airplane flight. Celebrate the accomplishments of astronauts such as Neil Armstrong, the first person to walk on the moon in 1969, and Sally Ride, the first American woman to fly in space in 1983 on the space shuttle *Challenger*.

Encourage your child to write a letter of appreciation to any trailblazer. In the letter, express thanks to the scientist for contributions to our world. Also include reasons why the scientist's accomplishments are important. If the selected trailblazer happens to be alive, mail the letter and hope for a response.

REQUIRED:
• Paper and pencil
OPTIONAL:
• Envelope and stamp

INCREDIBLE INVENTIONS

SKILLS: Brainstorming/Imaginative Thinking/Drawing & Constructing/Written Expression

February 11 is Inventor's Day, as well as the birthday of Thomas Alva Edison, one of our country's greatest inventors. Edison is responsible for the invention of the electric light and phonograph. He also contributed to the invention of the movie camera and telephone.

Discuss the job of an inventor. Brainstorm inventions that we use daily, including television, radio, bicycle, toothbrush, car, eyeglasses, flashlight, computer, paper, and pencil sharpener. Discuss what life would be like without some of these inventions. Encourage your child to think of something that has yet to be invented that could be used in everyday life.

Provide recyclable materials, glue, scissors, paper, crayons, and markers so your young inventor can draw or build a new invention. Encourage your child to write about the invention. Include details such as cost, instructions for usage, and jobs it does.

Whether the creation is an automatic homework helper, an electric page turner, or a battery-operated pencil, your child's invention is sure to be a hit!

REQUIRED:
• Paper and pencil
• Crayons/markers
• Recyclable materials
• Nontoxic glue
• Safety scissors

FIVE-SENSE RIDDLES

SKILLS: Imaginative Thinking/Asking Questions/Drawing Conclusions

Bring the five senses to life with Five-Sense Riddles. To begin, talk with your first grader about the five senses. Emphasize that we see with our eyes, hear with our ears, taste with our tongues, smell with our noses, and touch with our fingers. Ask your child to name things we see, hear, taste, smell, and touch. Then ask your child to solve a Five-Sense Riddle.

"I taste something sweet and juicy. It is red on the inside and green on the outside. I spit out the brown seeds. What do I taste?"

"You taste watermelon!"

"I see something fly by that is white and fluffy. It brings shade when it covers the sun. What do I see?"

"You see a cloud!"

"I hear a woof and a growl. What do I hear?"

"You hear a dog!"

"I touch something soft. I find it on the ground near a bird's nest. What do I touch?"

"You touch a feather!"

"I smell something salty and buttery. I'm at the movies. What do I smell?"

"You smell popcorn!"

Take turns creating and telling a Five-Sense Riddle and get the whole family to see, hear, taste, smell, and touch!

REQUIRED:
• Your time

FIVE-SENSE SURVEY

SKILLS: Observation/Surveying/Recording Data/Making Comparisons

Pick a place, any place, and let your first grader do a Five-Sense Survey. All you need is a clipboard, a pencil and paper, and your eyes, ears, nose, tongue, and hands. Divide the survey sheet into five columns labeled "See," "Hear," "Taste," "Smell," and "Touch." Then, wherever you are, look, listen, taste, smell, touch, and record.

Perhaps you'll walk around your yard or neighborhood. What do you see . . . tall trees, green bushes, tiny ants, stone walls, wooden benches? What do you hear . . . birds tweeting, horns honking, people talking, wind blowing, insects chirping? What do you taste? What do you smell? What do you touch?

Variation: Let each member of the family complete a Five-Sense Survey when you go to the grocery store, a movie theater, a restaurant, the library, an ice cream parlor, a baseball game. Then compare the results. You'll be amazed by how much you'll notice when you take the time to look, listen, taste, smell, and touch.

REQUIRED:
• Clipboard
• Paper and pencil
• Neighborhood walk

SCIENCE ACTIVITIES

THE NOSE KNOWS

SKILLS: Observation/Drawing Conclusions/Recording Data/Making Comparisons

What smells good and what smells bad? Does the nose know? Challenge your child to identify mystery smells. Divide a piece of paper into two columns, the first labeled "Cup #," the second labeled "Smell." Write "Cup 1," "Cup 2," and so on through "Cup 6" down column one and on six paper cups. Place an item in each cup, making sure to vary your choices. Suggestions include: baby powder, an orange slice, popcorn, cinnamon, a pickle, an onion slice.

Begin the smell check. Blindfold your child or cover each cup with a thin napkin held firm by a rubber band. Hold Cup #1 beneath your child's nose and ask, "What do you smell?" Record the response. Repeat the process for each cup. Then, invite your child to look in Cup #1 to confirm or correct the recorded response. Discuss and compare the characteristics of each smell, for example, sweet, fresh, spicy, sour. Repeat the experiment with different items to prove that The Nose Knows!

Variation: Play mystery taste and mystery touch.

REQUIRED:
- Cups
- Blindfold
- Paper and pencil
- Selection of smells

OPTIONAL:
- Napkins
- Rubber bands

TASTE TALLY

SKILLS: Brainstorming/Experimentation/Recording Data/Surveying

Why does maple syrup taste sweet, a lemon taste sour, a potato chip taste salty, unsweetened chocolate taste bitter, and pizza taste spicy? Ask your first grader to explain what he or she knows or believes to be true about why foods have different tastes. Explain that the tongue is like a taste detective that sends us clues about the foods we eat. Sample something sweet, sour, salty, bitter, and spicy to establish an understanding of each term. Then begin the Taste Tally.

Provide your child with a notebook or journal. Write, for example, "Emily's Taste Tally" on the cover. Label each page with a taste, "Sweet," "Sour," "Salty," "Bitter," "Spicy," and any other taste you choose. Begin the Taste Tally at meal or snack time. If the tacos are spicy, write "tacos" on the "Spicy" page. If the pickles are sour, write "pickles" on the "Sour" page. If the peaches are sweet, write "peaches" on the "Sweet" page. Encourage your child to survey other members of the family when they have a snack and add to the tally.

Variation: Try a Touch Tally, keeping a list of things that are soft, hard, bumpy, slimy, cold, or hot.

REQUIRED:
- Notebook or journal
- Pencil
- Foods

FIVE-SENSE READ

SKILLS: Observation/Recording Data

Pick a book, any book, and let your first grader do a Five-Sense Read. As you read, record the sights, sounds, smells, tastes, and touches that you find appealing in the story. Focus not only on the pictures when you talk about sight but also on the sights created by the words. Listen to the sounds and make them. Taste the tastes in actuality, smell the smells, and touch whatever is touched. Pay attention to the words the author uses to describe what we see, hear, smell, taste, and touch.

Enjoy a book such as *The Pea Patch Jig* by Thacher Hurd. Smell the sweet onions and see the tiny family that lives at the edge of the garden. Hear Father Mouse yell, "Timber," and listen to the big zucchini as it falls from the shelf, "Thwack!!!" Touch the warm, soapy water in Baby Mouse's bath. Observe red tomatoes like those in Farmer Clem's garden. Touch and examine the inside of a tomato just as Grandfather Mouse does. Taste the sweet peas the mice eat. Hear Farmer Clem snore. Listen to the sound of Grandfather's fiddle as you dance beneath the bright yellow moon!

REQUIRED:
- A book
- Paper and pencil
- Things to see, taste, hear, smell, and touch

OPTIONAL:
- Library/bookstore visit

ONE OF A KIND

SKILLS: Observation/Making Comparisons/Imaginative Thinking/Drawing

Astound your first grader with the fact that no two fingerprints are alike! Then challenge your young observer to check the validity of the statement. Start by providing a magnifying glass. Examine the right index finger of each family member. Then, use a stamp pad or paint to make fingerprints of the index fingers on a sheet of paper. Ask your child to examine the prints with his or her naked eye and with the magnifying glass. Point out differences among the prints and note that each is one of a kind. For added fingerprint fun, make fingerprint pictures. Press an inked or painted finger or thumb to paper. Allow to dry. Then, with a black felt tip pen, add simple lines, arcs, circles, dots, wiggles, and squiggles to create a menagerie of characters—a spider, a bird, a cat, a smiling face. Try to get your hands on *Ed Emberley's Great Thumbprint Drawing Book* for creative ideas and examples.

REQUIRED:
- Magnifying glass
- Stamp pad or paint
- Paper
- Felt tip pen

OPTIONAL:
- Library/bookstore visit

TAP-A-BONE

SKILLS: Brainstorming/Identifying/Recording Data

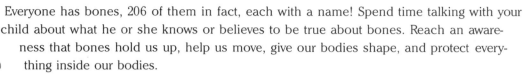

Everyone has bones, 206 of them in fact, each with a name! Spend time talking with your child about what he or she knows or believes to be true about bones. Reach an awareness that bones hold us up, help us move, give our bodies shape, and protect everything inside our bodies.

Then play the Tap-a-Bone Game. Take turns being the "caller." Say, for example, "Tap a toe bone." Your child taps his or her toe bone and you tap one of yours, too. Other calls might include a foot bone, an ankle bone, a shin bone, a calf bone, a kneecap, a thigh bone, a finger bone, a rib, an arm bone, a shoulder blade, your backbone (spine), your jawbone, your skull.

Make a list of all the bones you think of and add to the list each time you repeat the activity.

REQUIRED:
• Your time

NO BONES ABOUT IT

SKILLS: Observation/Imaginative Thinking/Drawing Conclusions

Make no bones about it, people need skeletons to hold them up and give their bodies shape. Without bones, people would flop about like wet noodles! Give your first grader the opportunity to make a dinosaur with and without bones to illustrate these facts. Before you begin, you may want to read about and look at pictures of dinosaurs in books such as *If the Dinosaurs Came Back* by Bernard Most or *Patrick's Dinosaurs* by Carol Carrick.

Supply your child with Play-Doh® and drinking straws cut into several 1″, 2″, 3″, and 4″ sections. Cover a work surface and challenge your child to make a tall dinosaur from Play-Doh®. The dinosaur may stand for a moment but will eventually, because of the lack of a skeleton, crumple or lose its shape.

Now make another tall dinosaur using straw sections for bones. Mold the Play-Doh® around the straw sections for legs and neck. Include as many "bones" as you wish. When complete, discuss why the dinosaur with bones stands while the dinosaur without bones falls.

REQUIRED:
• Play-Doh®
• Straws
• Safety scissors
• Work surface paper

OPTIONAL:
• Library/bookstore visit

A+ ACTIVITIES FOR FIRST GRADE

JOINT POINT

SKILLS: Observation/Identifying

Each and every bone in the human skeleton has at least one buddy! That is, each bone is connected to at least one other bone. Ask your child to make a fist. Observe the locations at which each finger bends. Point out that bones are connected at the "bending spots." These bending, turning, swiveling spots are called joints. Ligaments, acting like strong rubber bands, hold our bones together at the joints.

Play Joint Point. Bend your arm at the elbow and ask your child to point out and identify the joint. "Elbow joint!" Now your child bends a leg at the knee and asks you to point to and identify the joint. "Knee joint!" Continue in this fashion, pointing out and identifying other joints: ankles, hips, wrists, shoulders, spine, neck, and jaw.

Without joints, we wouldn't be able to do many everyday activities. Ask your child how joints help us hold a pencil, touch our toes, peel an orange, throw a ball, and play the trumpet. For fun, try to move without bending at the joints.

REQUIRED:
• Your time

DRINKING-STRAW SKELETONS

SKILLS: Observation/Identifying/Recording Data

Make Drinking-Straw Skeletons to help your first grader become familiar with the location of bones in the human skeleton.

Cut drinking straws to use as bones. For the upper body, cut 24 1″ sections for the vertebrae of the spine, 24 3″ sections for 12 pairs of ribs, two 3″ sections for collarbones, two 6″ sections for upper arm bones, and four 6″ sections for forearm bones. For the lower body, use six 7″ straws for calf bones, shinbones, and thighbones. Cut two 4″ sections for hipbones and 20 3″ sections for fingers and toes. Cut a skull from a sheet of paper, and draw a nose, eye sockets, and a mouth with teeth visible.

Construct your skeleton using a picture or model as a guide. Hold a 12″ × 18″ sheet of construction paper vertically. Glue the paper skull an inch from the top. Build the skeleton by gluing straw sections in appropriate locations. Upon completion, identify and label the bones.

REQUIRED:
• Straws
• Construction paper
• Nontoxic glue
• Safety scissors
• Skeleton picture or model

BONES, BONES, BONES

SKILLS: Observation/Identifying

Have you ever looked closely at the bones of a chicken wing or a steak, lamb, or pork chop? When you take the last bite of a turkey leg, don't miss a wonderful opportunity to get a good look at real bones.

The next time you have a meal that includes food with bones, take notice. Ask your child about the texture and color of the bone and its possible location in the body of the animal. Discuss your child's observations.

For further hands-on exploration, save the bones from a meal. Clean off the remaining meat and boil. When cool, remove the bones from the pot. Allow to dry. Observe each with your child.

At your next visit to the doctor, look at an old X-ray. Observe the X-ray and ask your child to guess which bones are pictured. Discuss why doctors sometimes need to see X-rays of our bones. Have fun exploring bones, bones, and more bones!

REQUIRED:
• Bones from dinner

OPTIONAL:
• X-ray

X-RAY EYES

SKILLS: Observation/Application/Drawing

In the book *Skeletons! Skeletons! All About Bones* by Katy Hall, young readers are given the opportunity to look at a picture of a skeleton, read a clue, and guess the animal to which the skeleton belongs. To confirm the response, the child holds the page up to the light to observe the skeleton inside the animal. Challenge your first grader to take this activity to the next level.

Look at pictures in magazines or books of animals—a dog, cat, frog, bird, snake, or monkey. Consider the appearance of the skeleton necessary to sustain the body of the animal. Focus on parts such as the skull, neck, back, abdomen, legs, feet, hands, fingers, wings, tail, and teeth. Use imaginary X-Ray Eyes to see the skeleton of a selected animal. Provide construction paper, nontoxic glue, safety scissors, a pencil, and wooden toothpicks. Manipulate the toothpicks to create the skeleton that fits the animal. Cut toothpicks as appropriate and glue to paper. Draw the skull. To enhance the structuring of the skeleton, your child can first draw the outline of the animal and fit the skeleton inside.

REQUIRED:
• Toothpicks
• Construction paper
• Nontoxic glue
• Safety scissors
• Animal pictures
• Pencil

OPTIONAL:
• Library/bookstore visit

THINK FAST

SKILL: Brainstorming

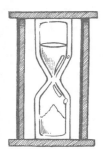

In all shapes and sizes, animals have been on Earth for hundreds of millions of years. They have survived by breathing oxygen and eating plants or other animals.

Get ready to think fast! Set a timer or use the second hand on a watch. Ask your first grader to name all the animals he or she can think of in two minutes. While your child calls out the animals, record the names. At the end of two minutes, ask your child to count and read all the names on the list. Save the recording sheet so that the next time you play, your child can try to beat the record.

For added fun, get the whole family involved. Provide everyone with paper and a pencil. Set the timer to two minutes and Think Fast. When time is up, read the lists, crossing out any animal that appears on more than one list. Award a point for each animal named on a list that no one else included. Tally the results to determine the winner.

REQUIRED:
- Paper and pencils
- Timer

HABITAT . . . LAND HO!

SKILLS: Brainstorming/Identifying/Sorting/Classifying/Drawing

Land animals roam the grasslands, polar lands, farmlands, woodlands, rain forests, jungles, deserts, mountains, backyards, and city parks. Ask your child to choose a habitat to draw and color on a paper plate. Label the finished plate with the name of the habitat. Brainstorm the kinds of animals that live in this habitat. Invite your child to draw a picture of each animal named and glue it to the plate. Write the name of the animal beneath its picture. Return to this activity often, each time selecting a different habitat. You may want to use a reference book to verify ideas. Before long you'll have lions, giraffes, rhinos, and zebras roaming a paper plate grassland; polar bears, penguins, whales, and caribou cavorting on a polar land plate; and cows, sheep, goats, and horses grazing on a farmland plate.

HABITAT/ANIMAL BANK:

Woodland:	deer, fox, bear, raccoon
Rain forest/Jungle:	monkey, parrot, sloth, iguana
Desert:	camel, roadrunner, desert tortoise, coyote
Mountains:	yak, bighorn sheep, golden eagle, cougar
Backyard:	dog, cat, robin, toad
City park:	pigeon, squirrel, chipmunk, field mouse

REQUIRED:
- Paper plates
- Markers/crayons
- Construction paper
- Safety scissors
- Nontoxic glue

OPTIONAL:
- Reference books

HABITAT ◆ ◆ ◆ FRESH & SALTY!

SKILLS: Brainstorming/Identifying/Sorting/Classifying/Drawing

Water animals live in both fresh water and salt water. Focus on lakes, rivers, ponds, and streams for a fresh water habitat and the ocean for a salt water habitat. Ask your child to draw and color a fresh water habitat on a paper plate. Label the finished plate "Fresh Water" and specify "Lake," "River," "Pond," or "Stream." Brainstorm the kinds of animals that live in this habitat. Invite your child to draw a picture of each animal named and glue it to the plate. Write the name of the animal beneath its picture. Return to this activity a second time to create the "Salt Water—Ocean" habitat. You may want to use a reference book to verify ideas. Display the habitat plates. Enjoy trout shimmering, beavers gnawing, geese honking, and frogs hopping in their fresh water habitat and sharks feeding, gulls fishing, lobsters clawing, and starfish basking in their salt water habitat.

REQUIRED:
- Paper plates
- Markers/crayons
- Construction paper
- Safety scissors
- Nontoxic glue

OPTIONAL:
- Reference books

HABITAT MATCH

SKILLS: Observation/Brainstorming/Sorting/Classifying

The world is filled with animals, those that live in water and those that live on land. Enhance your child's awareness of animal habitats by playing Habitat Match.

Look for pictures of water bodies and land areas in recyclable magazines. Cut out photos, paintings, or drawings of oceans, lakes, rivers, ponds, streams, mountains, meadows, pastures, fields, farmlands, deserts, forests, jungles, parks, polar lands, and grasslands. Anything goes! Ask your child to sort the pictures by water and land. Glue all water pictures on one large sheet of paper labeled "Water" and all land pictures on another labeled "Land."

Everyone in the family can participate as you brainstorm names of animals. Write each animal name on a small sticky tag or slip of paper. Place the posters on a table or floor. Call out the animal names as participants take turns matching the animal to the habitat by placing the sticky tag on the matching poster. For example, place the bear on the land poster and the octopus on the water poster. Add animals to the habitats at any time and talk about animals and where they live.

REQUIRED:
- Magazines
- Safety scissors
- Nontoxic glue
- Construction paper
- Sticky tags/paper

A+ ACTIVITIES FOR FIRST GRADE

YOU CAN'T SEE ME

SKILLS: Brainstorming/Observation/Drawing

One way that many animals protect themselves from their enemies is by blending with their surroundings. Some animals are naturally disguised or camouflaged with colors or markings. Others have the ability to change color to match different backgrounds.

Animals that blend with their surroundings include the deer, the polar bear, and the meadow frog. Animals that change their color to match the season include the arctic fox and the snowshoe rabbit. These arctic animals turn white in winter to blend with the snow. Animals that change color quickly include the chameleon and the gray treefrog.

Read any of Ruth Heller's *How to Hide A . . .* books to witness camouflage firsthand. Then ask your child to think of and choose any animal that blends with its surroundings. Draw the animal disguised in its natural habitat and see if any family members can find it.

REQUIRED:
- Paper and pencil
- Crayons/markers

OPTIONAL:
- Library/bookstore visit

MARVELOUS MAMMALS

SKILLS: Brainstorming/Recording Data/Making Comparisons

Marvelous Mammals are found all over the world. Although mammals differ in size, shape, color, mobility, behavior, habitat, and general appearance, they are alike in many ways. Mammals are warm blooded. They maintain a relatively constant body temperature regardless of climate. Mammals have hairy bodies. Some have thick fur; others, fine fur. Mammals have skulls and backbones. Mammals suckle their young.

Consider these facts when you read *Amos and Boris* by William Steig. Amos, a curious and inventive mouse, meets Boris, a helpful and kind whale. Amos is astounded to learn that they are both mammals. He wonders how a huge whale and a tiny mouse can possibly be members of the same animal group.

What is the same about a whale and a mouse? What is different? Make a Venn diagram by drawing two intersecting circles. Label the left section "Whale" and the right section "Mouse." Label the intersection "Both." Write facts specific to the whale in the "Whale" section, facts specific to the mouse in the "Mouse" section, and facts common to both in the "Both" section. Repeat the process for other pairs of mammals: giraffe and elephant, bat and bear, cat and dog, human being and porcupine.

REQUIRED:
- Paper and pencil

OPTIONAL:
- Library/bookstore visit

BODY PARTS

SKILLS: Observation/Making Comparisons/Imaginative Thinking/Drawing

Human beings are mammals! First graders are amazed to learn that they belong to the same group of animals as dolphins with fins, bats with wings, kangaroos with pouches, armadillos with shells, porcupines with spines, and lions with manes and tails.

Ask your child to observe a mammal in a book or magazine. Make a list of body parts that are common to the animal but not to a human being.

Now, read *Imogene's Antlers* by David Small. See the reaction one family has to its daughter's growing antlers. Ask your son or daughter to imagine waking up one morning with an animal body part. Write and illustrate a story to tell what body part grew and how life changed with the addition of this unusual appendage. What would happen if you woke up with the trunk of an elephant or the horns of a bull? How would you feel with the tail of a whale or the neck of a giraffe? What would you do with the tusks of a walrus or the hooves of a horse? Share your child's adventure and encourage other family members to write a Body Parts story, too!

REQUIRED:
• Paper and pencil
• Crayons/markers
• Animal pictures

OPTIONAL:
• Library/bookstore visit

BACKYARD ENTOMOLOGY

SKILLS: Observation/Collection/Making Comparisons

Become an insect observer right in your own backyard or neighborhood park. Your child can be an entomologist by collecting and observing any of the thousands of insects common to your area. As you and your child prepare for your bug hunt, discuss the proper and humane way to capture living creatures. Reinforce the need to be gentle. Provide your child with an appropriate container for collecting specimens. A medium-size plastic container is recommended. Poke small holes through the cover or use a piece of screen or mesh secured with a rubber band. Be sure to place soil, grass, leaves, and small sticks in the container so that the environment is suitable for short observation.

When your entomologist is satisfied with the collection, take time to observe the insects. Discuss any similarities and differences noticed between the specimens. When your observations are complete, free the insects in their natural environment.

REQUIRED:
• Medium-size plastic container with cover
• Soil, grass, leaves, small sticks

OPTIONAL:
• Piece of screen or mesh
• Rubber band

A+ ACTIVITIES FOR FIRST GRADE

BUG'S-EYE VIEW

SKILLS: Observation/Drawing/Making Comparisons/Written Expression

Did you ever wonder what the world looks like from a Bug's-Eye View? Invite family members to imagine that one morning you wake up as bugs in an open field. Talk about the kinds of bugs that crawl or hop in this habitat. Discuss how the world looks from the perspective of a tiny creature. Blades of grass look like tall trees. Small puddles appear as vast oceans. Flowers seem like gigantic colorful umbrellas.

Distribute paper, pencils, and markers or crayons to all participants. Work individually to draw the world from your bug's perspective. If you are a grasshopper, your drawing might be from the top of a rock or from the leaf of a bush. If you are an ant, your drawing might be from the base of a mushroom or from the entrance to your anthill. If you are a daddy longlegs, your drawing might be from the trunk of a tree or from the side of a stone wall.

Share completed illustrations, talking about the things you saw and how they looked from this different perspective. Compare your findings. Then, for added enrichment, do a family write, telling a story about your experience as a bug.

REQUIRED:
- Paper and pencil
- Crayons/markers

INSECT OR SPIDER?

SKILLS: Observation/Making Comparisons/Drawing

What are the differences between an insect and a spider? Adult insects have a body with three segments: head, thorax, and abdomen. Insects also have three pairs of legs, and a head with antennae, eyes, and mouthparts used for biting, sucking, piercing, or siphoning. Spiders have a body with two parts: abdomen and joined head and thorax. Spiders also have four pairs of legs, eight eyes, and pedipalps for guiding prey to the mouth.

Visit your library or bookstore to view books about insects and spiders. First, focus on the illustrations and photographs, noticing the number of legs, eyes, and body segments. Discuss the differences observed between insects and spiders. Provide paper and pencil and ask your child to draw an insect and a spider, using the books as a guide. Then, read to find out about the habits of each.

Books such as *Bugs* by Nancy Winslow Parker and Joan Richards Wright and *Monster Bugs* by Lucille Recht Penner are terrific examples that clearly show the differences between insects and spiders. Soon your child will be able to recognize and discuss the differences between insects and spiders.

REQUIRED:
- Library/bookstore visit
- Paper and pencil

SCIENCE ACTIVITIES

NOCTURNAL CRAWLER CATCH

SKILLS: Observation/Collection/Making Comparisons

Some bugs move about only at night. These nocturnal crawlers are difficult to catch because they are often light sensitive. They hide when a flashlight is used to find them. Nocturnal crawler traps effectively catch bugs such as centipedes, earwigs, wood lice, millipedes, beetles, and spiders.

Select a site to construct a nocturnal crawler trap. Place in a safe location to avoid disturbance. Use a spoon to dig a hole in the earth deep enough to accommodate an open jar with the rim flush to the surface of the ground. Traps containing "bait" often catch more bugs. You may want to put tiny pieces of meat, fish, cheese, and overripe fruit into the jar. Cover your trap with a small piece of wood raised on small stones to allow access for bugs as well as protection from rain and other elements.

Leave your trap at the site for one or two nights. Return to the site, remove the jar, and cover it. Were you successful at catching bugs? Observe the bugs' physical characteristics and behavior before returning them to their natural habitat.

REQUIRED:
- Jar
- Spoon
- Wood
- Stones

OPTIONAL:
- Bait

GLITTER ANTS

SKILLS: Brainstorming/Drawing

Glitter Ants are ants you'll invite to your picnic! Ask your child what he or she knows or believes to be true about ants. Discuss the fact that ants have three body segments, six legs, two antennae, two eyes, and a mouth.

Create a glitter ant on a sheet of construction paper. Work together to draw three connected ovals for the ant's body segments. Be sure that the head is the smallest oval, the thorax (midsection) a bit bigger, and the abdomen, the biggest. Looking down on the ant, draw three legs from each side of the thorax. Draw two antennae at the top of the head and add two eyes and a mouth. Trace over the ant with glue, and, before it dries, sprinkle glitter on the ant. Shake excess glitter into a container and lay flat to dry. Hang your Glitter Ant in a place for all to see!

Add to the glitter bug collection. Read Eric Carle's book, *The Very Quiet Cricket,* and make a glitter cricket, moth, dragonfly, praying mantis, mosquito, firefly, or spittlebug.

REQUIRED:
- Construction paper
- Pencil
- Glitter
- Nontoxic glue

OPTIONAL:
- Bookstore/library visit

BUG BOOKS

SKILLS: Connecting Science and Literature/Imaginative Thinking/Written Expression/Drawing

Bugs are often characters in children's literature. Through fantasy, authors provide insight into habits and behaviors of bugs. Visit your library or local bookstore to read Bug Books.

Join two youngsters as they spend an afternoon with ants in *Helping Bugs* by Rosemary Lonborg. Read *A Flea Story* by Leo Lionni and join two fleas as they travel from a dog's back to a porcupine's quills to a crow's wing. Marvel at the magic of fireflies in *Fireflies!* by Julie Brinckloe. Discover what's so bad about ants in *Two Bad Ants* by Chris Van Allsburg. Join the fun when two ladybugs meet on a leaf in search of breakfast in *The Grouchy Ladybug* by Eric Carle. Witness the life cycle of a butterfly in *The Very Hungry Caterpillar,* also by Eric Carle.

After reading, write and illustrate a story featuring a bug as the main character. Write about a horsefly's adventure on a farm or a walking stick's feelings when mistaken for a stick. Write about a spider who can't make a web or a ladybug who loses her spots. Invite your first grader to take the author's chair to share the bug book with the family.

> **REQUIRED:**
> • Library/bookstore visit
> • Paper and pencil
> • Crayons/markers

BUG JOURNAL

SKILLS: Observation/Collection/Recording Data/Written Expression/Drawing

Draw and write about insects and spiders whenever and wherever you meet them. Provide your child with a spiral notebook or sketch pad. On the cover, clearly print, for example, "Amy's Bug Journal." Remind your child to bring the journal and a pencil when walking in the park or woods.

Each time your first grader sees a bug, your young entomologist observes and sketches it in the journal. Ask questions and encourage your child to write about each bug observed. Write the name of the bug if known, words to describe the physical characteristics of the bug, and a few sentences to describe the behavior of the bug.

Give your child many opportunities to sketch and write in the journal, indoors and out, no matter what the weather or temperature. Talk about which bugs prefer a dry environment to a damp one, a cool environment to a warm one, the indoors to the outdoors. Whether your child decides to observe and sketch bug specimens in their natural environment or in captivity, your budding entomologist will always be able to use the journal as a personal bug reference.

> **REQUIRED:**
> • Notebook or sketch pad
> • Pencil

FANTASTIC FISH

SKILLS: Brainstorming/Observation/Making Comparisons

First graders are amazed to hear that approximately 20,000 kinds of fish inhabit the oceans, lakes, rivers, and ponds of our planet. While fish differ in size, shape, and color, they are alike in many ways. They are cold-blooded, with their body temperature dependent on the environment. Most fish have backbones and moist, waterproof, scaly skin. Fish have gills that absorb oxygen from the water to pass to the fish's body. Fins and tails propel fish through water. Most female fish lay thousands of small eggs that are often eaten by predators before they hatch.

Expose your young ichthyologist to fish. Visit a fish market, grocery store, aquarium, or, if you live near water, fishing docks. Make comparisons of the fish you see. Ask the proprietor to point out the gills, fins, flippers, scales, and mouth. Touch the fish if permitted. Then, visit your local library or bookstore. Enjoy the beauty of *The Rainbow Fish* by Marcus Pfister. Find sea creatures in *How to Hide an Octopus and Other Sea Creatures* by Ruth Heller. Celebrate the inventiveness of a fish in *Swimmy* by Leo Lionni. Discover the underwater world in *Big Al* by Andrew Clements.

REQUIRED:
- Market/aquarium visit
- Library/bookstore visit

FISH PRINTS

SKILLS: Observation/Painting

Next time you catch a fish, don't throw it back! Bring it home, put on aprons or smocks, and make fish prints. First observe the fish from head to tail. Supervise this exploration since parts of the fish may be sharp. Carefully lift the slits or flaps on either side of the head so that your child can examine the gills. Open the mouth to look inside. Examine the eyes, scales, fins, and tail.

Lightly paint one side of the fish with a paint roller. Gently lift the fish, turn it over, and press it to a sheet of white construction paper or newsprint. Use the fish repeatedly to make prints. Dry finished prints on a flat surface. Then mount and display the fish prints for all to admire.

Variation: Boil the fish, remove the meat, and gently clean and dry the skeleton. Then, roll paint carefully on the skeleton and repeat the printing process. Skeleton prints of the fish are equally fun to create!

REQUIRED:
- Fish
- Paint and roller
- Paper

PUFFY PAPER FISH

SKILLS: Brainstorming/Observation/Imaginative Thinking/Drawing & Painting

Recycle brown paper grocery bags into colorful fish. Challenge your first grader to match you, word for word, as you list every fish that comes to mind. Point out the enormous differences in the appearance of creatures like the shark, goldfish, seahorse, stingray, eel, catfish, pufferfish, flounder, salmon, and swordfish. Look at pictures of fish and other sea creatures in books and magazines.

Draw a fish on a brown bag. Fold the bag so that when your child cuts, two fish shapes result. Use an array of colors and designs to paint one fish. Then, while it is drying on a flat surface, paint the second fish to match. When both are dry, match the two fish, paint side out, and staple on three sides, leaving the top length of the creature open. Scrunch up the paper remnants of the bag and stuff inside the fish. Staple the remaining side. Punch a hole, if desired, attach string or yarn, and suspend your Puffy Paper Fish from the ceiling for all to see and admire.

REQUIRED:
- Brown grocery bags
- Pencil
- Paint/paintbrush
- Stapler
- Safety scissors

OPTIONAL:
- Hole punch
- Yarn/string
- Library/bookstore visit

REMARKABLE REPTILES

SKILLS: Brainstorming/Observation

Reptiles are remarkable in both fact and fiction. Discuss reptile facts with your young herpetologist. All reptiles have waterproof scaly skin. Reptiles live in warm climates. They are cold-blooded, with their body temperature dependent on their environment. Most reptiles live on land. Some live in water. Reptiles hatch from eggs.

Brainstorm a list of reptiles and do a reptile read. Find reptiles in *How to Hide a Crocodile* by Ruth Heller. Count crocs in *Counting Crocodiles* by Judy Sierra. Change color and shape with a lizard in *The Mixed-Up Chameleon* by Eric Carle. See how silly a tortoise can be in *The Foolish Tortoise* by Richard Buckley. Laugh at a selfish snake in *The Greedy Python* by Richard Buckley. See Paris from the eyes of a boa constrictor in *Crictor* by Tomi Ungerer. Grow up with a yellow sporty snake in *Verdi* by Janell Cannon. The reptiles in all of these books are truly remarkable.

REQUIRED:
- Library/bookstore visit

REPTILE HATCH

Crocodile, alligator
   I just hatched a crocodator
    Maybe it was an allidile
Looking at me with a silly smile!

     Encourage your first grader to hatch a reptile! Draw or paint a picture of a cracked reptile egg and the newborn that has emerged. Your baby reptile can assume any form, snake, lizard, dinosaur, turtle, tortoise, or a combination of two. Then make an official birth certificate for the "Reptilian Records." Include what kind of reptile it is, its name, the names of its parents, when it was born, where it was born, its color, weight, and length. For added enrichment, work with your first grader to use fact and fantasy to write a story about your new friend.

REQUIRED:
- Paper and pencil
- Crayons/markers

OPTIONAL:
- Paint/paintbrush

AMAZING AMPHIBIANS

Frogs, toads, newts, and salamanders are animals that spend part of their lives in water and part of their lives on land. Tell your child that animals that breathe underwater as babies but breathe on land when adults are called amphibians. Amazing Amphibians have moist, slimy skin. They live near fresh water, where the female lays thousands of eggs. Most amphibians change completely before they become adults. The changing process is called metamorphosis.

    To make comparisons between the two most familiar amphibians, the frog and the toad, share nonfiction books such as *Frogs* by Gallimard Jeunesse and Daniel Moignot, and any one of the *Frog and Toad* books, engaging fiction by Arnold Lobel. As you read the books, focus on the illustrations and descriptions of frogs and toads. What is the same about a frog and a toad? What is different? Make a Venn diagram of two intersecting circles. Label the left section "Frog" and the right section "Toad." Label the intersection "Both." From your observations, reading, and discussion, record facts specific to frogs in the "Frog" section, facts specific to toads in the "Toad" section, and facts common to both in the "Both" section.

REQUIRED:
- Library/bookstore visit
- Paper and pencil

FROG FACTS

SKILL: Sequencing

Share William Steig's *Gorky Rises,* a fantasy frog story, before asking your first grader what is true about real frogs. Frogs are amphibians that live both in water and on land. Frogs eat flies, spiders, and worms. Frogs are hunted by snakes and fish. Frogs use strong rear legs to jump. Male frogs sing noisy songs to attract female frogs. Female frogs lay eggs in the spring. Tadpoles hatch a few days later. Tadpoles breathe under water. By five weeks old, tadpoles have grown rear legs. At nine weeks, their tails start to shrink while their front legs grow. At twelve weeks, tadpoles have developed lungs and can breathe out of water.

Make an accordion book of the metamorphosis of tadpole to frog. Use three folded sheets of paper. Tape the right edge of the first folded paper to the left edge of the second and the second to the third. Fold accordion style. Label the cover, "Heather's Frog Book," for example. Illustrate and label five sequential pages to show frog eggs, tadpoles, tadpoles with rear legs, tadpoles with front legs and shrinking tails, frogs. Ask your child to explain the process of metamorphosis while sharing the book with the family.

REQUIRED:
- Paper and pencil
- Crayons/markers
- Tape

OPTIONAL:
- Library/bookstore visit

"CHEEPERS" BY THE DOZEN

SKILLS: Observation/Brainstorming/Describing/Recording Data

Birds wake us in the morning, visit us during the day, and serenade us at sunset. Walk about the neighborhood, observing and listening to the feathered friends that frequent your area. Discuss bird facts. All birds have wings and feathers even though some can't fly. Birds live all over the world in different habitats. Birds are warm blooded. They maintain a relatively constant body temperature regardless of the climate. Birds live alone, in small groups, and in large groups. Birds hatch from eggs of different sizes, shapes, and colors. Some birds swim while others don't. Birds have beaks or bills, talons, claws, or webbed feet. Welcome any information your young ornithologist shares.

Brainstorm a list of birds. Write each name on a plastic or paper egg along with a few facts. Focus on color, size, diet, and habitat. Use reference books if necessary. Penguin facts may include: black and white, swims, doesn't fly, big, cold habitat, eats fish. Robin facts may include: red-breasted, small, flies, eats worms, warm habitat.

Store fact eggs by the dozen in empty egg cartons. Review information and add eggs as ideas are generated.

REQUIRED:
- Plastic or paper eggs
- Fine point permanent marker
- Safety scissors
- Egg cartons

OPTIONAL:
- Reference books

SCIENCE ACTIVITIES

EGG BIRDS

SKILLS: Imaginative Thinking/Drawing & Painting/Written Expression

Since the eggs in your refrigerator don't hatch, turn an egg into a bird! Shake a room temperature egg carefully but vigorously to "scramble" the white and yolk inside the shell. Use a medium gauge sewing needle to poke a pinhole in one end of the egg. Carefully poke another hole at the other end of the egg, working the needle to enlarge the hole to about $^1/_{16}''$. Wash and dry the egg thoroughly. Sit at the kitchen table over a bowl or stand at the sink. Give your child the egg, emphasizing the need to handle it carefully. Gently blow into the smaller hole. If the contents of the egg don't begin to come out of the larger hole, make it just a little bigger. Blow until the egg is empty. Again, wash and dry the egg and your hands thoroughly.

Provide fine point markers, feathers, yarn, and other doodads to decorate the egg as a bird. Name the bird and write or tell a story about it. Store in a closed container. Your Egg Bird will last for years!

REQUIRED:
- One egg
- Fine point permanent markers
- Safety scissors
- Craft supplies
- Nontoxic glue
- Sewing needle

PEANUT BUTTER PINECONES

SKILLS: Collecting/Observation/Recording Data/Identifying/Making Comparisons/Drawing

By making Peanut Butter Pinecones, you can take a closer look at birds. Find a large pinecone. Cover it with peanut butter. Roll the pinecone in birdseed so that the seed sticks to the peanut butter. Hang the Peanut Butter Pinecone in a location where your child will be able to observe and compare the size, color, beak, and feeding patterns of birds. If you have binoculars, show your child the proper way to use them. Binoculars will certainly enhance observation. Encourage your child to draw and write about the birds observed. Look in books for help in identification.

Replace your Peanut Butter Pinecone periodically, and add others around your yard. Work together to determine which birds feed during which seasons. Soon, you and your first grader will know exactly which birds to expect for dinner.

REQUIRED:
- Pinecones
- Peanut butter
- Birdseed
- String

OPTIONAL:
- Paper and pencil
- Bird books
- Binoculars

THE BIG SEVEN

SKILLS: Brainstorming/Identifying/Classifying/Sorting

How do we keep track of the millions of animals that live on Earth? We divide them into related groups. The Big Seven includes mammals, insects, spiders/arachnids, fish, reptiles, amphibians, and birds. Work with your first grader to identify each group by naming one or two of its members. Mammals include human beings, lions, bats, and whales. Reptiles include snakes, turtles, lizards, and alligators. Amphibians are frogs, toads, salamanders, and newts. Fish include sharks, trout, seahorses, and eels. Birds are eagles, penguins, robins, and flamingos. Insects include butterflies, ants, bees, and crickets. Arachnids are scorpions, mites, and spiders.

Write the name of each animal group on an index card, shoe box, basket, or recycled container. Then make animal picture cards or animal word cards. Deal out the cards. Take turns naming the animal and placing it with its group. Share one fact that supports your choice. For example, "I put the frog with the amphibian group because it spends part of its life in water and part of its life on land." Add animals to the groups at any time.

REQUIRED:
- Index cards
- Pencil
- Crayons/markers
- Safety scissors

OPTIONAL:
- Seven containers

ZOOLOGIST AT WORK

SKILLS: Researching/Referential Writing/Drawing

A zoologist is a scientist who studies animals. Invite your first grader to work on your zoological team to research a favorite animal. Visit your local library. Meet with the librarian for suggestions of appropriate source materials. Use the card catalogue, too. Then find two or three books to bring home.

Before reading the books, brainstorm three to five questions to research. Write each question on an index card. Focus questions on specific information your young zoologist seeks, such as habitat, size, food, and enemies. Keep the topics limited and manageable. Take notes on each index card to answer the question posed. Work together to organize the cards so that the information is logically sequenced.

Develop a topic sentence that states the main purpose of the research, for example, "The elephant is an extraordinary animal." Then write the report, including the information gathered to support the main idea. Conclude with a sentence such as, "There can be no doubt that the elephant is an amazing mammal." Write the report in book form and encourage your child to draw an illustration, cut out and include pictures, or make a clay model of the animal.

REQUIRED:
- Library visit
- Index cards
- Paper and pencil

OPTIONAL:
- Crayons/markers
- Safety scissors
- Clay
- Magazines

SCIENCE ACTIVITIES

HELP THE ANIMALS

SKILLS: Brainstorming/Drawing/Drawing Conclusions/Written Expression

An animal species in danger of extinction is known as an endangered animal. Ask your first grader to brainstorm reasons why animals become endangered. Most often, the behavior of human beings is responsible. Many animals have been illegally hunted for their skins, tusks, and antlers. Others have become endangered from pollution of habitat or from destruction of forests and other areas where animals live, eat, and breed. These disruptions of nature have made it hard for many animals to survive.

Work with your child to help! First, create a poster to raise awareness about endangered animals. Get permission to display the poster in a public place. Next, explain that there are groups of caring people who work hard to find ways to protect animals. Write a letter to one of these groups. Ask how you can help. Then act upon the suggestions received. Organizations to consider include:

National Audubon Society
700 Broadway
New York, NY 10003
1-212-979-3000
Web site: www.audubon.org
E-mail: webmaster@list.audubon.org

World Wildlife Fund
1250 24th Street, NW
P.O. Box 97180
Washington, DC 20077
1-800-CALL-WWF
Web site: www.worldwildlife.org
E-mail: membership@wwfus.org

San Diego Zoo
P.O. Box 551
San Diego, CA 92112
Attention: Education Department
1-619-231-1515
Web site: www.sandiegozoo.org
E-mail: webmaster@sandiegozoo.org

The Nature Conservancy
4245 North Fairfax Drive
Suite 100
Arlington, VA 22203
1-703-841-5300
Web site: www.tnc.org
E-mail: comment@tnc.org

REQUIRED:
• Paper and pencil
• Markers/crayons/paint

A+ ACTIVITIES FOR FIRST GRADE

PROTECT THE ANIMALS

SKILLS: Brainstorming/Imaginative Thinking/Written Expression

Many countries have special areas set aside for animals. National parks and natural preserves provide areas where wild animals are protected in their natural habitats. Endangered animals get needed protection so they do not become extinct. Hunting in these areas is against the law. People may visit the animals but are not allowed to feed them.

Read about and observe pictures of endangered animals that live in protected areas. These animals include mammals such as the hippopotamus, elephant, rhinoceros, panda, lion, walrus, and whale, and certain breeds of the zebra. Endangered birds include the goldfinch, condor, and American bald eagle. Sea creatures include the hammerhead shark and the sea turtle.

Together, write a letter to one endangered animal. Tell the animal what you will do to protect it. For example, if you write to a manatee, promise to remind people to drive boats slowly and safely through the water. If you write to a dolphin, promise that you will remind people to buy only dolphin friendly tuna. Make a pledge to Protect the Animals.

REQUIRED:
• Paper and pencil

OPTIONAL:
• Library/bookstore visit

FAMILY METEOROLOGIST

SKILLS: Observation/Prediction/Gathering Information/Recording Data

What will the weather be tomorrow . . . warm or cold, sunny or cloudy, rainy or snowy? Give your first grader the opportunity to be Family Meteorologist.

Watch or listen to the weather forecast on television or radio to understand a meteorologist's responsibilities. Discuss the predictions that the meteorologist makes. Explain that the weather forecast helps us know how to dress, when to plan a picnic, when to go swimming, and when to stay indoors. The next day, go outside with your Family Meteorologist in the late afternoon before dark. Look at the sky. Is it cloudy or clear? Feel the air. Is it dry or damp, warm or cool? Is it windy or calm? Is it raining or snowing? Ask your child to use this data to forecast tomorrow's weather. Record your young meteorologist's prediction. When you wake up in the morning, check to see whether the forecast was correct.

Graph the frequency of different types of weather for a week, a month, or even a whole year! Your Family Meteorologist will be sure to keep you abreast of upcoming weather.

REQUIRED:
• Paper and pencil
• Television or radio

MOVE OVER METEOROLOGIST

SKILLS: Imaginative Thinking/Written Expression

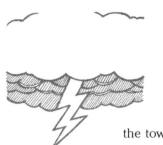

Use literature as a springboard for thinking about weather and writing forecasts. Experience a blizzard in *Katy and the Big Snow* by Virginia Lee Burton. See how Katy, the town plow, saves the day! Join Irene as she fights the wind and trudges through snow in *Brave Irene* by William Steig. Watch the clouds roll in and hear the thunder boom in *Tyler Toad and the Thunder* by Robert L. Crowe. Read weather poems in *Weather*, a poetry anthology by Lee Bennett Hopkins. Finally, visit the town of Chewandswallow where the weather comes three times a day—at breakfast, lunch, and dinner—in Judi Barrett's tall tale, *Cloudy With a Chance of Meatballs.*

Now ask your child to write a detailed weather forecast, real or fantasy! When the forecast is written, give your young meteorologist a spot on the family prime time news. If possible, videotape your child presenting the forecast. Or, make a television from a large empty box or piece of cardboard. Cut out a large rectangle for the screen and draw dials and switches beneath it. Gather the family around the "television" to hear the forecast.

REQUIRED:
- Library/bookstore visit
- Paper and pencil

OPTIONAL:
- Video camera
- Large box
- Piece of cardboard
- Scissors

CLOUD WATCHER

SKILLS: Observation/Making Comparisons/Recording Data

Expose your child to cumulus, cirrus, and cumulonimbus clouds. Cumulus clouds are white, puffy, and flat underneath. Cirrus clouds are white, thin, wispy, and high. Cumulus and cirrus clouds are fair weather clouds. They do not bring rain. Cumulonimbus clouds are gray, dark, and low. These clouds are the rain clouds. Review this information with your child.

Invite your Cloud Watcher to observe and record the different types of clouds seen in a week. Make a graph by dividing a piece of paper into three columns and seven rows. To the left of the first column, label each row with the days of the week, starting at the top with "Monday." Across the top, label the first column "Cumulus," the second, "Cirrus," and the third, "Cumulonimbus."

On Monday, ask your Cloud Watcher to observe the clouds. If your child sees a low, gray, dark cloud, fill in the column and row for "Monday, Cumulonimbus." On Tuesday, if your Cloud Watcher sees high, white, wispy clouds, fill in the column and row for "Tuesday, Cirrus." Follow this procedure for each day of the week. On Sunday, observe the data and discuss the clouds and the weather.

REQUIRED:
- Paper and pencil
- Crayon/marker

CLOUDSCAPES

SKILLS: Observation/Brainstorming

Look up and let your imagination soar with the Cloudscapes. Take a thermos of lemonade and a bag of cookies outside on a day when the sun is out, the sky is blue, and puffy clouds are flying. While looking up, ask your child what he or she knows or believes to be true about clouds. What is a cloud? Come to an understanding that a cloud is made from tiny drops of water or ice that float in the air.

Lie back on the grass and watch. What do you see in the clouds . . . a lion leaping, a dragon dancing, a giant jumping, a snake slithering, or a crocodile crawling? Find animals, objects, or shapes and point them out to each other.

To extend your child's knowledge and appreciation of clouds, visit your local library or bookstore on a rainy day and read books such as *Little Cloud* by Eric Carle, *Cloudland* by John Burningham, *It Looked Like Spilt Milk,* by Charles Shaw, or *Now I Know Clouds* by Roy Wandelmaier.

REQUIRED:
• Your time
OPTIONAL:
• Lemonade and cookies
• Library/bookstore visit

RAIN GAUGE

SKILLS: Observation/Measurement/Recording Data

Thin, light, white clouds hold only a little water. When we see them, we can expect fair weather. As millions of water droplets collect, clouds get bigger and become gray or even black. When we see these clouds, we can expect wet weather because the water droplets become too heavy to stay in the clouds. Cumulonimbus clouds bring the rain.

Construct a rain gauge so that when the cumulonimbus clouds roll in, you can measure the rainfall. Use a permanent marker to note ½″ intervals from bottom to top on an empty one-liter plastic bottle. Insert a funnel into the opening. Secure the funnel with packing or duct tape. Place the bottle outside in a clear area. Stabilize the base with rocks to prevent its blowing over in the wind. Then, go inside and wait for the rain to fall. At the end of the storm, read the rain gauge. How much rain fell? Record the results on a graph that shows date and measurement. Repeat the procedure each time it rains to keep track of rainfall for a designated time period.

REQUIRED:
• One-liter bottle
• Funnel
• Tape
• Permanent marker
• Rocks
• Paper and pencil

SNOWFLAKE MAKE

SKILLS: Observation/Cutting/Making Comparisons/Symmetry

High in the air, water vapor can freeze into crystals that fall to earth as snow. Amazingly, no two snowflakes are the same. Each snowflake forms a unique pattern. To illustrate that no two snowflakes are the same, invite family members to a Snowflake Make. Cover the work surface with dark construction paper. Give all participants a square or circle of plain white paper and safety scissors. Fold the square on the diagonal into a triangle. Then fold the triangle in half and then in half again. Fold the circle in half and then in half again. Keeping the shape folded, cut squiggles, triangles, arcs, zigzags, semicircles, loops, and curlicues into the folded shape. You can cut into the fold but be careful not to eliminate or sever it.

When everyone is done, unfold the snowflakes. Lay them out on the work surface. Oooh, aaah, and compare. Note the symmetry of design. See that no two snowflakes are the same. If you happen to live where snow falls, bring this experiment outside. Look closely at snowflakes as they fall on coats and mittens and witness the artistry of nature.

REQUIRED:
- White paper
- Dark construction paper
- Safety scissors

SNOWMAN CYCLE

SKILLS: Observation/Brainstorming/Drawing Conclusions

No matter how often the story is told, Frosty the Snowman always melts. The snowman in Raymond Briggs's book of the same title disappears. In Sylvia Loretan and Jan Lenica's book, *Bob the Snowman,* Bob discovers that even though he is doomed to melt, he'll certainly be back next year.

Illustrate the cycle of water to ice, ice to snow, and snow to water by making a blender snowman. Ask your first grader to fill an ice cube tray. Observe and discuss the characteristics of water: it is wet, I can't pick it up, it splashes. Put the tray in the freezer, explaining that, in time, the water will freeze in the cold temperature. At a later time, remove the tray from the freezer. Observe and discuss the characteristics of ice: it is hard, it is cold, I can pick it up, it doesn't splash or spill. Place the ice cubes into a blender. Grind or chop to make snow. Immediately, remove the snow and quickly build a tiny snowman on a rimmed plate. Watch the snowman melt. Pour the remaining water back into the tray, return to the freezer to make ice, and build another snowman anytime.

REQUIRED:
- Water
- Ice cube tray
- Blender
- Rimmed plate

OPTIONAL:
- Library/bookstore visit

CLINK TO SPLASH

SKILLS: Observation/Predicting/Measurement/Making Comparisons/Drawing Conclusions

When ice drops into a glass it clinks. When water is poured into a glass it splashes. Illustrate the differences between solid and liquid with this simple experiment.

Let your child drop six to eight ice cubes into a glass or jar . . . clink. Invite your child to measure the height of the ice in the container. Record the finding. Explain that ice is frozen water that will melt when the temperature rises above the freezing point, 32°F or 0°C. Ask your child to predict the height of the water that will be in the container after the ice melts in the warmth of the room.

Encourage your child to return to the glass periodically to check the progress of the melting ice. When the cubes are finally gone, ask your child to measure the height of the water. Compare the actual height of the water to the prediction made. Note that the liquid takes up less space than does the solid. Ask your child, "Where did the ice go?" Come to the conclusion that the solid, ice, is the liquid, water . . . splash!

REQUIRED:
- Ice cubes
- Glass container
- Ruler
- Paper and pencil

WHAT FLOATS?

SKILLS: Predicting/Observation/Experimentation/Drawing Conclusions/Recording Data/Drawing

In *Who Sank the Boat?* by Pamela Allen, five animals board a rowboat one by one. If you read the book, predict which animal will sink the boat. Discuss reasons for the prediction. Encourage your child to observe that the boat sinks a bit more each time an animal boards until finally, with the addition of a mouse, it sinks. The collective weight of the animals made the boat heavier than the water. It wasn't the mouse alone who sank the boat.

An object floats when it is lighter than water. Fill the kitchen sink. Collect items, some that are buoyant and some that sink. Ask your child to predict whether the item will float or sink and why. Then experiment with each item to test the prediction. Record the results by drawing a wavy water line across a sheet of paper. Above the water line, write the name or draw a picture of the objects that float. Below the water line, write the name or draw a picture of those that sink.

REQUIRED:
- Household items
- Kitchen sink
- Paper
- Crayon/marker

OPTIONAL:
- Library/bookstore visit

ITEM BANK: rock, feather, tennis ball, golf ball, quarter, stick, plastic spoon, steel spoon, sponge, apple, egg.

SINK THE SHIP

A buoyant object floats because it is lighter than water. Demonstrate this fact by conducting the experiment Sink the Ship.

Fill three-quarters of a two-quart pitcher with water. Use a 12-ounce glass as the "ship." Float the empty ship in the water. Ask your child why the ship floats. Now, submerge the ship to an inch above the water line. Point out that the partially filled ship floats because it is still lighter than the water in the pitcher it displaces. Estimate, in tablespoons, the amount of water needed to Sink the Ship.

Add a tablespoon of water to the floating ship. Did the ship stay afloat? Continue adding tablespoons of water to the ship. Count as tablespoons are added. When the ship finally sinks, compare the actual number of tablespoons needed to sink the ship to the estimated number. Was the estimate correct? Was it too high or too low? Why did the ship finally sink? The last tablespoon of water added to the water already in the ship made the ship heavier than the water in which it was floating.

REQUIRED:
- Two-quart pitcher
- 12-ounce glass
- Tablespoon

EVAPORATE? DEMONSTRATE!

What happens when the sun shines on oceans, rivers, lakes, ponds, pools, and puddles? As the water warms, it changes into a gas called water vapor. This gas rises and becomes an invisible part of the air. The water seems to disappear in this process called evaporation.

Experiment with evaporation at home. Cover the bottom of a saucer with water. Place the saucer on a sunny windowsill. Cover the bottom of a second saucer with water. Place this saucer in a closed cabinet. Ask your child to predict what will happen to the water in the sunny saucer and in the cabinet saucer. After a few days, observe the water level in each saucer. What has happened to the water in the sunny saucer? What has happened to the water in the cabinet saucer? Explain to your child, in simple terms, the process of evaporation. The water was warmed by the sun, changed into a gas called water vapor, rose into the air, and became invisible.

REQUIRED:
- Two saucers
- Water

COPYCAT

SKILLS: Experimentation/Observation/Drawing Conclusions

Play Copycat with your child to illustrate that shadows are formed when sunlight is blocked. Find an open, sunny place outdoors. Tell your child to observe your shadow as you hold one arm straight out like an airplane wing. Ask, "What did my shadow do when I held my arm out straight?" Your child responds, "Your shadow held its arm out straight, too!" Now move your arm back to your side and ask, "What happened to my shadow's arm?" Help your child recognize that shadows change as light is blocked by moving objects. Continue copycat shadow play. Hold both arms out. Observe and discuss the changes in your shadows. Jump up and down and watch your shadows do the same. Wave your arms, turn your heads, bend to the side, and stand on one leg.

For extra shadow fun, turn on a portable radio, stand a few feet from a wall in the sun, and dance with your shadows. These graceful dance partners will always imitate whatever you do!

REQUIRED:
• Your time

OPTIONAL:
• Music

SHADOW SHOW

SKILLS: Experimentation/Observation/Imaginative Thinking/Written Expression

Use your hands to block the light and put on a Shadow Show. Since light moves in a straight line, it can't pass through a solid object or shape. Set up your shadow show by shining a bright lamp or flashlight on a wall. Position yourselves so that you can safely move your hands in front of the light to block the light. Watch the wall as you manipulate your hands to create animals and shapes.

Invite everyone in the family to join in the fun as you try to guess which shadow creatures are roaming the walls of your home.

Variation: Add toys, stuffed animals, props, and a script to enhance your show.

REQUIRED:
• A light

OPTIONAL:
• Props
• A script from a book or your imagination

LIGHT LIST

SKILLS: Observation/Recording Data/Drawing

Find out what your child knows about light. Does your first grader know that the sun is the source of light and warmth for the earth, that we need light to see, that light is energy, that light flows in waves, that we see things in color when light hits objects, that animals and plants need light to live?

Think about all the different kinds of light you have seen. Consider sources of light that you see at home and in your neighborhood. Go for a "look for lights" walk. Discuss which lights are natural lights and which lights are made by people. Divide a piece of paper into two columns, label one "Natural Lights" and the other "People Lights." Then, work together to make a Light List. Encourage your child to draw a picture beside each light listed.

Variation: Make a family Light Logbook, listing a light with an illustration on each page.

Natural Lights: sun, lightning, fire, stars, meteor, aurora borealis or the Northern lights

People Lights: neon sign, fireworks, streetlight, flashbulb, traffic light, flashlight, match light

REQUIRED:
- Paper and pencil

OPTIONAL:
- Notebook or journal
- Neighborhood walk

ROY G. BIV

SKILLS: Experimentation/Observation/Drawing Conclusions

Who is ROY G. BIV? He's the acronym who helps us remember the colors of the rainbow: Red, Orange, Yellow, Green, Blue, Indigo, Violet. A rainbow is an arch of color in the sky formed when sunlight shines through raindrops. If the sun comes out during or immediately after a rain shower, stand with your back to the sun and look for a rainbow.

Look for rainbows in other places: in the spray from your sprinkler, in fountains, in bubbles, and in puddles. Then make a rainbow of your own. Fill a baking pan or casserole dish with water and place on a table by a sunny window. Partially immerse a mirror on an angle in the water so that the mirror is directly in the sun. Carefully manipulate the mirror to create a rainbow on the ceiling. Ask your child, "What made the rainbow?" Keep your explanation simple. A rainbow is made when sunlight passes through water.

REQUIRED:
- A pan of water
- A mirror
- A sunny day
- A table by a window

RAINBOW TOPS

SKILLS: Experimentation/Observation/Drawing Conclusions

New colors are formed when colors mix. Demonstrate this fact by making Rainbow Tops. Cut a 6″ circle from white card stock. Divide the circle into four equal sections. Color one section green, one orange, one blue, and one yellow. Work together to push a sharp pencil through the center of the circle. Move the circle halfway down the pencil. Then spin the rainbow top. What color or colors do you see? Make other tops, altering the number and pattern of colors used.

For more exposure to colors and mixing colors enjoy *Mouse Paint* by Ellen Stoll Walsh and *A Color of His Own* by Leo Lionni.

REQUIRED:
- White card stock
- Safety scissors
- Markers
- Sharp pencil

OPTIONAL:
- Library/bookstore visit

SEASON BOXES

SKILLS: Observation/Collecting/Classifying

No matter where you live, seasonal changes occur. Length of day, temperature, precipitation, plant growth, bird population, and insect population change. With four boxes, your child can capture the essence of spring, summer, autumn, and winter just as a field mouse does in *Frederick,* by Leo Lionni.

Use a small plain box and choose a season. For autumn, discuss the weather and temperature, the kinds of flowers and plants that grow, activities you do, constellations you see in the sky. Work together to decorate the box by drawing or painting autumn scenes and/or by attaching items common to autumn. One side could have a drawing of a pumpkin; another an acorn found in the yard; a third, a fallen leaf; and the last, a painting of a school bus. Throughout the season, you and your child put any and all items related to autumn into the box. When autumn ends, begin work on the winter box. Move to spring and finally summer. You and your child will have a special year beautifully stored in four Season Boxes.

REQUIRED:
- Four small boxes
- Crayons/markers/paint/ paintbrush
- Nontoxic glue
- Seasonal items

OPTIONAL:
- Library/bookstore visit

OUTDOOR LANDSCAPES

SKILLS: Observation/Drawing/Written Expression/Making Comparisons

What is your favorite season? Spring with the trees starting to bud? Summer with the flowers in full bloom? Autumn with its brilliant colors? Winter with snow falling by the inch? This activity shows your child that the world changes with the seasons.

Walk in your yard, neighborhood, or local park. Take paper and pencils, crayons, or markers with you. While walking, observe the landscape. What do the trees look like? Are the flowers in full bloom? Is snow covering the ground or can you see green grass? Find a place to sit while your child draws and colors the landscape as it appears. Label the picture with the name of the season or the month of the year.

At home, post the picture in a special place. During each successive season, return to the same spot to repeat the process. Discuss any changes observed.

Help your child write a description about the landscape after each observation. Place the illustrations and written descriptions in a three-ring binder, folder, or journal so that your child can review and compare the changes that have occurred over the course of a year.

REQUIRED:
- Paper and pencil
- Crayons/markers
- Binder, folder, or journal
- Neighborhood walk

NATURE DETECTIVE

SKILLS: Observation/Collecting/Identifying/Drawing/Recording Data

No matter where you live, each season provides new things to find and see for your first grader. Whether you explore your yard, a city park, a town forest, a public beach, a lakefront, a bird sanctuary, or a wildlife refuge, you can be a Nature Detective.

Take a bag, box, or basket along with you on your nature hike. Bring along water and fresh fruit as a snack. All along the way, be sure to supervise your young detective. Don't stand too near the bank of a stream or too close to the breaking waves at the shore. Observation is the first objective. Make note of all that is around you: birds, trees, plants, small animals, rocks, shells, seeds, flowers, leaves, spider webs, and insects. Don't take anything living, but do collect acorns, stones, shells, fallen leaves, pinecones, or feathers. Look for animal tracks, note the seasonal colors, observe the cloud formations, and note the position of the sun. Both your child and you should draw and record your observations in a naturalist's journal so that you have a record of your day.

REQUIRED:
- Basket/bag/box
- Pencil/crayons
- Journal or notebook
- Outdoor walk

A⁺ ACTIVITIES FOR FIRST GRADE

STONES AND SHELLS

SKILLS: Observation/Collecting/Imaginative Thinking/Painting

Stones and Shells invite endless possibilities for creative and imaginative thinking and design. Flat round stones are waiting to become ladybug, frog, or turtle paper-weights.

For the ladybug, paint the stone red with black spots. Paint two eyes at one end and three legs along each side. For the frog, paint the stone green. Use a nontoxic craft glue to attach two smaller stones as bulging eyes at the top and two at the base as feet. Paint the eyes green with a large black spot in the center. Paint the feet green. For the turtle, try brown paint crosshatched with black lines. Attach a small stone to one end for the head. Paint this stone brown with any color dot on either side for eyes. Two painted stones along each side serve as legs.

If you happen to live near the shore where you have access to shells, create a menagerie of creatures from the shells you find, following the same procedure as with stones.

In either case, take time to examine and appreciate the stones and shells in their natural shape and color before transforming them to meet the imagination.

REQUIRED:
- Stones or shells
- Paint/paintbrush
- Nontoxic glue

SEED READ

SKILLS: Researching/Experimentation/Observation/Making Comparisons/Drawing

Enjoy a Seed Read to learn more about how a seed grows. In *It's Pumpkin Time!* by Zoe Hall and in *Pumpkin Pumpkin* by Jeanne Titherington, you'll observe the stages of growth from seed to plant. In *The Carrot Seed* by R. Kraus, you'll witness the care necessary to make a plant grow. Talk about the essential ingredients—sunlight, soil, and water—that must be provided in order for a plant to grow.

Now experiment. Fill two small containers with soil. Plant kidney beans or popcorn kernels in each. Water and wait until the seeds sprout. Keep one plant in the light and place one plant in the dark. Water the plants as needed. Observe them each day. Discuss the effects of depriving the plant of light. Notice that the plant that grew in the dark is yellow and white while the one exposed to sunlight is green. Explain that the plant that had sunlight used the light to make food. Encourage your child to compare the two plants and to draw a detailed diagram of all observations.

As a variation, put both plants in the sunlight but deprive one of water. Follow the same experimental procedure.

REQUIRED:
- Seeds
- Soil and container
- Library/bookstore visit

CLEAN WATER WORKS

SKILLS: Brainstorming/Observation/Describing/Experimentation/
Predicting/Recording Data/Drawing Conclusions

Pour yourselves tall, cold glasses of water and discuss this refreshing drink. How do people use water? Why do animals and plants need water? Observe your drinking water. Ask your child to describe how it looks and tastes. Talk about the bodies of fresh water that are available to people, animals, and plants. Emphasize how important it is that we keep our rivers, lakes, ponds, and streams clean. Explain that some water can harm living things because it is very dirty or polluted. Ask what might pollute water?

Now set up the Clean Water Works experiment. Fill two empty, clean containers or milk cartons with soil. Label one container "Clean Water" and the other "Polluted Water." Plant a bean seed in each carton. Water one with clean water and one with water mixed with dish detergent and cooking oil. Make a prediction about what will happen to each bean. Record your predictions. Then observe the bean seeds over a number of days. Discuss the results of your experiment. Ask your child to draw a conclusion about the effect of polluted water on plant growth.

REQUIRED:
• Two containers
• Marker and labels
• Soil and water
• Bean seeds
• Dish detergent and oil
• Paper and pencil

DISSECT A SEED

SKILLS: Experimentation/Observation/Predicting/Drawing

Every seed has potential! Observe the baby plant inside a seed with Dissect a Seed. Soak a lima bean, kidney bean, or any large bean in water overnight. The next day, remove the bean from the water. As your child watches, gently cut into the bean, dissecting it lengthwise. Encourage your young botanist to examine the inside of the bean. If available, provide your child with a magnifying glass to heighten observation. Ask your child to draw a cross section diagram of the open bean. Then, working together, use your fingertips or the tip of a toothpick to remove the baby plant from the bean. Place the tiny plant on your work surface and examine. Again, ask your child to draw a diagram, this time of the baby plant. Talk about all observations. Predict what will happen to a bean when it is planted in soil.

REQUIRED:
• Large bean
• Container of water
• Knife
• Paper and pencil
• Crayons/markers

OPTIONAL:
• Magnifying glass
• Toothpicks

A+ ACTIVITIES FOR FIRST GRADE

KERNELS AND BEANS

SKILLS: Experimentation/Observation/Making Comparisons/Measurement/
Graphing/Recording Data/ Written Expression/Drawing

Make an indoor garden from Kernels and Beans so that your child can compare and
care for plants. Fill two small containers with potting soil. Ask your child to use a finger
to poke two shallow holes in the soil of each container. In one pot, drop a popcorn
kernel in each hole. Cover the kernels with soil, making sure to fill and tamp each
hole. Repeat the process in the second container, using two kidney or lima beans.

Discuss what your child needs to do to help the seeds grow. Emphasize that every
plant requires water and sunlight. On a daily basis,
check to see that the soil is *damp*, not wet. A spray
bottle works well and prevents overwatering. Caution
your child that too much water will harm the developing plant.

Observe the sprouting and subsequent growth of each plant. Measure
each plant two or three times per week, graphing the results. Make comparisons based on observations.

Variation: Write and illustrate a report that describes the growth of the
kernels and beans. Present the findings to the family.

REQUIRED:
- Two containers
- Potting soil
- Popcorn kernels
- Beans
- Paper and pencil

OPTIONAL:
- Crayons/markers

SEED AND ROOT, STEM AND LEAVES

SKILLS: Imaginative Thinking/Application/Drawing/Cutting

First graders recognize the seed, roots, stem, and leaves of a plant. They know that the
seed and roots are underground and that the stem and leaves are above ground. Let
your child's green thumb go to work to design and
draw a plant that sprouts from a seed.

Hold a sheet of white construction paper vertically. Using earth tones of crayon or construction
paper, cover the bottom quarter of the white paper
with "soil." Give your child any kind of seed to
glue underground. Provide thread, string, or yarn
for your young gardener to fashion into roots.

Finally, "grow" the plant from green construction paper, tissue, markers,
crayons, paint, or fabric, moving from Seed & Root to Stem & Leaves.
Display in the sunlight, but refrain from watering!

REQUIRED:
- Construction
  paper/tissue/fabric
- One seed
- Thread/string/yarn
- Crayons/markers/paint/
  paintbrush
- Nontoxic glue
- Safety scissors

GARDEN IN A BOTTLE

SKILLS: Observation/Drawing/Recording Data

Grow plants and flowers all year! Make a Garden in a Bottle with a two-liter plastic soda bottle, adult scissors, aluminum foil, potting soil, and seeds or tiny plants.

Cut off the bottom portion of the bottle along the base of the label. Keeping the bottle cap on, rinse the upper and lower portions of the bottle with hot water. Remove the label. Line the bottom portion of the bottle with aluminum foil and fill to three-quarters with potting soil. Plant bean seeds, dwarf variety flowers, or tiny plants. Water until the soil is moist. Now fit the upper portion of the bottle onto the soil-filled base. Seal with transparent tape and place in a sunny area. Because of condensation, you won't need to water the bottle garden again.

Encourage your child to observe the garden over the coming weeks and to draw and record observations and changes in a Garden in a Bottle log-book. Look at the soil, the plants, and the inner surface of the bottle. Your child will witness firsthand the rudiments of the life cycle of a plant and the cycle of water.

REQUIRED:
- Plastic two-liter soda bottle
- Scissors
- Aluminum foil
- Potting soil
- Transparent tape
- Paper and pencil/colored pencils
- Notebook/journal

SEED SEEKER AND SAVER

SKILLS: Observation/Collecting/Sorting/Making Comparisons/Recording Data

Seeds come from plants, from the fruits and vegetables we eat, and from our yards and neighborhoods, too. Encourage your child to be a Seed Seeker and Saver.

Look for seeds in vegetables. Cut into a green, red, or yellow pepper. Invite your child to examine the inside and remove and manipulate the seeds. Store the seeds in a sealed plastic bag labeled "Pepper Seeds." Sort through dry peas, kidney beans, lima beans, and popcorn kernels. Emphasize that peas, beans, and kernels are also seeds. Store these beans, seeds, and kernels in labeled bags. Do the same with fruit seeds, including apple, orange, grapefruit, tangerine, lemon, lime, pear, cantaloupe, watermelon, honeydew, grape, peach, plum, kiwi, and banana. Compare all seeds by shape, size, and color.

Seek and save seeds from outside, too. Find maple tree seeds to fly like helicopters and wear on your nose. Look for acorns, milkweed seeds, dandelion seeds, flower seeds, and grass seed. Talk about how seeds travel: some by air, some by water, some with the help of people and animals. Add to the seed bags at any time, and see your seed seeker's collection and knowledge grow.

REQUIRED:
- Plastic sandwich bags
- Marker and labels
- Seeds

FRUIT AND VEGGIE VIEW

SKILLS: Observation/Making Comparisons

In the hustle and bustle of our daily lives, we rarely, if ever, take time to examine the common components of our diet. Ready-made, prewashed salads come in bags that we tear open, dump in a bowl, dress, and serve. Think of all the learning that could occur in the kitchen if we were to take time to look at the food!

Next time you prepare a salad, vegetable side dish, or fruit dessert, invite your first grader to help. Wash the variety of salad leaves and spinach leaves, examining the colors, textures, and shapes. Slice the cucumber, zucchini, and tomato and point out the seeds. Pare the carrots, scrub the potatoes, shuck the corn, shell the peas, remove the celery strings, sort the sprouts, and slice the mushrooms while noticing and comparing the characteristics of each. Talk about how and where each grows.

Peel the bananas, oranges, and grapefruits; seed the cantaloupe, honeydew, and watermelon; slice the apples, pears, and peaches while letting your child participate by observing, touching, smelling, and tasting. Your child's curiosity and appetite can be sparked and satisfied with a Fruit and Veggie View.

REQUIRED:
- Fruits and vegetables
- Knife

THANKS, TREE!

SKILLS: Brainstorming/Recording Data/Written Expression

As you'll discover in *Treats from a Tree* by Susan Canizares and Mary Reid, we are given many treats from our trees! Ask your first grader to think of tree treats as you record all suggestions. The ideas shared may include fruits, nuts, spices, syrup, and chocolate. Invite your child to choose a tree treat to sample. Perhaps you'll enjoy tasty chocolate syrup on ice cream with a juicy cherry on top, pancakes dripping with sweet maple syrup, crispy cinnamon cookies, nutty pecan pie, or zesty apple muffins.

Whatever the tree treat, encourage your first grader to write a thank-you note to the tree that provided it. Include the greeting, "Dear Apple Tree"; the body, which includes your child's words of thanks; and the closing, "Your friend, Leah," for example. If the tree happens to be one that "resides" in your neighborhood, visit the tree. Ask your child to read the note to the tree in person. In either case, from the point of view of the tree, write a response to your child!

REQUIRED:
- A tree treat
- Paper and pencil

OPTIONAL:
- Library/bookstore visit

TREE SKETCH

SKILLS: Observation/Recording Data/Drawing/Making Comparisons/Identifying

Trees are big plants. They come in different shapes and sizes. Some are huge while others are small. Some are tall and pointed. Others are round. Some stand straight. Others droop. Some stay green all year. Others lose their leaves in the fall.

With clipboards, pencils, and crayons in hand, walk about your neighborhood, local park, or town forest. Look at the trees, observing height, shape, and color.

Examine the bark that covers the trunk and note the color. Comment on the size, shape, and texture of the leaves. Note any fruits, seeds, or cones observed. Sketch each kind of tree you see, jotting down notes about its characteristics.

Take the sketches with you the next time you visit the library. Compare your sketches to those found in source materials. Try to identify the name of each tree observed. Before long, you'll recognize the maples, willows, pines, birches, aspens, oaks, elms, or palms common to your area.

REQUIRED:
- Clipboards
- Paper and pencil
- Crayons
- Neighborhood walk

OPTIONAL:
- Library visit

LEAF EXPLORATION

SKILLS: Observation/Collecting/Making Comparisons/Sorting/Identifying/Symmetry

Tree leaves come in all sizes, shapes, and colors. Some stay on trees all year long, while others work to feed the tree all summer until their job is done in the fall. At that time their green disappears as they put on their autumn colors of red, orange, and yellow.

With basket or bag in hand, walk about your neighborhood, local park, or town forest. Gather a collection of leaves. If it happens to be autumn and you live in an area where the leaves change and fall, collect your supply from the ground. Otherwise, gently snip one leaf from each tree you pass.

At home, examine the leaves carefully, noting differences, making comparisons, and sorting. Group the wide leaves, narrow leaves, pointed leaves, and rounded leaves. Note the symmetry of their structure.

Take time to visit the library to check resources on leaves. Observe pictures to identify the leaves you found and familiarize yourself with others.

REQUIRED:
- Bag/basket
- Neighborhood walk

OPTIONAL:
- Library visit

LEAF ART

SKILLS: Observation/Collecting/Creative Thinking/Symmetry

Gather leaves and let creative ideas take over! First try leaf prints. Gently dip or brush one side of a leaf with paint. Press the leaf carefully to construction paper and lift gently. Dry on a flat surface. Note the symmetrical pattern of the leaf print and the shape of the leaf. Repeat the process with leaves of different sizes and shapes to create a leaf collage, leaf placemats, or leaf greeting cards.

Now try making leaf creatures by arranging leaves of varying sizes and shapes on construction paper to form real or imagined animals or objects. Glue the leaves to the paper, label the creation, and display for all to admire.

Finally, work with your child to preserve selected leaves by using a warm iron to press each leaf carefully between two sheets of wax paper. Tape or glue each waxed leaf to a piece of construction paper. Staple the sheets of construction paper together to make a leaf book. Label the cover with your child's name, for example, "Josh's Book of Leaves."

REQUIRED:
- Construction paper
- Nontoxic glue
- Paint/paintbrush
- Wax paper
- Iron
- Stapler

RECYCLING CENTER

SKILLS: Collecting/Sorting

Trash comes from factories, schools, stores, restaurants, construction sites, and homes. How much trash comes from your home? Consider all the papers, wrappers, boxes, aluminum cans, plastic bottles, and containers that your family throws away each week.

Discuss the need to recycle paper, aluminum, glass, and plastic. Machines shred, crush, melt, and wash these materials so that they can be recycled into new products. Amaze your child with the fact that eight small plastic bottles can be recycled into enough material to make a polar fleece scarf!

Work together to set up a recycling center in your home. Place four bins in a safe area. Label the bins "Paper," "Aluminum," "Glass," and "Plastic." Draw a picture or attach a small sample of the appropriate recyclable material on each bin as a visual aid for your first grader. Encourage family members to wash and then put recyclable materials in the appropriate bins. If your community provides a collection service, arrange for pick up. Otherwise, take your sorted recyclable materials to a community collection site. By setting up a recycling center in your home, your family will play an important role in conserving our resources.

REQUIRED:
- Four bins
- Marker
- Recyclable materials

RECYCLED ART

SKILLS: Brainstorming/Collecting/Imaginative Thinking/Constructing

Give your first grader's imagination another chance to blossom! Use recyclable household materials for art projects.

Set up a box in a place accessible to your young artist. Label the box "Recycled Art Materials." Brainstorm a list of materials that would be appropriate to use for art projects. Discuss the fact that all items must be safe and clean. Encourage all family members to contribute to the collection.

Your first grader should use the recycled art materials often, whether completing a book project for school or a work of art for home. Use Popsicle sticks or straws to build log cabins and skyscrapers. Use recycled fabric or discarded socks or panty hose to make puppets. Use buttons for noses and eyes. Use yarn or string for mouths and hair. Decorate an old egg carton for use as a school supply organizer on your child's desk. Turn an egg carton into an insect or spider using pipe cleaners for legs and antennae. Stuff a paper bag with newspaper, add a little paint and creativity, and you've got decorations for any occasion. Whatever the materials and whatever the ideas, recycle materials into masterpieces!

REQUIRED:
- Box
- Paper and pencil/paint/ paintbrush
- Markers
- Recyclable materials

NATURAL OR NOT?

SKILLS: Observation/Predicting/Recording Data/Experimentation/Drawing Conclusions/Making Comparisons

We sometimes see litter when driving through town, walking in a park, or swimming in a lake or pond. What happens to litter that does not get disposed of or recycled properly? If litter is natural, orange peels and apple cores, it decomposes into the ground. This means that natural litter is biodegradable, a term you may want to introduce to your first grader. If litter is people-made, bottles or cans, it does not decompose easily.

To demonstrate this concept, put natural litter, a banana peel or bread crust, and people-made litter, an old shoelace or bottle cap, into a sock. Bury the sock in a shallow hole. Mark the spot so that you can dig up the sock at a later date. Predict what will happen to the contents of the sock over time. Record all predictions.

In the next month or two, return to the spot and dig up the sock. What changes do you observe in the natural litter and what changes do you see in the people-made litter? Compare and discuss the results of the experiment. Were your predictions correct?

REQUIRED:
- Litter
- Sock
- Trowel
- Paper and pencil

A+ ACTIVITIES FOR FIRST GRADE

COMMUNITY CLEANUP

SKILLS: Brainstorming/Organization & Implementation/
Drawing & Painting/Sorting/Drawing Conclusions

ADOPT-A-
HiGHWAY

Although Earth Day is celebrated each year on the first day of spring, any time is a good time to promote your child's awareness of environmental issues. Brainstorm ways to help keep the earth beautiful. One way to help is by organizing a Community Cleanup.

Inform friends, family, and neighbors of the event. Create posters and flyers and, together, distribute them throughout your neighborhood. Remember to include the date, time, and location of the cleanup. Ask members of your neighborhood to donate a garbage bag or two for collecting litter. Work with friends to implement an efficient plan to sort recyclable materials. Encourage stores and businesses in the community to show support for the cleanup.

This process of initiating, organizing, implementing, and assessing results will give your child a wonderful sense of pride and accomplishment. It will also show the members of your neighborhood what can happen when people work together.

REQUIRED:
• Garbage bags

OPTIONAL:
• Paper and pencil
• Markers/crayons
• Paint/paintbrush

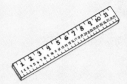

SOCIAL STUDIES

The world is our community, and what a marvelous community it is! The theme of the activities that follow, all interwoven, is that each of us is a valued member of the world community and that all of us together make up that community.

We begin with the child as an individual, focusing on self-confidence and self-esteem. You are invited to join your child in a celebration of self, one in which your first grader talks about, draws, and writes about all those qualities that make your child unique. The celebration then moves to the family, to the concept that, like links on a chain, family members fit together. After explorations of your heritage and history, we encourage you to explore families of all kinds, building respect through an awareness and understanding of diversity.

From the family, the community extends to the neighborhood. You are given the opportunity to reflect upon the special features of your neighborhood, its people, places, and services. From creating a No Place Like Home family book to drawing a neighborhood map, you will enhance your first grader's awareness of and pride in your community.

The exploration builds as you move to an awareness of the larger community that is our country. Set sail with Columbus, and join the Thanksgiving feast of the Pilgrims and Wampanoags. Meet Thomas Jefferson, and appreciate the gift of independence and the birthday of America. March with Dr. Martin Luther King, Jr., as you talk with your child and read about freedom, equality, and civil rights.

Finally, celebrate our world community. Explore with maps and globes to meet our world neighbors and develop an awareness of the vastness of our community. Write a letter to help a neighbor in need and make a collage of the faces of humanity. Complete your celebration of the world community by making a pledge to make the world more beautiful!

ALL ABOUT ME!

Self-confidence and self-esteem are two essential components to successful learning and living. In Nancy Carlson's book, *I Like Me,* the main character, a fanciful pig, calls herself her best friend. With easy-to-read text and fun-filled illustrations, Carlson shows the reader all the special qualities and activities of a young child.

Work with your child to write and illustrate an All about Me! book. Tell about and show the activities your child most enjoys, from bike riding to reading. Celebrate curly hair or straight, celebrate tall or short, celebrate brown eyes or blue. Whatever comes to mind, write about and illustrate each special quality on a separate sheet of paper. Make a cover including your child's name as author and illustrator. Staple or hole punch and tie into book form so that you can add this special book to your child's personal library.

REQUIRED:
- Construction paper
- Pencil
- Crayons/markers/colored pencils
- Stapler

OPTIONAL:
- Library/bookstore visit
- Hole punch
- Ribbon/yarn

CELEBRATE YOU

With sweeping text and magnificent illustrations, Sheila Hamanaka celebrates the diversity of children in her book, *All the Colors of the Earth*. The author/artist paints glorious images of children with her vivid description and exquisite art.

> Children come in all the colors of the earth—
> The roaring browns of bears and soaring eagles,
> The whispering golds of late summer grasses,
> And crackling russets of fallen leaves,
> The tinkling pinks of tiny seashells by the rumbling sea.

Join your child in drawing, coloring, and/or painting a self-portrait. Encourage the use of detail. Talk about the colors in nature that are similar to yours. On a separate sheet of paper, encourage your child to write, "I come in the colors of . . ." Guide your young artist/writer in the use of adjectives to describe those things in nature that best celebrate and describe who you are. Attach the description to the portrait. Invite all members of the family to make self-portraits to create a gallery that celebrates you!

REQUIRED:
- Construction paper
- Crayons/markers/colored pencils
- Stapler/nontoxic glue

OPTIONAL:
- Library/bookstore visit
- Hole punch
- Ribbon/yarn
- Paint/paintbrush

PERSON OF THE YEAR

SKILLS: Brainstorming/Imaginative Thinking/Drawing/Written Expression

What do you want to be when you grow up? In *Lilly's Purple Plastic Purse* by Kevin Henkes, an engaging young mouse dreams of one day being a teacher, a firefighter, a diva. Ask your child to imagine what the future holds. Talk about what occupations seem exciting. Then invite your child to be Person of the Year.

Encourage your first grader to draw a self-portrait as an adult. Include details that show the chosen occupation. If your child hopes to be an astronaut, wear a space suit; a baseball player, wear a uniform; a scientist, a lab coat. Attach the self-portrait to the cover of a magazine such as *Newsweek, Time,* or *Life.* Finally, work with your child to write a story to tell about his or her occupation and accomplishments.

REQUIRED:
- Paper and pencil
- Crayons/markers
- Recycled magazine
- Nontoxic glue

OPTIONAL:
- Library/bookstore visit

MY FRIEND AND I

SKILLS: Brainstorming/Making Comparisons/Written Expression/Drawing

In *Fly Homer Fly* by Bill Peet, an unlikely pair of birds become close friends. Homer, the country pigeon, is content with his quiet life in the country. Sparky, the city pigeon, is exhilarated by his fast-paced life in the city. While, as birds, Homer and Sparky have much in common, they also differ in a number of ways. Sharing, respecting, helping, and understanding are the basis of their friendship.

To build awareness of friendship, ask your child to complete a Venn diagram to compare him- or herself to a good friend. Draw two intersecting circles. Write your child's name inside the top of the left circle, a good friend's name inside the top of the right circle, and "Both" inside the top of the intersecting portion. Work together to brainstorm and record characteristics unique to your child in the left section, unique to the friend in the right section, and common characteristics in the "Both" section. Review the ideas generated. Then, encourage your child to write and illustrate a friendship story that highlights what friendship means. Be sure to share the finished story with the friend.

REQUIRED:
- Paper and pencil
- Crayons/markers

OPTIONAL:
- Library/bookstore visit

SOCIAL STUDIES ACTIVITIES

FIRST GRADE TIME CAPSULE

SKILLS: Collecting/Self-Awareness

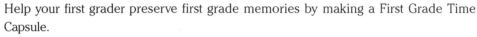

Help your first grader preserve first grade memories by making a First Grade Time Capsule.

Rinse out a recyclable cookie or potato chip canister. Set the lid aside. Cover the outside of the canister with colored construction paper. Provide your child with paper, crayons, markers, paint, recyclable magazines, stickers, glitter, and other materials to decorate the canister. As you approach the end of grade one, encourage your child to place small items in the canister. These items should be representative of your child's first grade experience. Items such as a special drawing, a class photograph, an award, and a story written by your first grader are some examples of what your child might choose to include.

On the final day of school, seal the canister. Ask your child to hide it in a secret place. Whenever your child decides to open the First Grade Time Capsule—in two weeks, two months, or two years—the special memories of first grade are sure to come rushing back!

REQUIRED:
• Empty canister
• Construction paper
• Safety scissors
• Nontoxic glue/tape
• Decorative materials
• First grade mementos

FAMILY LINKS

SKILLS: Family Awareness/Brainstorming

Like links on a chain, family members fit together! With this interactive and fun-filled family activity, you will build your child's awareness of who your family is and what makes your family special.

First prepare strips of colored construction paper approximately 8″ × 2″. Then, sit down with your child to talk about all those things that make your family special.

Generate a list of the names of family members and pets. List foods, activities, celebrations, traditions, and holidays you enjoy together. Include any words that come to mind as you think of the many experiences you share.

Write each name, word, or phrase on a paper strip. Join the two ends of the first strip with glue or tape. Then, to make a chain, insert the next strip into the finished link and join the two ends. Repeat the process until the chain is complete. Display the chain in your home and encourage your child or any family member to add to it at any time.

REQUIRED:
• Construction paper
• Safety scissors
• Tape or nontoxic glue
• Crayons/markers/pens/ colored pencils

PORTRAIT PAINTER

SKILLS: Brainstorming/Observing/Drawing & Painting

A family portrait is a picture that shows the likeness of each member of the family. Creating a family portrait will provide your first grader with the opportunity to observe the physical characteristics of family members.

Work with your child to brainstorm a list of physical characteristics on which to focus. Your list may include skin tone, eye color, hair color, hair length, height, weight, and facial characteristics. Ask your Portrait Painter to observe and discuss these characteristics as family members pose.

Supply your child with construction paper and crayons, markers, or paint. For more authenticity, pick up skin-tone crayons or skin-tone paint from your local craft shop or toy store. Encourage your child to be as accurate as possible, focusing on the physical characteristics observed. Remind your child to include him- or herself in the portrait. When the family portrait is complete, invite your young artist to unveil the work of art for the entire family to enjoy.

Variation: Encourage your Portrait Painter to make a self-portrait or a portrait of your extended family to include grandparents, aunts, uncles, and cousins.

REQUIRED:
- Paper and pencil
- Markers/crayons/paint/paintbrush

OPTIONAL:
- Skin-tone crayons/paint

I'LL NEVER FORGET

SKILLS: Brainstorming/Expressive Language

Relive some of your family's more memorable experiences! The next time you are in the car, whether on a long trip or in a traffic jam, reminisce as you play I'll Never Forget.

Think of an experience you had together that you'll never forget. Say, for example, "I'll never forget the time Sarah's ice cream flew off her cone and landed on Dad's head!" Then, ask someone else to take a turn. Patti says, for example, "I'll never forget the gingerbread house we made together when we visited Uncle Arthur last year." Encourage all family members to contribute to the game. Some memories shared will bring smiles while others may bring tears. I'll Never Forget is a terrific way to remember!

REQUIRED:
- Your time

FAMILY FLAG

SKILLS: Brainstorming/Imaginative Thinking/Drawing

Flags are designed and displayed to celebrate and acknowledge countries, states, organizations, and events. Make a list and talk about all the different flags you've seen. Then work together to create a Family Flag. What symbols are significant for you? While planning your flag's design, remind your child that the drawing and colors should stand for something unique to your family. Cite examples such as the American flag, which has fifty stars for fifty states, or the Canadian flag, which has one red maple leaf, the symbol of Canada.

Make your family flag on paper or cloth. Attach it with staples or glue to a dowel or pencil, and display it in a place of prominence. As an added activity, select a family bird and a family flower, both chosen to represent you!

REQUIRED:
- Paper/cloth
- Crayons/markers
- Dowel/pencil
- Stapler/nontoxic glue

FAMILY CREST

SKILLS: Brainstorming/Imaginative Thinking/Drawing & Painting

You don't have to live in the Middle Ages to have a coat of arms! Create a Family Crest to show what makes your family unique.

Explain that a family crest is an emblem designed to show what makes you special. Talk about characteristics unique to you. Record any and all ideas. On a large sheet of construction paper, draw a shield. Use a dark marker to divide the shield into quarters. Based on the recorded ideas, designate and label each quarter with a theme. Select from themes such as family members, traditions, celebrations, hobbies, occupations, and goals.

Invite family members to contribute to each section of the Family Crest with drawings, paintings, or words. When your Family Crest is complete, cut it out, mount it on cardboard or poster board, and display it with pride for all to see! As an option, you may want to visit the library to examine books on heraldry and view samples of a coat of arms or family crest.

REQUIRED:
- Paper and pencil
- Large sheet construction paper
- Safety scissors
- Markers/crayons/paint/paintbrush

OPTIONAL:
- Cardboard/poster board
- Nontoxic glue
- Library visit

A+ ACTIVITIES FOR FIRST GRADE

HERITAGE AND HISTORY

SKILLS: Cultural & Family Awareness/Drawing Conclusions

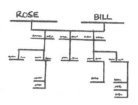

Ancestors are those people who came before us. Our names, traditions, and cultural heritage stem from our ancestors. Discovering ancestry is fascinating for both children and adults. Work together to learn more about your roots.

Using an atlas or world map, show your child where you live now. Then locate and view the countries or regions of your family's ancestors. If available, view and discuss photographs of your ancestors. Make a family tree to show

FAMILY TREE

generations of great-grandparents, grandparents, parents, and children. Talk about the impact your ancestors have had on your family.

If possible, visit the library or a museum to learn more about your country of origin.

For a real treat, celebrate your cultural heritage. Wear clothes and eat food particular to your family history. Play a game representative of your culture. Enjoy the music of your cultural roots. Whatever you choose to do to celebrate your cultural heritage, your first grader will benefit from being exposed to your family's special history.

> **REQUIRED:**
> • Items particular to your cultural heritage
>
> **OPTIONAL:**
> • Library/museum visit

FLY YOUR FLAGS

SKILLS: Observing/Drawing

What is the nationality of your ancestors? Talk with your first grader about the roots of your family. Use an atlas to show your child a map of the country where your family began. Explain that people sometimes move from one country to another to have a better life. Share facts about your country of ancestry. Then, in the atlas, find a picture of the flag of that country. If you are Native American, observe a flag or design a flag representative of your nation. Use crayons or markers to copy the flag onto an 8½″ × 11″ piece of paper. Staple or glue the flag to a dowel or pencil. Following the same directions, make a flag of your country of citizenship. Fly both flags together by standing them in a vase or glass.

> **REQUIRED:**
> • Atlas/maps
> • Crayons/markers
> • Dowel/pencil
> • Stapler/nontoxic glue
> • Paper
> • Vase or glass

MAGIC CARPET RIDE

Are your ancestors from India, Vietnam, Japan, or Pakistan? Are they from Russia, Poland, Ireland, or Scotland? From Ghana, Nigeria, Turkey, or Mexico? Are they Native Americans? Take a Magic Carpet Ride to a country or region of ancestry.

Spread a blanket, your magic carpet, on the floor. Tell participants that the carpet has the power to travel to the country or region of your ancestors. Name the country or region you will visit. Point it out on a map. Share any books, facts, pictures, or artifacts you may have from the country or region.

Write a story detailing your adventure. Ask questions to generate ideas. What did you see? Did you see the pyramids of Egypt or the Great Wall of China? Did you see the Great Plains of America or the sandy shores of Jamaica? Did you see farmlands or busy city streets? Did you see your ancestors? What did you say to them?

When text and illustrations are complete, bind or staple into a book. Share your Magic Carpet Ride and add this special volume to the family library.

REQUIRED:
- Blanket
- Paper and pencil
- Crayons/markers
- Yarn/ribbon
- Hole punch
- Stapler

OPTIONAL:
- Maps/books
- Pictures/artifacts

FAMILIES OF ALL KINDS

Children are exposed to all kinds of families. See unique and special qualities of individual families by reading stories that focus on Families of All Kinds.

Join an adopted child concerned about looking different from her parents in *Families Are Different* by Nina Pellegrini. Celebrate the love shared by Rosa, her mother, and grandmother in *A Chair For My Mother* by Vera B. Williams. Watch a baby bird search for its mother in *Are You My Mother?* by Philip Eastman. Anticipate the birth of a sibling with a young child in Lucille Clifton's *Everett Anderson's Nine Month Long*. Listen to a dad tell his young daughter what will change and what will stay the same after his new wife has a baby in *When I Am A Sister* by Robin Ballard. Take a sensitive look at how a dinosaur family deals with divorce in *Dinosaur's Divorce* by Laurene Krasny Brown and Marc Brown. Feel an extended family's warmth in *Shoes From Grandpa* by Mem Fox.

Visit your local library to find these and other books that send the message that the most important ingredient in a family is love.

REQUIRED:
- Library/bookstore visit

NO PLACE LIKE HOME

SKILLS: Observing/Brainstorming/Drawing/Written Expression

What makes your neighborhood special? Is it the storekeeper, the librarian, or the crossing guard? Is it the corner newsstand, the oak tree that shades the bus stop, the ten-story apartment building, the two-family home with the backyard swing, the field that rolls between farmhouses, or the gardens in the city park?

Work with your child to make an illustrated book of your neighborhood. Brainstorm a list of special people, places, and things that make your community unique. Encourage your child, along with all family members, to draw a picture to show that special person who helps you at the bank, that corner store where you go for sandwiches, that picnic table beside the brook where you have family barbecues. Write a caption just below the picture to tell about this special something. When all the illustrations and captions are complete, punch a hole in the top left-hand corner of each page and tie together with ribbon or yarn. Make a cover for your No Place Like Home family book.

Variation: Photograph the special people, places, and things to add to your book.

REQUIRED:
- Paper and pencil
- Crayons/markers
- Hole punch
- Ribbon/yarn

OPTIONAL:
- Camera
- Nontoxic glue

NEIGHBORHOOD NEWS

SKILLS: Observing/Note Taking/Written Expression/Drawing/Brainstorming

The Bluejays won the Little League game on Saturday! The Lewis family got a new car! Mrs. Benjamin planted tulip bulbs that are now in full bloom! City workers painted lines on Dolphin Road and put up the nets on the tennis courts in the park. The pizza shop added items to the menu, and the French bakery put tables outside!

What is news in your neighborhood? Encourage your Neighborhood News reporter to report neighborhood events that have occurred over the course of a week or two. Focus on anything you participate in or observe. Draw or photograph the new stoplight at the corner or the tree planted in the park. Then work together to put the ideas to print. Write a sentence for each news item on an index card. Glue the index cards to a sheet of construction paper to make a front page. Add illustrations or photos. Brainstorm possible names for your newspaper. Choose one and write it across the top of the completed page. Be sure to encourage your young reporter to share the news with the neighbors.

REQUIRED:
- Pencil
- Index cards
- Crayons/markers
- Construction paper
- Nontoxic glue

OPTIONAL:
- Camera

SIGN SURVEY

SKILLS: Observing/Interpreting Signs & Symbols/Drawing

To adults, interpreting traffic signs is second nature. To your first grader, however, many signs are unfamiliar. Help your child learn the meaning and importance of signs in your neighborhood by conducting a Sign Survey.

Equipped with a pad and pencil, walk through your neighborhood. Discuss signs that you see. Observe a stop sign and ask your first grader to draw it. Below the drawing, clearly print "Stop Sign." Take a close look at a pedestrian crossing sign. Again, ask your first grader to draw it. Below the drawing, clearly print "Pedestrian Crossing." Continue the sign survey. Discuss, draw, and label signs that indicate one-way streets, school zones, hospital zones, no parking, bus stops, taxi stands, deer crossing, bicycle zone, hidden driveway, yield, no turn on red, slow, left turn only, right turn only, no passing, curve.

Add to the survey as you travel about your town, city, state, or country.

REQUIRED:
- Paper and pencil
- Neighborhood walk

MAIL DELIVERY

SKILLS: Brainstorming/Exploring/Sequencing

What does your first grader know or believe to be true about mail delivery? Ask to find out. Then examine envelopes you have received. Point out the address and zip code that show postal workers where to send mail. Explain that the return address shows who sent the mail. Look closely at the stamp. Tell your child that the person who sends a letter or package has to pay. A stamp is purchased and placed in the upper right-hand corner of the envelope or package. Look at the postmark. Note the place from which the mail was sent and the date on which the mail was sent.

Finally, talk about the basic sequence followed when a letter is mailed. Mail is picked up by mail carriers from mailboxes; taken to the post office; postmarked and canceled so that stamps can't be reused; sorted by zip code; loaded on trucks, planes, or boats; taken to the local post offices; sorted again; and finally delivered!

To enhance understanding, arrange a visit to and tour of your local post office. Also plan a library visit to read *The Post Office Book, Mail and How It Moves* by Gail Gibbons.

REQUIRED:
- Incoming mail

OPTIONAL:
- Post office visit
- Library/bookstore visit

FROM ME TO YOU

SKILLS: Written Expression/Estimation/Experimentation

In *A Letter to Amy* by Ezra Jack Keats, a young boy mails birthday party invitations to his friends. In *The Jolly Postman* by Janet and Allan Ahlberg, favorite fairy tale characters delightfully receive mail. In "The Letter," from *Frog and Toad Are Friends* by Arnold Lobel, Toad bemoans the fact that he has never received mail!

Enjoy receiving mail by writing to each other! Start by mailing a surprise letter to your child. In the letter, write that you are interested in seeing how long it takes for a letter to get from the mailbox to the post office to your home. Ask your child to write back. Provide guidance in addressing, stamping, and mailing the letter from a roadside mailbox. When you put the letter in the mailbox, note the time of pick up. Ask your child to estimate how long it will take for the letter to get to the post office, be processed, and then be delivered to your home.

Allow your letter writer to check the mail on the following day(s). How close was your estimate to the actual delivery date? Read your mail and write back!

REQUIRED:
- Paper and pencil
- Envelope/stamp

OPTIONAL:
- Library/bookstore visit

STAMP SENSE

SKILLS: Observing/Collecting/Sorting/Classifying

Invite your child to become a philatelist, to join the ranks of those who engage in the world's most popular hobby, stamp collecting!

Explain to your child that stamps come in different sizes, designs, and values. They are placed on envelopes and packages to indicate that the sender has paid for postage. Tell your child that stamps, designed by artists, are often made to honor a person or organization. They are also designed to commemorate holidays, to celebrate nature, to display methods of transportation, or to raise money for a good cause.

Encourage your child to collect the canceled stamps that arrive on your mail. While stamps can be steamed off envelopes, be safe! Allow your child to cut stamps from discarded envelopes. Provide an album, journal, or notebook in which your young philatelist can glue the stamps, sorting by design, country, or cost. Label the categories. Ask friends and relatives to donate discarded envelopes with unusual stamps, too. This kind of "recycled" collecting could be the start of a lifetime hobby.

REQUIRED:
- Canceled stamps
- Safety scissors
- Nontoxic glue
- Journal/album/notebook
- Pencil/marker

DESIGN A STAMP

SKILLS: Brainstorming/Observing/Creative Thinking/Drawing & Painting

Postage stamps often commemorate or celebrate special people or events. Encourage your first grader to view the array of stamps that you use and those that appear on your mail. Brainstorm a list of famous people from sports, history, science, literature, or entertainment who might appear on a stamp. Think about and list favorite or endangered animals that deserve a place on a stamp. Consider friends and family members, neighborhood heroes, plants, animals, toys, or games that warrant notice. List holidays, special events, or beautiful places that could be celebrated on a stamp. Finally, list any causes you feel could benefit from being honored on a stamp.

Now encourage your child to choose one idea from the many you've generated. Design, draw, paint, or color a stamp on construction paper. Include the cost of the stamp and country of origin.

REQUIRED:
- Stamp samples
- Paper and pencil
- Crayons/markers/ paint/paintbrush

STATION VISITS

SKILLS: Brainstorming/Observing/Describing/Written Expression

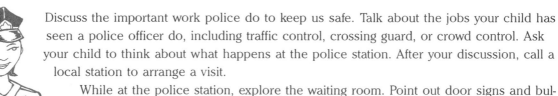

Discuss the important work police do to keep us safe. Talk about the jobs your child has seen a police officer do, including traffic control, crossing guard, or crowd control. Ask your child to think about what happens at the police station. After your discussion, call a local station to arrange a visit.

While at the police station, explore the waiting room. Point out door signs and bulletin board announcements. Observe officers at work. Ask your child to observe and describe the uniform of a police officer. If the station is quiet, introduce yourselves to the officer at the front desk. Explain the purpose of your visit. Ask the officer to take a few moments to talk to your child about the importance of police work. Before leaving, request a card with emergency numbers to keep by your phone. Work with your first grader to memorize 911 and other emergency numbers. At home, write a thank-you note to your police force for the work that they do.

On another day, follow the same procedure in order to learn more about the firefighters in your area and the work they do.

REQUIRED:
- Your time
- Police station visit

OPTIONAL:
- Paper and pencil
- Envelope/stamp
- Fire station visit

A+ ACTIVITIES FOR FIRST GRADE

COMMUNITY DIORAMA

SKILLS: Brainstorming/Observing/Imaginative Thinking/Drawing & Painting

There are many people and places that help keep a community running smoothly. Ask your child to brainstorm places that are important to your community. Choose one of the places named, such as the library, park, hospital, drugstore, post office, supermarket, fire station, bank, police station, school, or recreation center. Name people and activities that are particular to this place. Ask your child why this place is important to the community. Visit this place to observe people and characteristic activity.

Make a diorama of the interior or exterior of this location inside a shoe box. Hold the shoe box horizontally with the opening facing you. Use all interior and exterior surfaces of the box to depict the scene.

Be creative! Use Popsicle sticks, colored tissue, foil, straws, string, construction paper, Styrofoam, anything. Draw, paint, or color. Emphasize detail and design as your first grader recreates a miniature of a community location.

REQUIRED:
- Shoe box
- Safety scissors
- Nontoxic glue
- Construction paper
- Markers/crayons/paint/ paintbrush
- Recyclable materials
- Community visit

COMMUNITY CARTOGRAPHY

SKILLS: Observing/Drawing/Imaginative Thinking/Mapping

First graders may see maps in the classroom, in the car, in magazines, or in brochures of the places you visit. Ask your young cartographer about maps. What are they used for and what do they show? Explain that maps can show the outline of an area, streets, landmarks, lakes, mountains, and rivers.

Now choose a book from your child's collection that has characters moving from one place to another. For example, in *The Bee Tree* by Patricia Polacco, people chase a bee from a garden to the woods. Ask your child to pretend to chase a bee, a squirrel, a cat, or a dog, for example, through your yard or neighborhood. Outline the imaginary route followed around the tree, beside the garden, over the wall, through the meadow, up the hill, over the stream, across the blueberry patch to the tree. Draw and label each landmark imagined as you move from one place to another.

REQUIRED:
- Paper
- Felt tip pens or colored pencils
- Book

OPTIONAL:
- Library/bookstore visit

NEIGHBORHOOD MAP

SKILLS: Observing/Drawing/Mapping

Maps are tools used by people for many reasons. Maps help us find places. Firefighters and police use maps to find the fastest route to an emergency. Meteorologists use maps to display weather patterns. Tourists use maps to locate points of interest. Expose your child to maps by sharing a map of your city or town. Find a map in your local phone book or library. Point out and name streets, ponds, parks, and landmarks. Indicate the location of hospitals, schools, your city or town hall, libraries, bus stations, and police and fire stations.

To prepare for map making, walk around your neighborhood to observe places and landmarks that your child feels are important. Then, at home, provide materials for your young cartographer to make a neighborhood map that includes the places or landmarks observed.

Share the map when it is complete. Encourage your child to point out all details included. Challenge your child to make other maps of places such as the inside of your home, the route to school, or the way to a friend or relative's home. You may want to collect the maps and bind as a personal atlas.

REQUIRED:
• Local map
• Paper
• Crayons/markers
• Neighborhood walk

OPTIONAL:
• Stapler
• Yarn/ribbon
• Hole punch

TEA AND TREASURE

SKILLS: Imaginative Thinking/Drawing/Mapping/Brainstorming

Imagine that your yard or neighborhood park was once home to pirates who buried their treasure hundreds of years ago. Make up your own treasure map, complete with labels and landmarks.

To make your treasure map look old, use heavy watercolor paper, available at art or craft shops. Fold the paper into halves, quarters, eighths, until it is a small square. When you unfold the paper, it will be crinkled. Brush the paper lightly with cold tea, using a paintbrush or the tea bag itself. While the paper is drying, paint over sections to create a splotchy and old effect. Blot damp spots with a paper towel to enhance the antique appearance.

When the paper is completely dry, draw the outline of the yard or park in brown pencil or fine tipped marker. Add imagined rocks, mountains, streams, trees, caves, swamps, waterfalls, or hazards. Brainstorm catchy names for each such as "Never Return Rocks," "Mighty Monster Mountains," "Cracked Root Tree," and "Icy Ridge Stream." Make an *X* to mark the spot of the treasure.

REQUIRED:
• Watercolor paper
• Felt tip pens or colored pencils
• Tea and tea bag
• Paintbrush

A+ ACTIVITIES FOR FIRST GRADE

DREAMVILLE

SKILLS: Brainstorming/Imaginative Thinking/Drawing

Create the town of your dreams. Imagine the materials you could use to build buildings, and think of the products that might grow in gardens or on trees. Build a library with a gumdrop roof so that you can have a treat while reading. Put a swimming pool that is filled with melted chocolate in the park. Fill your school with books that have talking and walking characters. Plant gardens of gigantic vegetables and trees with juicy drinks.

Supply your first grader with construction paper, markers, or crayons to make a map of Dreamville. Encourage your child to be creative! When the fun is done, your young town planner can give colorful and fanciful names to the delightful landmarks created.

You may want to visit your library or bookstore to read *The Big Orange Splot* by Daniel Manus Pinkwater, a story of personal dreams and dream houses.

REQUIRED:
- Large sheet construction paper
- Crayons/markers

OPTIONAL:
- Library/bookstore visit

SETTING SAIL

SKILLS: Brainstorming/Imaginative Thinking/Drawing/Written Expression

Ask your young historian about Christopher Columbus. Then share basic facts to enhance your child's background knowledge. Columbus believed that he could sail west from Spain to reach India. He did not know that by sailing west, he would come ashore on lands that would later be known as the West Indies. Columbus organized crews and sailed west on three ships, the Nina, the Pinta, and the Santa Maria. Despite the long and difficult journey, Columbus and his crews landed in the New World on October 12, 1492.

After discussion, ask your child to imagine what it would have been like to sail with Columbus. Ask, "How did you feel when Columbus asked you to sail with him?" "On which ship did you sail?" "What were the hardest things about the voyage?" "What responsibilities did you have on the ship?" "What were your sleeping quarters like?" "Did you miss your family?" Now, encourage your young explorer to draw a picture of him- or herself aboard one of the ships. Then write a story telling of the time he or she sailed with Columbus.

REQUIRED:
- Paper and pencil
- Crayons/markers

TELL THE TALE

On the fourth Thursday in November, people across the United States celebrate Thanksgiving. What does your child know or believe to be true about Thanksgiving? Explain that long ago, before the United States was born, a group of people known as the Pilgrims left a country called England and sailed across the Atlantic Ocean on a small ship called the *Mayflower*. They left England to find freedom in a new home. Point out England and the Atlantic Ocean on a map.

The Pilgrims came ashore in an area of the New World that is now the state of Massachusetts. Point out Massachusetts. There the Pilgrims built a village called New Plymouth. They made friends with the people who lived in the New World. These people were the Wampanoag Indians. The Wampanoags taught the Pilgrims how to plant corn, fish, and hunt. To give thanks for their new home and their new friends, the Pilgrims made a huge feast to share with the Wampanoags.

Invite your child to retell the story of the first Thanksgiving to another member of the family, pointing out on a map the start and finish of the voyage of the Pilgrims.

REQUIRED:
• World map/globe

TABLE TRIMMINGS

As the celebration of Thanksgiving approaches, share a story with your first grader, such as *A Turkey for Thanksgiving* by Eve Bunting. In this engaging story, Mr. and Mrs. Moose have a turkey for Thanksgiving . . . as a guest along with all their other friends. In *Thanksgiving at the Tappletons'*, by Eileen Spinelli, a series of mishaps results in the family's sharing a modest meal and realizing that being together on this special day is all that matters.

As a follow-up to any Thanksgiving story you read or tell, invite your child to set a paper table with all the trimmings and surround it with friends and family. Use a 12″ × 18″ sheet of white paper as the background. Cut a paper table from brown paper and glue to the background. Then, brainstorm a list of foods for the feast and cut each from construction paper to glue to the table. Finally, make a list of guests who will attend the meal and draw or paint each one beside or behind the table. Display your child's Table Trimmings for all to see.

REQUIRED:
• Construction paper
• Crayons/paint/paintbrush/ colored pencils
• Nontoxic glue
• Safety scissors
• Library/bookstore visit

FREE TO BE ME

SKILLS: Brainstorming/Written Expression/Drawing

More than two hundred years ago, in 1776, a famous American named Thomas Jefferson wrote an important paper called the Declaration of Independence. This paper said that a new country, the United States of America, had been created. Thomas Jefferson spoke for all the people of this new country when he wrote that all people have the right to be free.

Talk with your first grader about what it means to be free. Tell your child about the Declaration of Independence, keeping your explanation simple and understandable. Then invite your first grader to write a Free to Be Me book.

Fold a piece of paper in half. Hold the paper like a card with the fold on the left. Ask your child to put the title, author, and a self-portrait on the cover. Then, on the inside facing pages and on the back page, encourage your child to draw pictures and write sentences that show and tell what being free means to him or her. Encourage each family member to make a Free to Be Me book to share.

REQUIRED:
- Paper and pencil
- Crayons/markers

HAPPY BIRTHDAY, USA!

SKILLS: Brainstorming/Drawing/Written Expression

Happy birthday, dear U.S.A., happy birthday to you! Ask your child why we celebrate the Fourth of July. Why do we have picnics, parades, concerts, and fireworks? Explain that July 4 is the day that is set aside for Americans to celebrate the birthday of the United States of America. Tell your child that on the Fourth of July, we think about the Americans of long ago who worked hard to gain freedom for all of us who live in the USA.

Talk about the ways we celebrate our birthdays, with parties, cards, and presents. Now work together to make a birthday card for the USA. Brainstorm ideas for a patriotic design and an appropriate message. Then, fold a piece of paper in half to form the card, and let imaginations soar! You may want to provide glitter glue or glitter markers along with crayons and standard markers to create a festive design.

On the Fourth of July, be sure to have your child share the card and sing Happy Birthday to the USA as part of the festivities of the day!

REQUIRED:
- Paper and pencil
- Crayons/markers

OPTIONAL:
- Glitter glue or glitter markers

THE GRAND OLD FLAG

SKILLS: Brainstorming/Counting/Drawing

Talk to your child about the American flag. Ask why a country has a flag. Explain that the flag stands for a country or is a symbol of a country and the people who live there.

Work together to make a list of all the places where we see the American flag. You will probably include front yards, schoolyards, classrooms, public buildings, parks, stadiums, airplanes, ships, trains, and uniforms. Look closely at the American flag or at a picture of the flag. Count the stars.

REQUIRED:
- Picture of the American flag
- Paper and pencil
- Markers

OPTIONAL:
- Permanent ink markers
- Pillowcase, dishtowel, or T-shirt
- United States map

Explain that there is one star for each of the fifty states. You may want to show your child a map of the United States and count the states for confirmation. Next count the stripes. Explain that the thirteen stripes stand for the first thirteen colonies/states that were part of the United States. Finally, make an American flag on paper, on the front of a white T-shirt, on a dishtowel, or on a pillowcase. If you use fabric, use permanent ink markers. Fly or wear your flag with pride!

I PLEDGE ALLEGIANCE . . .

SKILLS: Vocabulary Development/Comprehension

None of us can take for granted that children, and sometimes even adults, know the meaning of memorized songs, pledges, or poems. In the well-loved children's book *Ramona the Pest,* by Beverly Cleary, Ramona Quimby comes home from school, telling her mother that she really liked learning the "dawnzer" song. What Ramona referred to was actually the American national anthem, *The Star Spangled Banner.* Ramona, like most children her age, was asked to learn a song by rote. She didn't have the necessary language skills to identify the individual words in the line, ". . . by the dawn's early light." In the same way, your child has probably been asked to recite or learn the Pledge of Allegiance. Ask your child what he or she knows about the Pledge of Allegiance. Ask what the words "pledge" and "allegiance" mean. Why do we put our right hand over our heart when we say the Pledge of Allegiance? Continue the discussion so that your child understands that a pledge is a promise and allegiance is loyalty or devotion.

REQUIRED:
- Your time

A+ ACTIVITIES FOR FIRST GRADE

CIVIL RIGHTS READ

SKILL: Drawing Conclusions

Throughout time, people have fought for civil rights. These rights ensure that all people are treated equally despite differences. Not too long ago, Martin Luther King, Jr., led a nonviolent campaign to gain equal rights not only for African-Americans but for all people. King was not alone. Many people, including Rosa Parks and Ruby Bridges, contributed to the fight for civil rights. More than one hundred years ago, Harriet Tubman and countless others helped slaves find freedom. Expose your child to these important people with a Civil Rights Read.

Witness the life and leadership of Martin Luther King, Jr., in *A Picture Book of Martin Luther King, Jr.* by David A. Adler. Discover the consequences when Rosa Parks refused to sit in the back of the bus in *A Picture Book of Rosa Parks,* also by David E. Adler. Empathize with the first African-American child to attend an all-white school in Robert Coles's *The Story of Ruby Bridges.* Escape slavery in *Aunt Harriet's Underground Railroad in the Sky* by Faith Ringgold and *The Drinking Gourd* by E. N. Monjo. These stories, and many others, will raise your child's consciousness about the need for equality!

REQUIRED:
• Library/bookstore visit

"I HAVE A DREAM . . ."

SKILLS: Brainstorming/Written Expression/Drawing

Martin Luther King, Jr.'s famous speech at the March On Washington in 1963 included the powerful and memorable phrase, "I have a dream. . . ." Martin Luther King, Jr., was a renowned civil rights advocate whose dream was for our world to acknowledge all people as equals despite their differences. Discuss this dream with your first grader. Find out what your child knows or believes to be true about Martin Luther King, Jr. Record any ideas presented.

Work with your child to make a book of dreams. Encourage your first grader to write and draw about personal dreams, dreams for family and friends, and dreams for the world. Perhaps your first grader will draw a picture of one person helping another, with the caption, "My dream is that all people are kind to one another." Maybe your child will include an illustration of people shaking hands, with the caption, "My dream is that people will solve problems using words." Encourage all family members to write a page in the book. When all entries are made, decorate a cover, print the title *"Our Book of Dreams,"* bind with ribbon or yarn, and add to the family library.

REQUIRED:
• Paper and pencil
• Crayons/markers
• Ribbon/yarn
• Hole punch

SOCIAL STUDIES ACTIVITIES

CIRCLE GAME

SKILLS: Ordering/Self-Awareness/Community Awareness

Ask, "What is the name of our city?" or "What is the name of our state?" Your first grader may not know the answers!

Build your child's awareness of community with the Circle Game. Cut seven concentric circles from seven colors of paper. Begin with a 2″ circle, making each successive circle 2″ larger than the preceding one. Label the smallest circle "My House, Apartment, Condo." Write along the top of each remaining circle, for example, "My Neighborhood—Cabot Street," "My City—Newton," "My State—Massachusetts," "My Country—United States of America," "My Continent—North America," "My Planet—Earth."

Place the "Earth" circle on the table. Work back in sequential order to "My House," centering each circle on the preceding circle. Keep all writing visible. Let your child "travel" the circles. Pick up the smallest one. Say, "This is my house." Pick up the next. "It is in the Cabot Street neighborhood." "My neighborhood is in the city of Newton." "My city is in the state of Massachusetts." Continue in this manner through all circles.

Variation: Place the circles from left to right, smallest to largest or largest to smallest.

REQUIRED:
• Construction paper
• Markers
• Safety scissors

NEIGHBORS EVERYWHERE

SKILLS: Observing/Map Skills

Neighbors are all around us. Some of us get to know next door neighbors, neighbors across the street, and neighbors behind us. Others meet neighbors down the hall, neighbors across the hall, and neighbors upstairs. Explain that your city or town, state, and country have neighbors as well. The United States has two neighbors, one above us to the north, Canada, and one below us to the south, Mexico.

Look at a map of your state or region. Point out and name your city or town and its neighboring communities. Now, look at a map of the country. Point out and name your state and its neighboring states. Introduce your first grader to the term "border" as you use a finger to trace the border of your state. Finally, look at a world map or a map of North America. Point out and name the United States and its neighbors, Canada and Mexico. Again, ask your child to use a finger to trace the border of our country. Exposure of this kind enhances your child's understanding that we have Neighbors Everywhere.

REQUIRED:
• Maps

WHERE IN THE WORLD?

SKILL: Map skills

Where in the World is a hands-on game that exposes your child to the seven continents and four oceans of the earth. Your young geographer will want to play for hours!

Put a large world map on the wall at eye level or open to a world map in an atlas. Travel the world by pointing out and naming each continent and ocean. Ask your child to touch the map at any point with eyes closed. Then, with eyes open, see Where in the World you are.

Ask, "Are you in the water?" Your child answers, "Yes." Respond in an animated way, for example, "You are in the Pacific Ocean! Be on the lookout for whales!" Ask, "Are you on land?" Your child responds, "Yes." You say, "Wow, you're in Asia, the biggest continent!" or "Brrrr, put on your snowsuit! It's freezing in Antarctica!" Lead your child in observation of the map by asking questions such as, "What color is the water on the map?" "What colors are used to show land?" Let your child's prior knowledge of and exposure to maps and globes determine the nature of your discussion.

Variation: Use a globe instead of a map.

REQUIRED:
• World map
OPTIONAL:
• Globe

A LETTER TO HELP

SKILL: Written Expression

We all need food to live. Food keeps us healthy. Food gives us energy. Food helps us grow. Let your first grader know that not all the people in the world are as lucky as you. There are many people in our country and in countries around the world who don't have enough to eat. Explain that there are groups of caring people who work hard to find ways to provide food for the needy.

Work with your child to write a letter to a charitable organization to find out how you can help. Then act upon the suggestions received. Organizations to consider include:

CARE
151 Ellis Street
Atlanta, GA 30303
1-404-681-2552
Web site: www.care.org
E-mail: info@care.org

Oxfam America
26 West Street
Boston, MA 02111
1-800-77-OXFAM
Web site:
www.oxfamamerica.org
E-mail:
info@oxfamamerica.org

UNICEF Headquarters
UNICEF House
3 United Nations Plaza
New York, NY 10017
1-212-326-7000
Web site: www.unicef.org
E-mail:
netmaster@unicef.org

REQUIRED:
• Paper and pencil
• Envelope/stamp

CELEBRATE THE PEOPLE

SKILLS: Observing/Respecting Human Differences

Celebrate our diversity by making a collage of people of the world. Talk about how exciting it is to know, meet, and live and work with people of different cultures and backgrounds. Then spend time looking through recyclable magazines for faces that represent the people of the world community. Cut out and collect pictures of children and adults—black, white, yellow, and red; people at work, people at play. When you have a wide and representative sample, make a Celebrate the People collage on a large piece of poster board or construction paper. Arrange the pictures to cover the entire paper, leaving space across the top for the heading. Glue the pictures to the paper and Celebrate the People!

REQUIRED:
- Poster board/ construction paper
- Marker
- Magazines
- Safety scissors
- Nontoxic glue

MAKE THE WORLD MORE BEAUTIFUL

SKILLS: Brainstorming/Observing/Recording/Written Expression/Drawing/Applying

In *Folks Call Me Appleseed John* by Andrew Glass, a man makes the world more beautiful by planting apple seeds. John Chapman comes to be known as Johnny Appleseed. In *Miss Rumphius* by Barbara Cooney, a woman makes the world more beautiful by planting lupine seeds. Alice Rumphius comes to be known as the Lupine Lady. Whether in fact or fancy, both Johnny Appleseed and Alice Rumphius set a wonderful example for all. Each gives unselfishly to add to the beauty of the environment and bring joy to people.

Ask your child to think about something to do to make the world more beautiful. As you travel about your community and beyond, observe everything around you. Keep a running list of possibilities. Then, select one and encourage your child to write and illustrate a Make the World More Beautiful pledge. Over time, help your child to implement the pledge. Plant a garden, help a neighbor, share with a friend.

REQUIRED:
- Paper and pencil
- Crayons/markers

OPTIONAL:
- Library/bookstore visit

# BIBLIOGRAPHY

Adler, David A. *A Picture Book of Martin Luther King, Jr.* New York: Holiday House, Inc., 1991.

Adler, David A. *A Picture Book of Rosa Parks.* New York: Holiday House, Inc., 1997.

Ahlberg, Janet & Allan. *The Jolly Postman or Other People's Letters.* Boston: Little, Brown and Company, 1986.

Allen, Pamela. *Who Sank the Boat?* New York: Coward-McCann, Inc., 1982.

Axelrod, Amy. *Pigs On a Blanket.* New York: Simon & Schuster, 1996.

Axelrod, Amy. *Pigs Will Be Pigs.* New York: Simon & Schuster, 1977.

Ballard, Robin. *When I Am a Sister.* New York: Greenwillow Books, 1998.

Barrett, Judi. *Cloudy With A Chance of Meatballs.* New York: Macmillan Publishing Company, 1978.

Beck, Ian (illustrator). *Five Little Ducks.* New York: Henry Holt and Company, Inc., 1992.

Bradbury, Judy. *One Carton of Oops.* New York: Learning Triangle Press, 1977.

Bridwell, Norman. *Clifford's Birthday Party.* New York: Scholastic Inc., 1988.

Briggs, Raymond. *The Snowman.* New York: Random House, 1978.

Brinckloe, Julie. *Fireflies!* New York: Aladdin Books, 1985.

Brown, Marc. *Arthur's Tooth.* Boston: Little, Brown and Company, 1985.

Brown, Margaret Wise. *The Runaway Bunny.* New York: Harper Collins, 1972.

Buckley, Richard. *The Foolish Tortoise.* New York: Scholastic Inc., 1985.

Buckley, Richard. *The Greedy Python.* New York: Scholastic Inc., 1985.

Bunting, Eve. *A Turkey for Thanksgiving.* New York: Scholastic Inc., 1991.

Burningham, John. *Cloudland.* New York: Crown Publishing Group, 1996.

Burton, Virginia Lee. *Katy and the Big Snow.* Boston: Houghton Mifflin Company, 1943.

Canizares, Susan, and Mary Reid. *Treats From a Tree.* New York: Scholastic Inc., 1998.

Cannon, Janell. *Stellaluna.* New York: Harcourt Brace & Company, 1993.

Cannon, Janell. *Verdi.* New York: Harcourt Brace & Company, 1997.

Carle, Eric. *The Grouchy Ladybug.* New York: HarperCollins, 1986.

Carle, Eric. *Little Cloud.* New York: Scholastic Inc., 1996.

Carle, Eric. *The Mixed-Up Chameleon.* New York: Harper Trophy, 1975.

Carle, Eric. *Today Is Monday.* New York: Scholastic Inc., 1993.

Carle, Eric. *The Very Busy Spider.* New York: Putnam Publishing Group, 1985.

Carle, Eric. *The Very Hungry Caterpillar*. New York: Scholastic Inc., 1987.

Carle, Eric. *The Very Quiet Cricket*. New York: Putnam Publishing, 1990.

Carlson, Nancy. *I Like Me*. New York: Penguin Books, 1988.

Christelow, Eileen. *Five Little Monkeys Sitting in a Tree*. Boston: Houghton Mifflin, 1991.

Cleary, Beverly. *Ramona the Pest*. New York: Avon Books, 1968.

Clements, Andrew. *Big Al*. New York: Scholastic Inc., 1988.

Clifton, Lucille. *Everett Anderson's Nine Month Long*. New York: Henry Holt & Company, 1978.

Coerr, Eleanor. *The Josefina Story Quilt*. New York: Harper, 1986.

Coles, Robert. *The Story of Ruby Bridges*. New York: Scholastic Inc., 1995.

Cooney, Barbara. *Miss Rumphius*. New York: Viking Penguin Inc., 1982.

Crews, Donald. *Ten Black Dots*. New York: Scholastic Inc., 1986.

Cristaldi, Kathryn. *Even Steven, Odd Todd*. New York: Scholastic Inc., 1996.

Crowe, Robert L. *Tyler Toad and the Thunder*. New York: E. P. Dutton, 1980.

Day, Alexandra. *Good Dog, Carl*. Hong Kong: Green Tiger Press, 1985.

DePaola, Tomie. *Pancakes for Breakfast*. New York: Harcourt Brace Jovanovich, Publishers, 1978.

DePaola, Tomie. *Strega Nona*. New York: Scholastic Inc., 1975.

Eastman, Philip. *Are You My Mother?* New York: Beginner Books, 1976.

Emberley, Edward R. *Ed Emberley's Great Thumbprint Drawing Book*. New York: Scholastic Inc., 1977.

Flournoy, Valerie. *The Patchwork Quilt*. New York: Dial, 1985.

Fox, Mem. *Possum Magic*. New York: Harcourt Brace, 1990.

Fox, Mem. *Shoes From Grandpa*. New York: Orchard Books, 1992.

Gackenbach, Dick. *Harry and the Terrible Whatzit*. New York: Clarion Books, 1977.

Galdone, Paul. *The Three Bears*. New York: Clarion Books, 1972.

Gibbons, Gail. *The Post Office Book . . . Mail and How It Moves*. New York: HarperCollins Publishers, 1982.

Glass, Andrew. *Folks Call Me Appleseed John*. New York: Bantam Doubleday Dell Books for Young Readers, 1995.

Guarino, Deborah. *Is Your Mama A Llama?* New York: Scholastic Inc., 1989.

Hall, Katy. *Skeletons! Skeletons! All About Bones*. New York: Scholastic Inc., 1991.

Hall, Zoe. *It's Pumpkin Time*. New York: Scholastic Inc., 1994.

Hamanaka, Sheila. *All the Colors of the Earth*. New York: Morrow Junior Books, 1994.

Heller, Ruth. *How to Hide a Crocodile and Other Reptiles*. New York: Grosset & Dunlap, 1986.

A+ ACTIVITIES FOR FIRST GRADE

Heller, Ruth. *How to Hide a Meadow Frog and Other Amphibians*. New York: Grosset & Dunlap, 1986.

Heller, Ruth. *How to Hide An Octopus and Other Sea Creatures*. New York: Grosset & Dunlap, 1985.

Heller, Ruth. *How to Hide a Parakeet and Other Birds*. New York: Grosset & Dunlap, 1986.

Heller, Ruth. *How to Hide a Polar Bear and Other Mammals*. New York: Grosset & Dunlap, 1985.

Henkes, Kevin. *Chrysanthemum*. New York: Greenwillow Books, 1991.

Henkes, Kevin. *Julius: The Baby of the World*. New York: Mulberry Books, 1990.

Henkes, Kevin. *Lilly's Purple Plastic Purse*. New York: Greenwillow Books, 1996.

Henkes, Kevin. *Owen*. New York: Greenwillow Books, 1993.

Hoban, Russell. *Bread and Jam for Frances*. New York: Harper Trophy, 1986.

Hopkins, Lee Bennett. *Weather*. New York: Harper Collins Publishers, 1994.

Hulme, Joy N. *Sea Sums*. New York: Hyperion Books, 1996.

Hurd, Thacher. *The Pea Patch Jig*. New York: Harper Collins Publishers, 1986.

Hutchins, Pat. *The Doorbell Rang*. New York: Mulberry Books, 1986.

Jeunesse, Gallimard, and Daniel Moignot. *Frogs, A First Discovery Book*. New York: Scholastic Inc., 1994.

Keats, Ezra Jack. *A Letter to Amy*. New York: Harper & Row, 1968.

Krasny Brown, Laurene, and Marc Brown. *Dinosaur's Divorce*. Boston: Little, Brown & Company, 1988.

Kraus, R. *The Carrot Seed*. New York: Harper Collins, 1945.

Leedy, Loreen. *Measuring Penny*. New York: Henry Holt & Company, 1997.

Lester, Helen. *Me First*. Boston: Houghton Mifflin, 1992. ·

Lionni, Leo. *A Busy Year*. New York: Scholastic Inc., 1992.

Lionni, Leo. *A Color of His Own*. New York: Scholastic Inc., 1975.

Lionni, Leo. *A Flea Story*. New York: Pantheon Books, 1995.

Lionni, Leo. *Frederick*. New York: Alfred A. Knopf, 1967.

Lionni, Leo. *Inch by Inch*. New York: Mulberry Books, 1960.

Lionni, Leo. *Swimmy*. New York: Random House, 1973.

Lobel, Arnold. *Days With Frog and Toad*. New York: Scholastic, 1979.

Lobel, Arnold. *Frog and Toad All Year*. New York: HarperCollins Publishers, 1976.

Lobel, Arnold. *Frog and Toad Are Friends*. New York: Harper & Row, 1970.

Lobel, Arnold. *Frog and Toad Together*. New York: Scholastic, 1971.

Lonborg, Rosemary. *Helping Bugs*. Scituate, MA: Little Friend Press, 1995.

London, Jonathan. *Froggy Gets Dressed*. New York: Viking, 1992.

Loretan, Sylvia, and Jan Lenica. *Bob the Snowman*. New York: Scholastic Inc., 1988.

Mathews, Louise. *Bunches and Bunches of Bunnies*. New York: Scholastic Inc., 1978.

McGrath, Barbara Barbieri. *M & M Counting Book*. Watertown, MA: Charlesbridge Publishing, 1994.

McMillan, Bruce. *Jellybeans for Sale*. New York: Scholastic Inc., 1996.

McMillan, Bruce. *Time To . . .* New York: Scholastic, Inc., 1989.

Medearis, Angela Shelf. *The 100th Day of School*. New York: Scholastic Inc., 1996.

Monjo, E. N. *The Drinking Gourd*. New York: HarperCollins, 1991.

Nikola-Lisa, W. *One Hole In the Road*. New York: Henry Holt & Company, 1996.

Parish, Peggy. *Amelia Bedelia*. New York: Harper & Row, 1963.

Peet, Bill. *Big Bad Bruce*. Boston: Houghton Mifflin Company, 1977.

Peet, Bill. *Fly, Homer, Fly*. Boston: Houghton Mifflin Company, 1969.

Pellegrini, Nina. *Families Are Different*. New York: Holiday House, Inc., 1991.

Pfister, Marcus. *The Rainbow Fish*. New York: North-South Books, 1992.

Pinczes, Elinor J. *One Hundred Hungry Ants*. Boston: Houghton Mifflin Company, 1993.

Pinczes, Elinor J. *A Remainder of One*. Boston: Houghton Mifflin Company, 1995.

Polacco, Patricia. *The Bee Tree*. New York: Philomel Books, 1993.

Polacco, Patricia. *The Keeping Quilt*. New York: Simon & Schuster, Inc., 1988.

Polacco, Patricia. *Some Birthday*. New York: Simon & Schuster, Inc., 1991.

Ransom, Candice. *The Big Green Pocketbook*. New York: Harper Collins Publishers, 1993.

Recht Penner, Lucille. *Monster Bugs*. New York: Random House, 1996.

Richards Wright, Joan, & Nancy Winslow Parker. *Bugs*. New York: Mulberry Books, 1988.

Ringgold, Faith. *Aunt Harriet's Underground Railroad in the Sky*. New York: Crown Publishing Group, 1995.

Sendak, Maurice. *Where the Wild Things Are*. New York: Harper & Row, 1963.

Shaw, Charles. *It Looked Like Spilt Milk*. New York: Harper Collins, 1947.

Shaw, Nancy. *Sheep In A Jeep*. Boston: Houghton Mifflin Company, 1986.

Sierra, Judy. *Counting Crocodiles*. New York: Scholastic, Inc., 1997.

Small, David. *Imogene's Antlers*. New York: Scholastic Inc., 1985.

Spinelli, Eileen. *Thanksgiving at the Tappletons'*. New York: HarperCollins Publishers, 1982.

Steig, William. *Amos and Boris*. New York: Farrar, Straus, Giroux, 1992.

Steig, William. *Brave Irene*. New York: Farrar, Straus, Giroux, 1986.

Steig, William. *Gorky Rises*. New York: Farrar, Straus, Giroux, 1980.

Titherington, Jeanne. *Pumpkin Pumpkin*. New York: Scholastic Inc., 1986.

Trapani, Iza (illustrator). *Itsy Bitsy Spider*. Dallas: Whispering Coyote Press, 1997.

Ungerer, Tomi. *Crictor*. New York: Harper & Row, 1958.

Van Allsburg, Chris. *Two Bad Ants*. Boston: Houghton Mifflin Company, 1988.

Waber, Bernard. *Ira Sleeps Over*. Boston: Houghton Mifflin Company, 1972.

Walsh, Ellen Stoll. *Mouse Paint*. New York: Harcourt Brace Jovanovich, Inc., 1989.

Wandelmaier, Roy. *Now I Know Clouds*. New York: Troll Associates, 1985.

Ward, Cindy. *Cookie's Week*. New York: Scholastic Inc., 1988.

Wells, Rosemary. *Noisy Nora*. New York: Puffin Pied Piper, 1973.

Westcott, Nadine. *The Lady with the Alligator Purse*. Boston: Little Brown and Company, 1988.

Westcott, Nadine. *Skip to My Lou*. Boston: Houghton Mifflin Impression, 1995.

Williams, Vera B. *A Chair For My Mother*. New York: William Morrow & Company, 1984.

Ziefert, Harriet. *Bears Odd Bears Even*. New York: Penguin Books, 1997.

RESOURCES

Contact any of the resources provided below to enhance and extend exploration, discovery, and environmental awareness.

National Audubon Society
700 Broadway
New York, NY 10003
1-212-979-3000
Web site: *www.audubon.org*
E-mail: *webmaster@list.audubon.org*

The Nature Conservancy
4245 North Fairfax Drive Suite 100
Arlington, VA 22203
1-703-841-5300
Web site: *www.tnc.org*
E-mail: *comment@tnc.org*

San Diego Zoo
P.O. Box 551
San Diego, CA 92112
Attention: Education Department
1-619-231-1515
Web site: *www.sandiegozoo.org*
E-mail: *webmaster@sandiegozoo.org*

World Wildlife Fund
1250 24th Street, NW
P.O. Box 97180
Washington, D.C. 20077
1-800-CALL-WWF
Web site: *www.worldwildlife.org*
E-mail: *membership@wwfus.org*

Contact any of the resources below to enhance awareness of the world community.

CARE
151 Ellis Street
Atlanta, GA 30303
1-404-681-2552
Web site: *www.care.org*
E-mail: *info@care.org*

Oxfam America
26 West Street
Boston, MA 02111
1-800-77-OXFAM
Web site: *www.oxfamamerica.org*
E-mail: *info@oxfamamerica.org*

UNICEF Headquarters
UNICEF House
3 United Nations Plaza
New York, NY 10017
1-212-326-7000
Web site: *www.unicef.org*
E-mail: *netmaster@unicef.org*

# ABOUT THE AUTHORS

Naomi E. Singer has been a teacher in Newton, Massachusetts, for more than twenty years. In her role as language arts and reading specialist, she teaches in kindergarten through grade five at the John Ward School and the Cabot School. Naomi also works with faculty and staff to coordinate and integrate the language arts program into all other areas of the curriculum. Additionally, she facilitates parent meetings that focus on early literacy acquisition. Naomi is the coauthor of *A+ Activities for Second Grade,* the author of several literature units for grades two through five, and the coauthor of a number of literature enrichment programs for kindergarten through grade three. Naomi holds a bachelor of arts degree with a major in English from the University of Connecticut and a master's degree in education from Lesley College in Cambridge, Massachusetts.

Matthew J. Miller has been a primary grade teacher in Newton, Massachusetts, since 1993. Matt was nominated for the 1998 Massachusetts Teacher of the Year Award. Currently, he is a member of the Cabot School Council, working with teachers, parents, and community members on this advisory committee to the principal. Matt is one of the authors of the Cabot School Web site and is a developer of curriculum at the first grade level. Matt is the coauthor of *A+ Activities for Second Grade.* He holds a bachelor of science degree with a major in education from Springfield College in Springfield, Massachusetts.